McA
006.74
HTML

to Do
thing
with

HTML &
XHTML

W9-DHW-684

ING
24.99

FRAMINGHAM PUBLIC LIBRARY

JAN 0 5 2006

Praise for *How to Do Everything with HTML:*

"I'm sure you have heard this a hundred times.....but I just love your book....I have a Web site that cost me a fortune in programming—it was way out of my league, so I don't regret the money—however, now, thanks to your book, I am able to 'tweak' it without having to go through the aggravation and expense for every little change."—Cathie D'Agostino

"Thanks for what already appears to be a very helpful book because, after just two chapters, I've completed & tested my first web page!"—Jerry Williams

"Your book, *How to Do Everything with HTML*, has really been a BIG help for me. I was using a Web page–building program (okay, so it was a cheap one) to build a site and became frustrated with its limitations. There were things I wanted to do with HTML that I couldn't. So I went out and bought your book and read it over and over and over! It's completely changed the way I work with HTML and I love the way I have control over how my code looks orderly and 'readable.'"—Kelvin Kolman

Amazon.com reviews:

"As an avid book reader, I can honestly say, without a doubt, that James H. Pence is one of the very best writers that I have ever encountered. This book, with its easy-to-understand language, gave me the courage and confidence to try creating a Web site....This book is the next best thing to taking an actual college course."

"Do not buy any other book until you have read this book and gone through it. Take it from somebody who did not know anything about building Web sites to one who built his own Web site in two weeks flat! This is the very best book in the world."

About the Author

A full-time freelance writer with a broad diversity of writing experience, James strives for excellence in all his work. James is the author of *Cascading Style Sheets: A Beginner's Guide*, published in 2001 by McGraw-Hill/Osborne. Also a novelist, James's first suspense/thriller novel, *Blind Sight*, was published in 2003 by Tyndale House Publishers. He has contributed op-ed pieces to the *Dallas Morning News* and has been published in *Writer* magazine and the 2001 edition of *The Writer's Handbook*. James is a 2003 graduate of Dallas Theological Seminary, where he trained in creative writing and journalism. He is an accomplished speaker and teacher, having served as an ordained minister for more than 20 years. James is also a gospel chalk artist and vocalist. He uses these talents in reaching out to inmates in the Texas prison system.

For more information about James Pence's writing, his prison ministry, or his other creative endeavors, visit www.jamespence.com or e-mail him at jim@jamespence.com.

FRAMINGHAM PUBLIC LIBRARY

JAN 0 5 2006

How to Do *Everything* with

HTML & XHTML

James H. Pence

McGraw-Hill/Osborne

New York   Chicago   San Francisco   Lisbon
London   Madrid   Mexico City   Milan   New Delhi
San Juan   Seoul   Singapore   Sydney   Toronto

The McGraw·Hill Companies

McGraw-Hill/Osborne
2100 Powell Street, 10th Floor
Emeryville, California 94608
U.S.A.

To arrange bulk purchase discounts for sales promotions, premiums, or fund-raisers, please
contact **McGraw-Hill**/Osborne at the above address. For information on translations or book
distributors outside the U.S.A., please see the International Contact Information page immediately
following the index of this book.

How to Do Everything with HTML & XHTML

Copyright © 2003 by The McGraw-Hill Companies. All rights reserved. Printed in the United
States of America. Except as permitted under the Copyright Act of 1976, no part of this publication
may be reproduced or distributed in any form or by any means, or stored in a database or retrieval
system, without the prior written permission of publisher, with the exception that the program
listings may be entered, stored, and executed in a computer system, but they may not be reproduced
for publication.

34567890 FGR FGR 01987654

ISBN 0-07-223129-7

Publisher	Brandon A. Nordin
Vice President &	
Associate Publisher	Scott Rogers
Acquisitions Editor	Megg Morin
Project Editor	Jennifer Malnick
Acquisitions Coordinator	Athena Honore
Technical Editor	George Semerenko
Copy Editor	Andrea Boucher
Proofreaders	Susan Carlson Greene, Jennifer Malnick
Indexer	Jack Lewis
Composition	Lucie Ericksen, John Patrus
Illustrators	Michael Mueller, Kathleen Fay Edwards, Melinda Moore Lytle
Series Design	Mickey Galicia
Cover Illustration	Tom Willis

This book was composed with Corel VENTURA™ Publisher.

Information has been obtained by **McGraw-Hill**/Osborne from sources believed to be reliable. However, because of the possibility of
human or mechanical error by our sources, **McGraw-Hill**/Osborne, or others, **McGraw-Hill**/Osborne does not guarantee the accuracy,
adequacy, or completeness of any information and is not responsible for any errors or omissions or the results obtained from the use of
such information.

This book is lovingly dedicated to

My wife, the love of my life, Laurel. You believed in me, even
when I refused to believe in myself.

Robert Key. I write to support my outreach into the Texas prison system
and, humanly speaking, you are why I am doing that. Thank you for
inviting me in, brother.

And SDG

Contents at a Glance

Contents

Acknowledgments

John Donne wrote that no man is an island unto himself. That is certainly true when it comes to writing a book. Many more have played a part in this book than space will allow me to mention, but some deserve special recognition.

Megg Morin, my acquisitions editor, gave me the opportunity of a lifetime—again! Thank you for all your help and encouragement as we've seen the second edition of this book become a reality.

Jennifer Malnick was a great help as my project editor. Thanks for helping to keep me on track, organized, and focused.

Andrea Boucher did a superb job as my copy editor. Thanks for smoothing out all my "rough spots" and helping me shape this book into something great.

My good friend and tech editor extraordinaire, George Semerenko, deserves a big thank you. Thanks for your attention to detail and for catching all the little things that I tend to miss.

Finally, my agent, Barbara Rosenberg, deserves credit for negotiating another great contract. Thanks, Barbara; I'm looking forward to many more projects.

By the way, thank you Sherry and John for suggesting I develop a seminar in HTML. If it hadn't been for you, I'd have never written this book.

Introduction

The title *How to Do Everything with HTML & XHTML* is an ambitious one indeed. It is something akin to titling a book *How to Do Everything with English.* Better yet, how about *How to Do Everything with Algebra?* The obvious question is: How do you know when you can do *everything* with any of the above?

HTML and XHTML are languages, and there are different ways to learn a language. Have you ever seen a book that promises to teach you Japanese in 30 days? Generally, what you get with those books are some basic phrases you can use if you travel to those places. As a rule, you don't learn a great deal about the language. Although you might be able to order in a restaurant or ask directions, you definitely can't do *everything* with it. On the other hand, you could buy a hefty book on Japanese grammar that expounds the language to the smallest detail. If you make it all the way through one of these reference books, you might have read everything *about* the language, but you still would not know how to do everything *with* it.

Books on HTML and XHTML work about the same way. You can buy books that are great for figuring out how to do specific things with XHTML—kind of like those "learn Japanese in 30 days" books. In these books you'll find instructions that are so focused and pointed that you can practically cut and paste the code into your own pages. Other volumes are large, intimidating tomes that literally tell you everything about XHTML. However, these are not the kind of books a beginner will find helpful.

You see, doing *everything* with Japanese, Algebra, English, or XHTML doesn't mean learning a few stock phrases, formulas, or lines of code. Neither does it mean you must digest an entire reference book of material. It doesn't even necessarily mean that you are fluent. Doing *everything* in this context means you are functional and competent—that is, you understand how the language works and you know how to use it without pulling a handbook out every five minutes. That's what this book is all about. *How to Do Everything with HTML & XHTML* is aimed at teaching you how to do Web pages by helping you understand XHTML and how it works. While this book won't bring you to a point where you never need reference books, it can help you gain a strong enough command of XHTML so that you don't need to design Web sites with a reference book open the whole time, or cut and paste someone else's code into your site. *How to Do Everything with HTML & XHTML* can give you the satisfaction of being able to develop your own site and know that it is *yours!*

A second area where this book will help you is in understanding the differences between HTML and XHTML. The world of Web authoring is changing, and if you want your Web site to stay current with the technology of the day, you need to be learning XHTML. This book will help you understand the reasons behind the shift from HTML to XHTML and the importance of learning to write standards-compliant pages. You will also learn, step-by-step, how to write pages in XHTML.

Who Should Read this Book

This book is designed for anybody who has ever wanted to do a Web site, but just hasn't got any idea where to start. You're not a "techie" and definitely wouldn't consider yourself a computer expert, but you're comfortable with your PC. You know how to find your way around your computer, transfer files, change directories, install software, create and save files, and so on. In other words, you're past the stage of being afraid that your system might self-destruct if you do something wrong. You're also willing to learn and not afraid of trying something new. Most important, you really *really* want to be able to design and build your own Web pages. If the "want to" is strong enough, you'll be willing to work through the examples and teach yourself this new skill of Web authoring.

How to Read this Book

If you've already worked with HTML and have done some Web authoring, you should have no problem plugging in to any chapter at random and working with that chapter's subject matter. However, if you have never worked with HTML before, you might want to keep some things in mind as you work through this book. While many HTML books are reference-oriented (you already know what you want to do and find out how to do it by looking it up in the index), this one is tutorial-oriented. The goal of *How to Do Everything with HTML & XHTML* is to help you write XHTML by learning how the language works. Therefore, you might keep some of the following suggestions in mind as you read:

- **Each chapter builds on the preceding one.**   Work through the book chapter by chapter. That way you'll be able to use what you learned in earlier chapters as you develop new skills progressively through the book.

- **Work through the projects; don't just read them.**   With any skill, you need to practice. Web authoring with XHTML is no different. If you only read about it, you'll never learn it.

- **Modify the examples for your own use.**   You'll learn faster and have a better understanding of how HTML works if you experiment with the examples rather than just typing them in as is. As you play with the code and see the results of your experiments, go back to the text and try to think through why you got the results you did.

- **Make use of the online resources.**   All of the code, images, and examples created for this book are available for download, either from the author's Web site—www.jamespence.com—or from Osborne's Web site at www.osborne.com. By downloading the resources, you will be able to reproduce exactly the illustrations you find in the book. This will make it much easier to understand and apply the principles you are learning

- **Download the free online appendixes.**   Three free appendixes are also available online through the author's or Osborne's Web site. These appendixes provide added details about Cascading Style Sheets, Module-Based XHTML, and Character Entities. By downloading and using them you can enhance your experience in learning XHTML.

- **Ask questions.**   Don't hesitate to e-mail the author if you have a question or problem. James welcomes e-mail contacts from readers and will do his best to answer your questions. You can reach him at jim@jamespence.com.

Help You'll Find in this Book

As you read through *How to Do Everything with HTML & XHTML*, you'll find some helpful resources mixed in with the regular text. These special icons and text boxes will give you additional information related to the topic at hand. These helpful conventions and their names are as follows:

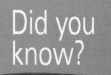

About These Boxes

Did You Know boxes give you interesting and helpful background information that is related to the topic at hand.

Utilize These Boxes

How To text boxes add special tips and tricks and other fun things you can do.

NOTE   *Notes provide additional information that is related to the particular discussion but are not necessarily action-oriented.*

TIP   *Tips contain additional tidbits of information that will make things easier—how to make the best use of software features, and so on.*

 *Shortcuts offer time-saving steps and suggestions for easier ways to perform particular tasks.*

 *Look to Cautions for information about pitfalls to avoid, workarounds to employ, and "gotchas" to be aware of.*

How this Book Is Organized

How to Do Everything with HTML & XHTML is organized into three parts. Each part focuses on a different aspect of XHTML and Web design. Part I, Chapters 1–7, takes you through the basics of HTML and XHTML and how to build a Web site. These chapters show you everything you need to know to get a site up and running. Part II, Chapters 8–10, focuses on style, how to structure your pages, and how to make them look good. Beginning with tables and then moving to frames and Cascading Style Sheets, you'll learn how to craft your site and make it distinctively yours. Part III, Chapters 11–16, shows you how to add bells and whistles to your pages. With audio and video, animations, forms, JavaScript, and even such advanced topics as XML, you can learn how to make your pages fly. The online appendixes provide reference guides designed to help you put some of the things you learn into practice—without having to reread the text.

One final recommendation for working through this book and developing your own Web site: Have a great time!

Part I

HTML Basics: Everything You Need to Build a Web Site

Chapter 1

Get Your Feet Wet with HTML

How to...

■ Understand HTML

■ Create and display a simple Web page

■ Create a working template

■ Convert text to HTML

■ Add comments to HTML

■ Create a home page for a Web site

The World Wide Web: you've just got to be a part of it. You've surfed the Net for years and have always wondered what it would be like to put up your own site, but you've got a nagging fear that writing Web pages is too difficult for you. After all, you're not a programmer or a "techie." Relax. You don't need to be a techie to learn how to do Web pages. If you can create and save a text file, know how to use a Web browser, and have some basic experience with the Internet, you have all the skills you need to create Web pages.

So where do you start? Perhaps the best place to begin is by understanding HTML, the original language of the World Wide Web.

Understand HTML

You may be asking yourself, "What about XHTML?" Although this book is titled *How to Do Everything with HTML & XHTML,* that's a pretty big chunk to take in at one time. You'll find it much easier to understand XHTML if first you learn a few basics about HTML. Besides, there are many similarities between the two languages; learning about one will help you grasp the other.

HTML stands for *Hypertext Markup Language*, and it is the language in which, until recently, virtually all Web pages were written. Now, don't break out in hives when you hear the word "language." You don't need complex logical or mathematical formulas to work with HTML, and you don't need to think like a programmer to use it. Computer programmers must think through the tasks that they want their programs to perform, and then develop an elaborate (and usually complicated) series of instructions to tell the computer what to do. Although you do need to do some thinking and planning when you use HTML, it is not nearly that difficult. So, how *does* Hypertext Markup Language work?

Hypertext refers to the way in which Web pages (HTML documents) are linked together. When you click a link in a Web page, you are using hypertext. It is this system of linking documents that has made the World Wide Web the global phenomenon it has become.

Markup Language describes how HTML works. With a markup language, you simply "mark up" a text document with tags that tell a Web browser how to structure it. HTML originally was developed with the intent of defining the structure of documents (headings, paragraphs, lists, and so forth) to facilitate the sharing of scientific information between researchers. All you need to do to use HTML is to learn what type of markup to use to get the results you want.

Markup 101: Four Key Concepts

The first step toward understanding and working with HTML is learning the basic terms that describe most of the functions of this language. You will come across these terms repeatedly as you use HTML and if you understand them, you will have progressed a long way toward comprehending HTML, not to mention XHTML.

Elements

All HTML pages are made up of *elements*. Think of an element as a container in which a portion of a page is placed. Whatever is contained inside the element will take on the characteristics of that element. For example, to identify a heading on a page, you would enclose it in a *heading* element <h1> </h1>. If you want to create a table, you put the table information inside the *table* element <table> </table>. To construct a form, you need the *form* element <form> </form>.

Tags

Often, you'll find the terms *element* and *tag* used interchangeably. It's fairly common, but not strictly accurate. An element is made up of two tags: an opening tag and a closing tag. Although it might seem somewhat picky to make this distinction, when you begin to work with XHTML (*Extensible Hypertext Markup Language*), it will be a very important difference to remember. If you get into the habit of distinguishing elements and tags from the very beginning, you'll save yourself some confusion down the line.

All tags are constructed the same way. The tag begins with a "less than" sign (<), then the element name, followed by a "greater than" sign (>). For example, an opening tag for the *paragraph* element would look like this: <p>. The only difference in a closing tag is that the closing tag includes a slash (/) before the element name: </p>. Your content goes between the tags. A simple paragraph might look like this:

```
<p>This is an HTML paragraph.</p>
```

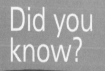

Where the *X* in XHTML Comes From

Extensible (the *X* in XHTML) means that the language can be modified and *extended*, unlike HTML, which is fixed. Because of the explosive growth of the Internet, HTML is being stretched far beyond its capacity. For example, if musicians want to create a Web page with markup for musical notation, they are out of luck—HTML does not have the ability to accommodate this kind of specialization. However, as you'll learn in this book, XHTML will eventually make it possible for music page authors—and many other specialists—to create specialized extensions that will address their particular needs. Extensibility will enable XHTML to adapt to the growing and changing needs of the future.

Some elements do not use closing tags because they do not enclose content. These are called *empty elements*. For example, the line break element <br> does not require a closing tag. In the case of empty elements, add a closing slash after the element name, like this: <br />. When a browser sees the slash, it will recognize the element as one that does not need a separate, closing tag.

*When writing an empty element, it's important to add a space between the element name and the closing slash. Correct:
 Incorrect:
*

Attributes and Values

Attributes are another important part of HTML markup. An attribute is used to define the characteristics of an element and is placed inside the element's opening tag. For example, to specify the size of an image or graphic on your page, you would use the *image* element <img /> along with the *height* and *width* attributes:

```
<img height=" " width=" " />
```

Be sure to notice that an equals sign and a set of quotation marks follow both the height and the width attributes. That's because attributes need *values* to go with them. In the case of the preceding illustration, you might add a value of 200 to cause your image to display at a size of 200 x 200 pixels:

```
<img height="200" width="200" />
```

The preceding <img /> element is incomplete because it also requires an attribute that specifies which image you want inserted in your page. To find out more about inserting images, check Chapter 6.

Values work together with attributes to complete the definition of an element's characteristics. An easy way to think of how attributes and values work together is to compare them with nouns and adjectives. A noun names something; an adjective describes it. An attribute names a characteristic; a value describes it. Imagine that you are trying to identify a person's hair color with a markup language. *Hair* would be the element, *color* the attribute, and *red* the value. You might write such a description as follows:

```
<hair color="red">Red-headed Person</hair>
```

Always enclose values in quotation marks.

Nesting

Often you will want to apply more than one element to a portion of your page. An essential concept to understand is *nesting*. Nesting simply means that elements must never overlap. Properly nested elements are contained inside one another, as in the following:

```
<a> <b> <c> </c> </b> </a>
```

Sometimes it's easier to understand the concept if the elements are displayed vertically, like this:

```
<a>
   <b>
      <c>
      </c>
   </b>
</a>
```

The following elements, on the other hand, are overlapping:

```
<a>
   <b>
</a>
      <c>
   </b>
      </c>
```

Web browsers displaying an HTML page can be pretty forgiving if your elements are not properly nested; however, overlapped elements can create garbled results, particularly if you are trying to construct frames or tables. Also, when you become familiar with XHTML's stricter standards, you'll discover that overlapping elements are an absolute "no-no."

Now that you have a handle on the basic concepts behind HTML, it's time to roll up your sleeves and create your first Web page.

Project 1: Create and Display a Home Page

Creating a Web page is so easy, you'll wonder why you waited this long to learn how to do it. All you need are a simple text editor, such as Windows Notepad, and a Web browser to view the page and you're off and running.

Create a Home Page in Notepad

To create your first Web page, use Windows Notepad or another text editor. Although you could use Word, WordPerfect, or any other word processor to create HTML documents, it's easier to start with a simple text editor. (For more about HTML authoring tools, see Chapter 7.)

Understand Document Elements

The elements listed in the following could be called *document* elements because they describe and define your HTML document. You won't use all of these right now, but it's good to know them and understand what they do.

- **<html> </html>**   Defines the beginning and end of the document.
- **<head> </head>**   This is the document header. It works like a storehouse of important information about the document. This information generally is not displayed in the document.
- **<title> </title>**   The title element is nested inside the header. It displays a page title in the title bar at the top of the browser.

- **<body> </body>**   Contains the main body of the Web page.
- **<!-- Enclose comments here -->**   Enables you to add hidden comments and explanatory notes to your code. This will make it easier for you (and others who may have to edit your pages in the future) to decipher your code.

TIP   *Choose your <title> carefully. One way search engines find, categorize, and list a page is by its title. So, if you want people to find you, be sure that every page on your Web site has a title that concisely and accurately describes that page's contents. The better your title choice, the more likely your page will come up high on a search engine's results.*

At this point, you need to concern yourself with only the following elements: <html>, <head>, <title>, and <body>. These are the elements you will find in virtually all HTML pages. Strictly speaking, you can get away without using any of them. To see for yourself, just open Notepad and type "This is an HTML page." Then save the document as test.htm. When you display it in a browser, you'll discover that the browser recognizes and displays the page just fine. So, why use HTML? HTML enables you to define the structure of your page or document. If you display a page of text without adding any markup, you'll discover that it displays as one large mass. However, as you learn to use HTML and XHTML, you will learn how to use elements, attributes, and values to add structure to that body of text.

Create an HTML Template

An HTML *template* is simply a file that has all the basic elements for a Web page already written. It's a good starting place to learn how to create an HTML document. An added benefit is that it saves you the trouble of typing these elements every time you want to create a new page. To create an HTML template, follow these steps:

1. Open Notepad or another text editor.
2. At the top of the page type **<html>**.
3. On the next line, indent five spaces and now add the opening header tag: **<head>**.
4. On the next line, indent ten spaces and type **<title> </title>**.
5. Go to the next line, indent five spaces from the margin and insert the closing header tag: **</head>**.
6. Five spaces in from the margin on the next line, type **<body>**.
7. Now drop down another line and type the closing tag right below its mate: **</body>**.
8. Finally, go to the next line and type **</html>**.
9. In the File menu, choose Save As.
10. In the Save as Type option box, choose All Files.
11. Name the file *template.htm*.
12. Click Save.

You have created a template that you can use whenever you want to make a new Web page. Your HTML code should look something like this:

```html
<html>
    <head>
        <title> </title>
    </head>
    <body>
    </body>
</html>
```

Incidentally, you could just have easily written the tags all on the same line. Web browsers don't really care. It's better, though, if you try to write your code so that you can understand what the different elements are doing. If it's all jumbled together, you might find yourself confused when you go back in and modify your page. Besides, if others have to edit your page someday, they will find it much easier to decipher your HTML if you have put the tags on separate lines and indented them, as in the preceding code. By writing your pages this way, you can make sure that your elements are properly nested, and you can make it much more convenient for anyone who is trying to "debug" your code.

Creating different templates for your Web pages will speed up your work considerably. When you have designed a page, save it as a template before you begin adding content. Then you can perfectly reproduce the layout every time you want to use that design.

Create a Home Page

Now that you have a template to work with, it's time to see just how easy it is to create your own Web page. In this step you will open your template and save it as *index.htm*. This is because Web servers require that a Web site's home page have a special name. This enables the server to automatically direct visitors to the main page of your site. Generally, index.htm is preferred; however, some servers will also allow you to use *default.htm*.

1. Open template.htm in Notepad.
2. Before you do anything else, save the page as *index.htm*.
3. In between the <title> tags, type **My Home Page**.
4. In between the <body> tags, type (***Your name***)**'s Home Page**.
5. Drop down two lines and type: **This is my very first Web page**.
6. Save the page.

Always save the file with either an .htm or .html extension. If you allow Notepad to save your file as a text (.txt) file, a Web browser will not be able to read it. Also, it's a good idea to be consistent in using .htm and html extensions, because web servers will treat index.htm *and* index.html *as two different files. To avoid confusion, stick with one or the other.*

Your finished HTML code should look something like Figure 1-1.

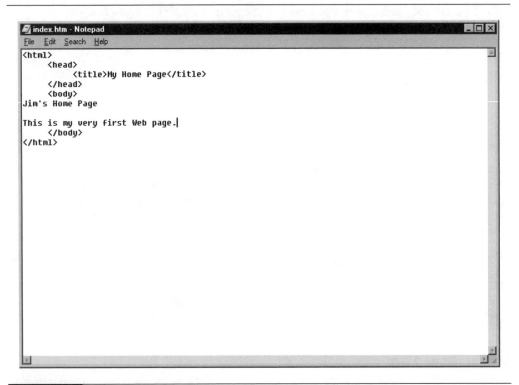

```
index.htm - Notepad                                      _□×
File  Edit  Search  Help
<html>
      <head>
            <title>My Home Page</title>
      </head>
      <body>
Jim's Home Page

This is my very first Web page.
      </body>
</html>
```

FIGURE 1-1   A basic HTML page in Notepad

View Your Page in a Web Browser

Once you have saved your page, it's time to see what it looks like. To display your page, follow
these steps:

1. Open your favorite Web browser and click the File menu.

2. Depending on which browser you are using, you should find an option that reads Open,
   Open Page, or Open File. Select that option.

3. A dialog box will open and display your computer's filing system. Use that box to
   navigate to the directory where you saved index.htm. If you are using Internet Explorer,
   you will also need to click the Browse button that comes up after you click Open.

4. When you find your file, click its icon.

5. Click OK or Open, whichever choice your browser gives you. Your file should be
   displayed in the browser and should look like the sample in Figure 1-2.

You've created your very first Web page! It's as simple as that. As you progress through the
rest of the book, you will learn to build on that simple skeleton, creating Web pages that you will
be proud to display for the world.

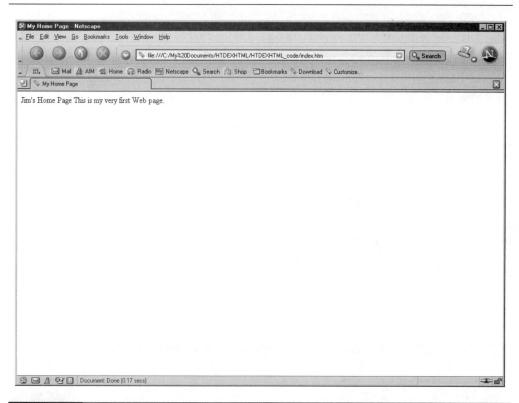

Jim's Home Page This is my very first Web page.

FIGURE 1-2   Your first Web page

Convert Text to HTML

As you begin to think about what you would like to put on your Web site, you might be wondering about material that you already have written but that is not "Web ready" yet. Maybe you have some recipes or short stories you've written. Or you might want to put your company's employee manual online. Will you have to retype all that information? Not if you learn how to convert it to HTML. Although it's possible to have a word processor save a file in HTML format, it's not a great idea. Word processors tend to generate messy HTML. Besides, it's quite easy to convert text to HTML.

Import Text into an HTML Page

Importing text into your HTML document is as easy as using the cut and paste options in Windows. However, when you import your text, you will notice that it has lost all of its formatting. You will learn in Chapter 2 how to use HTML elements to redefine the structure of your text.

   1. Open template.htm in Notepad.

2. Open the document you want to import in your word processing program.

3. Select the text you want to import and copy it to the clipboard.

4. In Notepad, paste the text in between the <body> tags and then save the document under a different file name (so you don't ruin your template).

5. Now, display the page in your browser.

When you import text into an HTML document, it loses any formatting it originally had. It will simply appear as a solid block of text. If you want the material you imported to be organized or structured in some way, you'll have to do it with HTML elements. In the next couple of chapters, you'll learn how to take your text and shape it up with text elements.

Convert a Page of Text to HTML

Another way to transform material you already have into a Web page is to simply save the file as a text file (but using an HTML extension). Then add the necessary HTML tags (see Figure 1-3). The main thing to remember is that you must save the file as a plain text file, not as a word processor file. Otherwise, the word processor's codes will interfere with your HTML.

1. Open the file you want to convert to HTML.

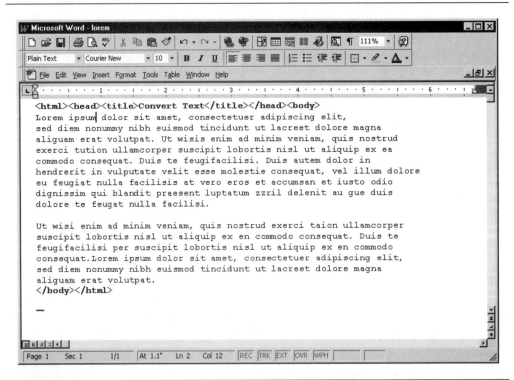

FIGURE 1-3   A word processor document with HTML tags added

2. At the top of the document, type **<html><head><title>Convert Text</title> </head><body>**.

3. At the end of the document, type **</body></html>**.

4. From the File menu, choose Save As.

5. Choose Save As Text and name the file *convert.htm*.

6. Open the file in your browser.

Add Comments to Your HTML Document

Although the first HTML pages you write will be fairly simple, they can get complicated in a hurry. As your pages become more detailed and complex, you might find it difficult to remember what a particular section of code is supposed to do. The easiest solution is to add comments to your HTML source code. Comments function as little notes to yourself (see Figure 1-4). Web browsers will ignore the comments completely, but they will come in very handy if you are writing a complex page with many lines of HTML.

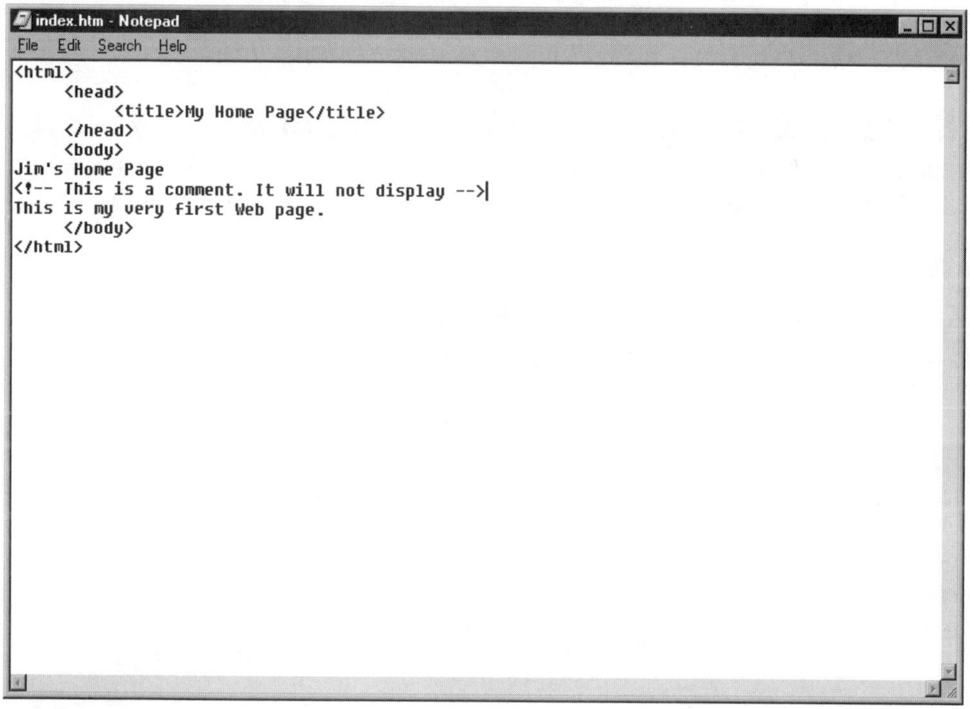

```
<html>
    <head>
        <title>My Home Page</title>
    </head>
    <body>
Jim's Home Page
<!-- This is a comment. It will not display -->
This is my very first Web page.
    </body>
</html>
```

FIGURE 1-4   HTML code with a comment added.

Adding comments to your HTML is easy. Just enclose your comment between comment tags: <!-- *Add your comment here* -->.

To add a comment to the Web page you just created, follow these steps:

1. Open index.htm in Notepad.

2. Anywhere between the <body> </body> tags, type the first comment tag: **<!--** (a "less than" sign, followed by an exclamation point and two dashes).

3. Type **This is a comment**.

4. Type the closing comment tag: **-->** (two dashes followed by a "greater than" sign).

5. Your completed comment should look like this:

```
<!-- This is a comment -->
```

If you save and display the page in a browser, and you have entered the comment tags correctly, the comment should not display. If you see it, check your comment tags to make sure you wrote them correctly.

| TIP | *Comment tags are useful for more than putting little notes in your code. When you want to use JavaScript to add some special effects to your page, you can hide the script in comment tags to hide it from older browsers that can't use JavaScript. Older browsers then will ignore your script, whereas JavaScript-enabled browsers will execute it. To learn more about using JavaScript in your pages, read Chapter 15.* |

Quick Reference: Creating HTML Documents

As you have already seen, creating a Web page is a relatively simple task. However, the more you learn of HTML and XHTML markup, the more difficult it will be to remember everything. The purpose of this section is to help you remember what you've learned and to provide a quick reference as you begin to develop your own Web pages.

To Do This	Use This
Create an HTML document	```<html> <head> <title> </title> </head> <body> </body> </html>```
Save an HTML document	.htm or .html
Name the home page for a Web site	index.htm or default.htm (Most servers prefer index.htm for your home page's file name.)
Assign a title to a page	`<title>Insert title here</title>`
Add comments	`<!-- Enclose comments here -->`

Chapter 2

Work with Text and Lists

How to...

- Designate headings
- Identify text
- Create bulleted lists
- Build numbered lists
- Create definition lists
- Add special characters

In Chapter 1 you learned how to create a basic Web page. In this chapter you'll have the chance to put something more than raw text on your page. You'll also learn about a key issue in using HTML and XHTML: the importance of content versus presentation.

Chances are that if you want to create Web pages, your primary concern is how your Web pages will *look*. In other words, you are interested in *presentation*. However, to be able to work with XHTML, you need to understand that *content* comes first. In fact, HTML was originally developed to assist scientists in linking and transmitting research documents over a computer network. Thus, as you'll see in this chapter, the elements are designed to reflect their content. Working with headings, simple text elements, and lists is a great way to begin learning this aspect of HTML. These elements are simple, straightforward, and uncomplicated, but they give you good practice for working with tags. Creating lists will allow you to experiment with the concept of nesting covered in the last chapter. *Nesting* (placing HTML elements inside one another) is an important practice in HTML; it is essential in XHTML. Lists will also provide the opportunity to learn about another important part of working with XHTML, the problem of *deprecated* elements and attributes. However, before tackling that problem, you'll find it easier to work with something easy, like headings.

Designate Headings with <h#> </h#>

The purpose of the heading element is to indicate different heading levels in a document. The tags are made up of an *h* with a number following it. For example, to specify a level one heading, you would write:

```
<h1>This is a level one heading.</h1>
```

A level two heading would look like this:

```
<h2>This is a level two heading.</h2>
```

HTML includes six heading levels: <h1>, <h2>, <h3>, <h4>, <h5>, and <h6>. Try typing the following HTML code to see how the six heading levels will display on a Web browser:

```
<html>
    <head>
        <title>The Heading Element</title>
    </head>
    <body>
        <h1>This is a level one heading.</h1>
        <h2>This is a level two heading.</h2>
        <h3>This is a level three heading.</h3>
        <h4>This is a level four heading.</h4>
        <h5>This is a level five heading.</h5>
        <h6>This is a level six heading.</h6>
    </body>
</html>
```

SHORTCUT   *Remember the file you created in Chapter 1 named* template.htm? *That file can save you the trouble of retyping the basic page elements every time you create a new page. Just open* template.htm, *then save it with a new name and, presto, you have a new HTML page ready to work with.*

Now, save this file as *headings.htm* and open it in your Web browser. Figure 2-1 shows you what you should see when you display your page.

As you can see, the text displays in a range of different sizes, from very large to quite small. In fact, it has become commonplace to use the heading elements as an easy way to control font size. However, as you begin to learn to use HTML and XHTML, you will be wise to avoid this shortcut. The reason for this is that it defeats the purpose of the markup, which is to *describe* the content of your page. The <h#> elements were created to identify different divisions within a document, not to display different font sizes. To understand this concept further, consider how the *text elements* work.

Use Text Elements to Describe Text

Text elements derive their names from the intended function or purpose of the text. For example, the <strong> element stands for strongly emphasized text. Generally, browsers will display <strong> text with a bold typeface, indicating that it is *strongly emphasized.*

Identify Text with Text Elements

As you will see, each of the following elements not only displays text, but also says something *about* the text it contains:

- ■ **<em> </em>**   The *emphasis* element is an element used for emphasizing important portions of a document. It generally displays italicized text.

- ■ **<strong> </strong>**   The *strong* element indicates stronger emphasis than does <em> and usually displays as bold text.

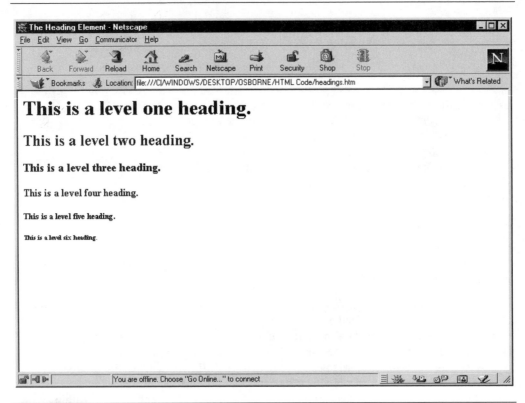

FIGURE 2-1 The six heading levels of HTML

- **<kbd> </kbd>** Standing for *keyboard*, this element identifies its contents as user input through a keyboard. Generally, it displays as a monospaced font. Some browsers also might display it as bold.

- **<cite> </cite>** The *citation* element identifies a portion of your document as a reference to an outside source.

- **<var> </var>** This element indicates a *variable*, as might be used in computer code.

- **<dfn> </dfn>** The <dfn> element identifies a portion of text as a *defining instance* of a term. It also generally displays in italic.

- **<code> </code>** This element not only displays in a courier, fixed-width font, but also indicates that the text is a portion of computer code.

- **<samp> </samp>** The <samp> element identifies its contents as *sample output*, for example, from a computer program, most often rendering text in a monospaced font.

- **<abbr> </abbr>** Identifies an abbreviation; for example, TX instead of Texas.

- **<acronym> </acronym>**   This element identifies text as an acronym, such as S.C.U.B.A. or N.A.S.A.
- **<address> </address>**   You would use this element to set apart your address or personal information at the bottom of a Web page. The <address> element also adds a line break before and after the address.

To see each of these elements in action, copy the code listing that follows and save it as *text.htm*. To save time, open template.htm and save it as text.htm. Then just add the lines in between the <body> </body> portion of the code to get the results shown in the following illustration:

```
<html>
    <head>
        <title>Using Text Elements</title>
    </head>
    <body>
        The <em>Emphasis element</em><br />
        The <strong>Strong element</strong><br />
        The <kbd>Keyboard element</kbd><br />
        The <cite>Citation element</cite><br />
        The <var>Variable element</var><br />
        The <dfn>Definition element</dfn><br />
        The <code>Code element</code><br />
        The<samp>Sample output element</samp><br />
        The <acronym>Acronym element</acronym><br />
        The <address>Address element</address><br />
    </body>
</html>
```

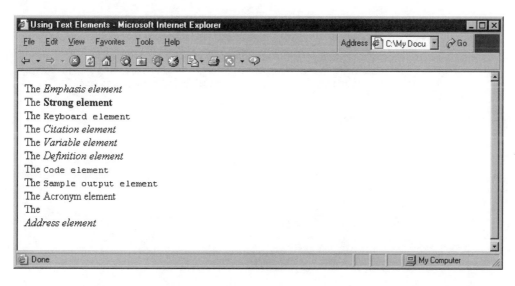

 *The line break <br /> element at the end of each line in the preceding code causes the browser to create a new line of text.*

Why are there so many different ways to describe text? Because HTML is not primarily concerned with what someone sees when they view a Web page. Hypertext Markup Language is aimed at defining the content of a document, not its appearance. Do you need to use all of these different elements in your Web pages? Not necessarily, but keep in mind that the World Wide Web didn't get that name for nothing. As your knowledge of HTML and XHTML grows and you become more concerned with making your pages accessible to as many people as possible, you will develop an appreciation for these elements.

Add Superscripts and Subscripts with <sup> and <sub>

The superscript and subscript elements are reflective of the need to add footnotes for sources as well as the need to be able to write chemical formulas. They are also useful tools for the Web page author. Perhaps you'll need to document a source on your Web site by inserting a footnote reference at the end of a quotation. For this, you'll use the <sup> element. Or perhaps you're a science nut and want to describe the molecular structure of water or carbon dioxide. Then you can create a subscript with the <sub> element.

- ****   This element creates a superscript.
- ****   This element forces text to display as a subscript.

To see these elements in action, use your template to create a new document, saving it as *sup.htm*. Then insert the following line in between the <body> </body> tags. It will create a line with both superscripts and subscripts, as in the following illustration:

```
<html>
    <head>
        <title>Superscript and Subscript</title>
    </head>
    <body>
    The <sup>superscript</sup> and <sub>subscript</sub> elements
raise and lower text.
    </body>
</html>
```

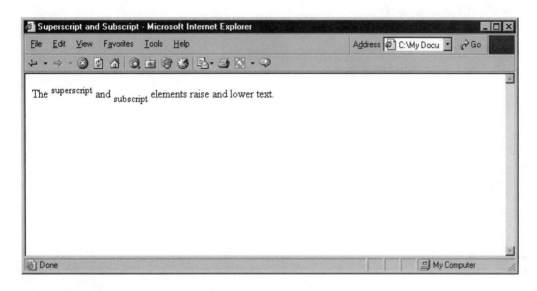

Identify Deleted and Inserted Text with <del> and <ins>

Perhaps no elements better illustrate HTML's document-oriented roots than the <del> and <ins> elements. In the process of editing and rewriting manuscripts, deleted text is displayed with a line through the middle (strikethrough), and newly added text is displayed as underlined. That way, the writers and editors of a document can clearly discern the changes that are being made. HTML's <del> and <ins> perform the same function, causing text to display as strikethrough or as underlined.

- ■ **<del> </del>** The *deleted text* element indicates (by a strikethrough) that the text has been deleted but left in the page.
- ■ **<ins> </ins>** The *inserted text* element is a logical element that indicates new text has been inserted since the document was written.

Create an HTML file like the one that follows and save it as del.htm. Then display it in your browser to see the <del> and <ins> elements in action. Your page should resemble the following illustration:

```
<html>
    <head>
        <title>Deleted and Inserted Text</title>
    </head>
    <body>
To identify text as <del>deleted</del> or <ins>inserted</ins>
use the deleted and inserted text elements.
    </body>
</html>
```

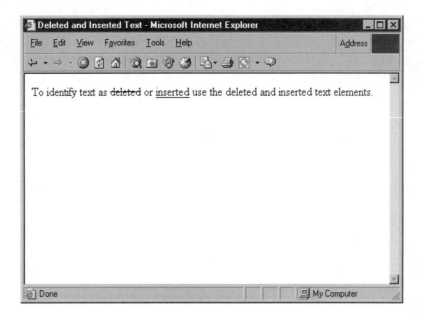

Retain Text Formatting with <pre>

If you try converting large blocks of text from a word processor into HTML, you will notice that all formatting, spacing, line, and paragraph divisions are lost in the process of conversion. As you'll learn in the next chapter, style sheets will enable you to re-create that formatting. However, HTML does provide an element that preserves line breaks, spacing, and white space. Using the *preformatted text* element, <pre>, you can instruct a browser to display your text exactly as you enter it. Simply enclose the text between the <pre> </pre> tags, and the browser will leave it as is. The downside of this element is that the browser will also display the text in a typewriter-style or monospaced font. However, in the next chapter you'll learn how to use style sheets to override this and instruct the browser to use a different font.

To see how <pre> works, create and save a page, naming it *pre.htm*. Then type in the following code. As you can see in the illustration that follows, the browser retains whatever spacing you gave the characters:

```
<html>
    <head>
        <title>Preformatted Text</title>
    <head>
    <body>
<pre>This is a sample of preformatted text:
```

```
Thirty days hath September,
     April, June, and November.
          All the rest have thirty one,
Save February and it has twenty eight.</pre>
     </body>
</html>
```

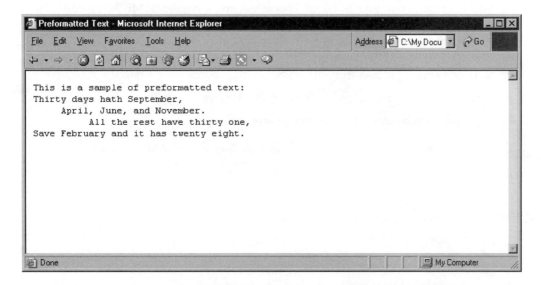

The text elements give you limited influence over how your text is displayed. In the next chapter you will expand that influence. But before moving into that arena, it will be helpful for you to learn a simple way to structure the information you put on your Web pages.

Organize Your Content with Lists

HTML lists are a great way to organize content on your Web site. Whether you want to list the ingredients of your favorite recipe, create a page of links with their descriptions, or offer step-by-step instructions for washing a dog, you can use list elements to put your material in order. Another benefit that comes from working with lists is that it will give you some experience in nesting your elements.

Create Unordered Lists with <ul> and <li>

An *unordered list* is what you might know as a bulleted list. The items in the list are not organized by number or letter. Rather, each item has a small symbol (bullet) in front of it. In HTML, you can create unordered lists that have a solid disc, a circle, or a square.

Use <ul> and <li> to Create an Unordered List

You need two elements to create an unordered (bulleted) list:

- ■ **<ul> </ul>**   The *unordered list* element creates the list.
- ■ **<li> </li>**   You specify individual items on the list with the *list item* element.

Use your template to create a new HTML document. Save it in your HTML reference directory as *ulist.htm.* Then, in between the <body> </body> tags:

1. Type an opening *unordered list* tag: **<ul>**.

2. Next, add a set of *list item* tags: **<li> </li>**.

3. For each new list item, add another set of **<li> </li>** tags.

4. When the list is complete, type a closing **</ul>** tag.

The code for a simple unordered list might look something like what you see here:

```
<html>
    <head>
        <title>Unordered Lists</title>
    <head>
    <body>
        <ul>
            <li>This is the first item</li>
            <li>This is the second item</li>
            <li>This is the third item</li>
        </ul>
    </body>
</html>
```

When you display your page in a browser, it will produce a bulleted list, like the one in the illustration here:

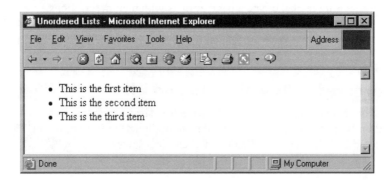

Did you
know?

W3C Stands for World Wide Web Consortium

The W3C is an international organization responsible for setting the standards concerning the Internet, World Wide Web, HTML, XHTML, and any other related technologies.

You'll notice when you display the list that your browser supplies a solid disc as the bullet for each item. If you would prefer a circle or a square, you can specify it by using the *type* attribute. However, before you begin experimenting with different bullet types, you need to understand something about the type attribute and why the W3C doesn't want you to use it.

Understand Deprecated Elements and Attributes

Over the years since HTML was developed, browser companies (specifically Netscape and Internet Explorer) have *extended* it to include what might be known as *presentational elements*. For example, Netscape introduced the <blink> element, which causes text to blink on and off. Internet Explorer introduced the <marquee> element, which makes text scroll across the screen like a movie marquee. Some of these *proprietary elements* were supported only by their respective browsers; others were eventually incorporated into the HTML standard. For example, frames are a Netscape innovation that ultimately became part of HTML. However, as more and more presentational elements were added, HTML moved farther and farther away from its original purpose—describing document content.

The W3C has been working for several years to eliminate any HTML markup that governs appearance. The reasons for this move, and the alternative method for addressing presentation (Cascading Style Sheets), will be introduced in Chapter 3, but it's important to understand now that certain elements and attributes have been officially *deprecated* by the W3C. Deprecated is just a fancy way of saying that they don't want you to use those elements and attributes anymore. Don't worry, though. Nobody from the "Web Police" will knock on your door if you use these deprecated portions of HTML. However, the possibility exists that browsers may eventually stop supporting them. If your Web pages are built on those elements and attributes, you might find yourself having to redo them down the line.

Use the *type* Attribute to Specify Different Bullets (Deprecated)

The *type* attribute enables you to choose between a disc, circle, or square as the bullet for your list items. Even though this attribute has been deprecated in favor of Cascading Style Sheets, you'll find it helpful to learn how to use it. Just as working with lists will help you understand the concept of nesting, using the type attribute will enable you to become acquainted with attributes and how they work.

There are two different ways you can use the type attribute in a list: globally (the entire list) or individual list items. To specify the bullets for an entire list, put the attribute inside the opening <ul> tag:

- To specify a square: **<ul type="square">**
- To specify a circle: **<ul type="circle">**
- To specify a disc: **<ul type="disc">**

You also can control the type of bullet for each separate item by putting the attribute inside the <li> tag. For example, the following code will supply a different bullet for each item.

```
<ul>
    <li type="square">This supplies a square.</li>
    <li type="circle">This supplies a circle.</li>
    <li type="disc">This supplies a disc.</li>
</ul>
```

Project 2: Create a Multilevel List

To create a list with multiple levels, you simply nest one or more unordered lists inside each other. Save ulist.htm with the new name *ulist2.htm*. Now make a multilevel list from it:

1. Change the <title> to read **Multi-Level Unordered Lists**.

2. In the first <ul> tag, just below the body tag, enter **type="square"**.

3. Inside the first set of <li> tags, type **<ul>**.

4. Inside this new <ul> tag, enter **type="circle"**.

5. Add a line that says **<li>This is a sub point.</li>**.

6. Add another line that reads: **<li>This is a sub point.</li>**.

7. Close out the sublist with **</ul>**.

8. Add a set of subpoints to the second main point. Use **type="disc"** to specify the disc bullet.

9. Add a set of subpoints to the third main point. Use **type="square"** to specify the square bullet.

Your list should look like this:

```
<html>
    <head>
        <title>Multi-Level Unordered Lists</title>
    <head>
    <body>
        <ul type="square">
```

```
<li>This is the first item
    <ul type="circle">
        <li>This is a sub point</li>
        <li>This is a sub point</li>
    </ul>
</li>
<li>This is the second item
    <ul type="disc">
        <li>This is a sub point</li>
        <li>This is a sub point</li>
    </ul>
</li>
<li>This is the third item
    <ul type="square">
        <li>This is a sub point</li>
        <li>This is a sub point</li>
    </ul>
</li>
        </ul>
    </body>
</html>
```

If you want to add another level of sub points, you can do it by nesting another complete list inside each <li> </li> element where you want the next level. A multilevel list such as the one rendered here will resemble the following illustration:

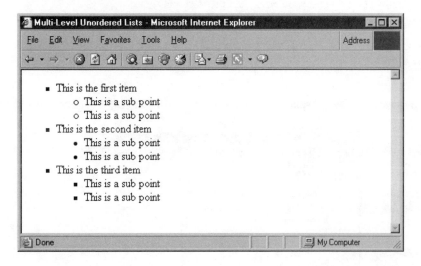

 *You can get away with putting your sublist below the list item to which it applies instead of inside the tags. Most browsers will still display it properly. However, it's sloppy HTML and will not meet the more stringent standards of XHTML.*

Create Ordered Lists with <ol> and <li>

What if you want to display an outline with numbers and letters delineating the various points? Or perhaps you want to create a list of instructions in numbered sequence. Lists that arrange items in sequence by number or letter are called *ordered lists* in HTML and are quite similar in their structure to unordered lists. To create an ordered list, you need the following:

- ■ **<ol> </ol>** This is the ordered list element.
- ■ **<li> </li>** This is the list item element.

Use <ol> to Create a Numbered List

You can create a simple numbered list by enclosing a series of list items inside the ordered list element, as in the following sample page. Use your template to open a new HTML page and save it as *olist.htm.* Then type in this code:

```
<html>
    <head>
        <title>Ordered Lists</title>
    </head>
    <body>
        <ol>
            <li>Ordered lists display items with numbers.</li>
            <li>But HTML doesn't sort the items.</li>
            <li>It only numbers them.</li>
            <li>You have to do the arranging yourself.</li>
        </ol>
    </body>
</html>
```

After you save your page, display it in your browser. You should see a numbered list like this:

When you display this in a browser, you will notice that the list is numbered in sequence. The actual format depends on the browser you use, but normally it is a simple list with Arabic numerals. One important difference with numbered lists is that if you nest the lists to create multiple levels, the browser uses the same numbering system throughout; it does not automatically change to a different style with each level. You must use the type attribute or Cascading Style Sheets to specify any changes you want.

Use the type Attribute to Specify Numbers or Letters (Deprecated)

Just as you can instruct the browser to use different types of bullets in an unordered list, you can tell the browser what types of letters or numbers to use. This is very useful if you want to produce an outline in HTML, as you have a nice range of choices available. You specify numbers or letters with the *type* attribute, just as you did for unordered lists.

- **<ol type="I">**   Capitalized Roman numerals
- **<ol type="i">**   Lowercase Roman numerals
- **<ol type="1">**   Numbers (default)
- **<ol type="A">**   Capital letters
- **<ol type="a">**   Lowercase letters

As with unordered lists, if you place the type attribute inside the <ol> tag, you can specify your preferences for the entire list. If you place the attribute inside a <li> tag, it will change only that particular list item.

Use the *start* Attribute to Choose a Starting Number (Deprecated)

What if you want to begin a list at a point other than 1 or A? All you need to do is include the *start* attribute at the point where you want to change the number or letter. The browser will start the list at the number you choose and continue numbering from that point. For example, if you want to start a list at the number 23, you might do it this way:

```
<ol type="1" start="23">
```

Create a new HTML document and save it as *olist2.htm*. Now, try typing the following code and displaying it in your browser to see what a list like this might look like if you did it with Roman numerals, starting at number 10:

```
<html>
    <head>
        <title>Ordered Lists</title>
    </head>
    <body>
        <ol type="I" start="10">
            <li>Item ten</li>
```

```
            <li>Item eleven</li>
            <li>Item twelve</li>
            <li>Item thirteen</li>
        </ol>
    </body>
</html>
```

When you display this in your browser, the list will begin with the Roman numeral "X," as in the following:

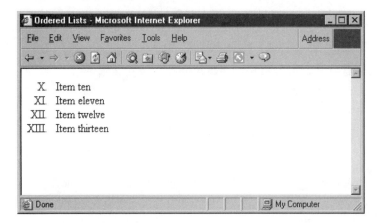

 Beware of a little quirk with the start attribute. It makes no difference whether you are using numbers, letters, or Roman numerals in your list. To specify a starting point, you always do it with Arabic numbers (1, 2, 3), not the characters that will display in the outline. If you modify the preceding code to use the Roman numeral for 10, start="X", you'll find the browser ignores the instruction entirely.

Project 3: Create an Outline with <ol>

To present material in outline format in HTML takes a bit more thought and planning than it does with an average word processor, but it will produce satisfying results. The following sample HTML code will produce a 2-point Roman numeral outline with lettered subpoints. Save it as *olist3.htm*:

```
<html>
    <head>
        <title>A Sample Outline</title>
    </head>
    <body>
        <ol type="I">
            <li>Major point
```

```
        <ol type="A">
            <li>Sub point</li>
            <li>Sub point</li>
        </ol>
    </li>
    <li>Major point
        <ol type="A">
            <li>Sub point</li>
            <li>Sub point</li>
        </ol>
    </li>
  </ol>
 </body>
</html>
```

The following illustration shows how an outline would look on your Web browser:

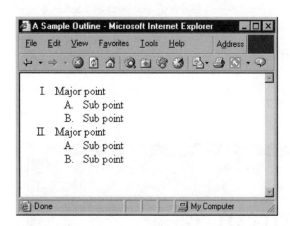

TIP   *Make sure you have properly nested your tags. Your subpoint list should be placed in between the list item tag it relates to. If you overlap them or leave out a closing </ol> tag, your outline will not display the way you want it to.*

Create Definition Lists with <dl>, <dt>, and <dd>

Perhaps the most versatile type of list is the definition list. Originally developed as a means of creating glossaries in a document, this type of list lends itself most readily for use on Web sites. You will use a different set of elements to create this type of list:

- **<dl> </dl>**   The *definition list* element creates the list.
- **<dt> </dt>**   The *definition term* element identifies the term to be defined.
- **<dd> </dd>**   The *definition description* element sets off the definition.

To see how a definition list works, try typing in the following code and displaying it in your browser. Save the file as *dlist.htm.* Notice that the code also includes some of the text formatting elements covered earlier in this chapter:

```
<html>
    <head>
        <title>Definition Lists</title>
    </head>
    <body>
        <h1>HTML Terms</h1>
            <dl>
                <dt>HTML</dt>
                <dd>HyperText Markup Language</dd>
                <dt>Element</dt>
                <dd>Describes document content.</dd>
                <dt>Attribute</dt>
                <dd>Identifies a characteristic of an element</dd>
                <dt>Value</dt>
                <dd> Gives details of a specific attribute</dd>
            </dl>
    </body>
</html>
```

Displayed in a browser, a definition list will look similar to the one in the following illustration:

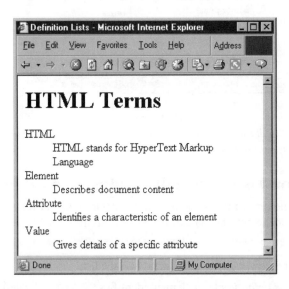

As you can see, this type of list can be very useful; you could use it to provide a page of links, with a special paragraph explaining each link. It also might be used to create a directory (often called a *site map*) of your Web site. The possible uses of the definition list are limited only by your imagination.

Insert Special Characters on Your Page

Have you ever seen the copyright notice at the bottom of a Web page and wondered where they found the © symbol? After all, it's not on the keyboard. How did they get it onto the page? Let's say you're doing a mathematical formula and you want to place a < or > sign on your page. If you just type in the characters, the Web browser will interpret them as HTML markup. Not only will the characters not appear, they very likely will cause your page to display incorrectly. The same holds true with marks like the ampersand (&) and quotation marks. If you have JavaScript or another scripting language on your page, browsers can misinterpret these characters, too. So how do you instruct a Web browser to display special characters rather than ignoring them or treating them as code? Perhaps you want to include a word from a foreign language and you need a special symbol or accent. What do you do? The way around this and similar problems is through the use of *entities*.

Understand Entities

Simply put, an *entity* is a character that either is not accessible through your keyboard or one that will be incorrectly interpreted by the browser. However, these characters are resident in your computer's system, and you can access them through the use of special codes.

The source for entity codes is the ISO-Latin1 character set. ISO stands for the *International Standards Organization*. The rest of the term denotes that this character set is derived from the Latin (or Roman) alphabet. Of course, there are many other character sets, derived from different alphabets. But the one you are most likely to use is ISO Latin-1; this also is the default character set for the Web.

NOTE
Entities described by numbers are called numeric entities. Entities described by descriptive terms are called character entities. Many special characters are represented by both types. For example, the copyright symbol © can be written either as a numeric entity, ©, or as a character entity, ©. Whichever you use, a Web browser will recognize it as the entity for the copyright symbol and display the symbol in its place.

An entity must be constructed properly for the browser to recognize it. It always begins with an ampersand (&) and closes with a semicolon (;). In between, you insert either a numeric code or a logical descriptive term. In addition, numeric entities must have the number symbol (#) preceding the entity number. Also, entities are case sensitive; always type them in exactly as you see them on a reference chart. Incidentally, some older browsers might not recognize particular character entities. It's always a good idea to test your page in different browsers to be sure of its compatibility.

 *For an extensive chart of numeric and character entities, download Appendix C from the author's Web site at www.jamespence.com.*

Insert an Entity in a Web Page

A practical way to experiment with entities is by adding a copyright notice to your Web page. To use the entity for the copyright © symbol, follow these steps:

1. Open template.htm and save it as *entity.htm*.

2. In the <body> section of the document, type **Copyright 2015**.

3. After the word *Copyright*, type the ampersand character, **&**.

4. Enter either the numeric or character code. For example, for the copyright symbol you would type **copy** or **#169**.

5. Close out the code by typing a semicolon. Your text should look like this:

```
Copyright &copy; 2015 or Copyright &#169; 2015
```

However, on a Web browser it will display this way: Copyright © 2015. Try it out on a sample page. Remember to put the entities in the actual text of your Web page, not in the tags. It would be incorrect to write <h6 ©>Copyright 2015</h6>. If you do put the entity in the wrong place, the browser will just ignore it. Type in the following code for a demonstration of how entities work and for a sample of what shows up when they are entered correctly:

```
<html>
    <head>
        <title>Sample Entity Display</title>
    </head>
    <body>
        Copyright &copy; 2015
        My Trademark &#174; is a registered trademark.
    </body>
</html>
```

When you save and display this page, you'll notice, as in the illustration that follows, that the code for your entity is replaced by the special character that it represents:

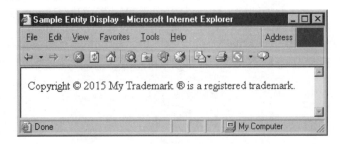

Quick Reference: Text, Lists, and Entities

In this chapter you have learned how to use headings, text elements, lists, and entities. More important, you have mastered the concept of nesting and have learned how to use elements, attributes, and values in a Web page. As you practice these techniques, use the following reference charts to help you remember what you have learned.

Work with Text

The elements which allow you to work with text are straightforward and easy to use. To cause text to display using the elements listed in the table below, simply enclose it between the proper set of tags. For example, to emphasize text, place it inside the <em> element like this: <em>Emphasized Text</em>.

To Do This	Use This
Indicate a heading	<h#> </h#> (may use #1–6)
Emphasize text	<em> </em>
Strongly emphasize text	<strong> </strong>
Identify text as keyboard input	<kbd> </kbd>
Identify text as a citation	<cite> </cite>
Identify text as a variable (as in a computer program)	<var> </var>
Identify text as a defining instance (of a term)	<dfn> </dfn>
Identify text as sample output	<samp> </samp>
Identify text as an acronym	<acronym> </acronym>
Identify text as an abbreviated term	<abbr> </abbr>
Set apart a portion of text that contains author information	<address> </address>
Identify text as computer code	<code> </code>
Create a superscript	
Create a subscript	
Preserve your spacing and formatting	<pre> </pre>
Indicate inserted text	<ins> </ins>
Indicate deleted text	<del> </del>

Create Lists

Lists are easy to create and provide a useful tool for menus, site directories, lists of links, and outlines. There are three different types of lists to choose from: ordered (numbered), unordered (bulleted), and definition (glossary). The trick to doing lists well is remembering to nest your elements properly. The elements necessary for creating lists are included in the following table:

To Do This	Use This
Create an ordered (numbered) list	`<ol> </ol>`
Create an unordered (bulleted) list	`<ul> </ul>`
Create a definition list	`<dl> </dl>`
Add a list item	`<li> </li>`
Add a definition term (definition list only)	`<dt> </dt>`
Add a definition description (definition list only)	`<dd> </dd>`
Specify a starting number (ordered list only)	`start="#"` (Deprecated)
Specify a bullet type (unordered list only)	`type="disc	circle	square"` (Deprecated)
Specify a number type (ordered list only)	`type="a	A	i	I	#"` (Deprecated)
Set the value for a particular list item	`value="#"` (Use Arabic numerals only, no matter what type of numbering is used in the list.) (Deprecated)

Insert Entities

In the following table are some entities that you might be likely to use. Notice that some have both numeric and character versions, while others only are represented by numeric codes. This list is not complete, but includes some of the most common characters. Download Appendix C for a more extensive list (www.jamespence.com).

To Display This	Use This Numeric Entity	Use This Character Entity	This Character Will Display
Exclamation	&#33;		!
Quotation	&#34;	&quot;	"
Number	&#35;		#
Dollar	&#36;		$
Percent	&#37;		%
Ampersand	&#38;	&amp;	&
Apostrophe	&#39;		'
Asterisk	&#42;		*
Plus sign	&#43;		+
Comma	&#44;		,
Hyphen	&#45;		-
Period	&#46;		.
Slash	&#47;		/
Colon	&#58;		:
Semicolon	&#59;		;

To Display This	Use This Numeric Entity	Use This Character Entity	This Character Will Display
Less than	&#60;	&lt;	<
Equal sign	&#61;		=
Greater than	&#62;	&gt;	>
Question	&#63;		?
"At" sign	&#64;		@
Left bracket	&#91;		[
Backslash	&#92;		\
Right bracket	&#93;		]
Left curly brace	&#123;		{
Right curly brace	&#125;		}
Tilde	&#126;		~
Copyright	&#169;	&copy;	©
Trademark	&#174;	&reg;	®

2

Chapter 3

Modify Text with Text Elements and CSS

How to...

- Create Line and Paragraph Breaks
- Indent Text
- Position and Align Text
- Choose Fonts
- Control Font Sizes and Colors

Thus far, you have used HTML to create a Web page and add basic text and list elements. You've also probably noticed that your results aren't very exciting. In fact, drab might be the description that comes to mind. Very likely you'd prefer that your text look fancier, with a variety of fonts, sizes, and colors. In this chapter you will learn how to control text flow with a few additional text elements. You will also learn how to use Cascading Style Sheets to indent text, specify different fonts, and control font size, position, and color. You also will be introduced to XHTML and to one of the most important issues in Web design—content versus presentation. However, before you begin to work with style, you'll find it helpful to experiment with a few more basic page elements.

Control Text Flow with Text Elements

If you pasted a text file into your sample Web page in Chapter 2, you noticed instantly that text loses even the simplest formatting when brought into an HTML document: indents; paragraph breaks, and line spacing all are gone. However, HTML provides several elements for creating paragraphs and identifying breaks in your text.

Create Line Breaks with <br /> and Paragraphs with <p>

The *line break*
 and *paragraph* <p> elements are structural in nature and help you control how your text will be divided on the page. The difference between the line break and the paragraph elements is that when you use <br /> you're telling a browser to simply insert a line break and go to the next line, like this:

```
To insert a line break, use the line break element.<br />
```

On the other hand, the <p> element will drop down an extra line before it starts your new paragraph, as in the following:

```
<p>Use the paragraph element to identify paragraphs.</p>
```

What Is the Difference Between Block Level and Inline Elements?

Elements that start a separate division of the page, such as the <p> and <h#> elements, are *block level elements*. Elements that do not create separate divisions on the page, for example: <em> and <strong>, are *inline elements*.

Insert Ruler Lines with <hr />

Have you ever noticed how some Web pages are divided into sections by horizontal lines? You can create these with the *horizontal rule* element, <hr />. This element will draw a horizontal line all the way across the page. Notice also that this is an empty element. Because it has no content, it doesn't require a closing tag. For example, if you want to put a dividing line beneath the preceding example, you would write it this way:

```
<p>Use the paragraph element to identify paragraphs.</p>
<hr />
```

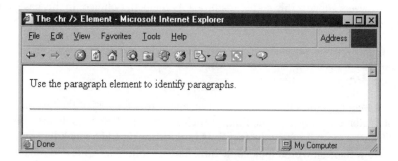

Identify Quotations with <q> and <blockquote>

Some other text elements are designed to identify short and long quotations. If you want to identify a short "inline" quotation, you could use the <q> element, as in the following line of markup:

```
<p>Use the paragraph element to identify paragraphs.<br />
Author James H. Pence says, <q>This is a very important
element.</q> </p>
```

A problem with the <q> element is that Internet Explorer does not support it. If you type the preceding line into an HTML document and view it in Internet Explorer 6 (IE), you'll discover that the <q> element does not change the appearance of the quotation at all. However, if you view it in Netscape 7 or Opera 7, this element adds a set of quotation marks to the line, as in the following illustration:

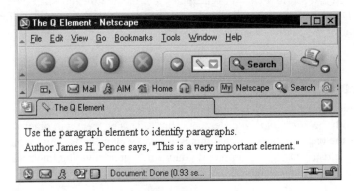

Thus, the <q> element is not your best choice when identifying a short quotation on your page.

The other way to insert quotation marks around an inline quote is by using the " entity. Since all three browsers support this entity, it's probably the better choice. In this case your HTML would look like the markup that follows:

```
<p>Use the paragraph element to identify paragraphs.<br />
Author James H. Pence says, &quot;This is a very important
element.&quot;</p>
```

If you have a long quotation that you want to set apart from the rest of the text on your page, the <blockquote> element will help you. Simply enclose your quotation inside the <blockquote> tags and the Web browser will indent the text from both sides and add a blank line before and after the quote. Your markup would look something like the following code and illustration:

```
<p>This sentence represents the main text of a Web page.<br />
    <blockquote>These sentences are an extended <br />
quotation. These sentences are an extended <br />
quotation. These sentences are an extended <br />
quotation. These sentences are an extended quotation.
    </blockquote>
The main body of text continues with this sentence.</p>
```

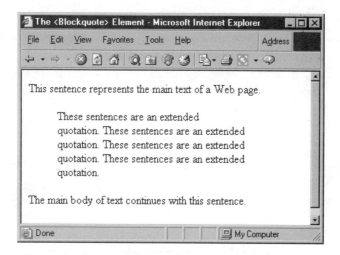

Project 4: Use Text Elements to Format Content

Before you move on to using CSS, it will be helpful for you to apply some of the elements you have learned in this section. In this project you'll be using the <h#>, <br />, <p>, <hr />and <blockquote> elements to give structure to an unformatted body of text. When you have finished, your Web page should look something like Figure 3-1.

For this project, you'll need a fairly large block of unformatted text. If you have a word processing program such as Microsoft Word or WordPerfect, just open up any of your files, then click on File, Save As, and choose *text* or *.txt*. The program will save your file as plain text, without any formatting codes.

TIP   *If you don't have access to a file you can convert to plain text, you can download lorem.txt (a plain text, gibberish file) from the author's Web site at www.jamespence.com.*

Once you have your text file ready, perform the following steps:

1. Open your text file in Notepad and save it as *text-format.htm*. Don't forget to select the "All Files" option in the Save As dialog box.

2. Add the <html> tag at the beginning of the document, and the </html> at the end.

3. Inside the first <html> tag, add the <head> and <title> elements. Don't forget to nest the <title> element inside the <head> element.

4. Add a title to your page: <title>**Text Formatting**</title>

5. Create a heading by enclosing the first sentence of your text inside the <h1> element.

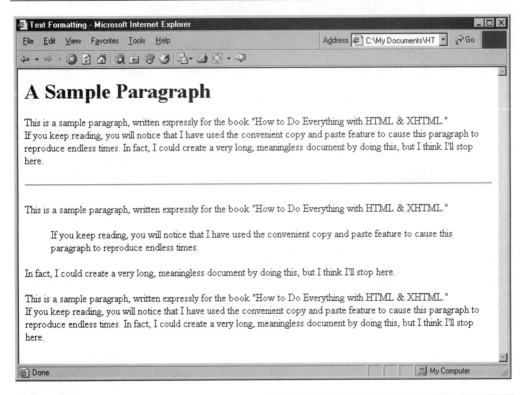

FIGURE 3-1 Text structured by means of text elements

6. Divide your text into three paragraphs using the <p> element. Each paragraph should be enclosed inside one set of <p> </p> tags.

7. Add a dividing line by inserting the <hr /> element between the first and second paragraphs.

8. Try adding a few line breaks by placing the <br /> element wherever you want a line to break.

9. Set off a sentence from your center paragraph by enclosing it in between the <blockquote> tags.

10. Save your page and load it in your Web browser. Your results should be similar to Figure 3-1.

If you are having problems with this project and want to look at the HTML for Figure 3-1, you'll find it at the end of this chapter.

Understand Content Versus Presentation

Now that you have practiced working with text elements, you are ready to add style. You might be wondering how to do that, particularly since the W3C discourages the use of elements and attributes related to presentation. For example, the <font> element, used widely to control font color and size, is one of many elements and attributes that have been officially deprecated by the W3C. Because the word "deprecate" literally means to express disapproval for something, you might wonder why the W3C is expressing disapproval for its own HTML elements. To understand the answer to this question, you must learn a bit of HTML history.

HTML Originally Defined Structure

When Tim Berners-Lee developed HTML in 1989, the Internet was a very different place. It was used mostly by the government and universities and existed primarily for the exchange of scientific or scholarly information. The material transmitted was documentary and looked more like term papers than Web pages. In other words, when HTML was created the main concern was document content. HTML served to identify the different parts of a page's content. For example, the <h1> through <h6> elements defined heading levels one through six. The paragraph element defined a paragraph, the list element a list, and so on. Thus, in early HTML documents structure was everything; however, the arrival of the World Wide Web and graphical Web browsers changed all that.

HTML Extended to Address Presentation Issues

When the Web came on the scene, the academic world of HTML became a world of color, pictures, and design almost overnight. Prior to this, a document's layout was virtually a nonissue. But advances in graphics moved presentation to the front. This created a problem. Because HTML was never intended to deal with design issues, Web page authors found themselves struggling with questions of how to create pleasing designs while maintaining some control over how their documents appeared when viewed online. Because HTML didn't provide the tools they needed, they developed "workarounds," applying HTML markup in ways its authors never intended. Eventually, browser companies Microsoft and Netscape extended HTML to include "proprietary" elements, supported only by their browsers. Some of these, such as frames and tables, were later incorporated into the official HTML recommendation. Thus, over time HTML was nudged away from its original purpose and into the design arena. Unfortunately, HTML's inherent limitations make it a very inadequate design tool. That's where Cascading Style Sheets enter the picture.

Use Cascading Style Sheets for Layout and Design

The W3C has been working for some time to solve the problems created by HTML's limitations. One key step was introducing *Cascading Style Sheets (CSS)*. CSS provide a means of controlling a page's design apart from HTML markup. This enables the Web page author to separate content (HTML) from presentation (CSS). The W3C's wish is that you use HTML as it was intended, to

Why Are Certain Elements Deprecated?

If an element or attribute is deprecated, the World Wide Web Consortium (W3C) discourages its use because there is a preferred alternative, generally CSS. Even so, most browsers still support the deprecated elements and attributes, and probably will do so for many years to come.

define your document's structure; and use CSS to specify its presentation. For that reason, the W3C is phasing out (deprecating) many of the elements that were developed as extensions to HTML. So, what can you do with CSS? A lot!

Cascading Style Sheets are easy to learn. However, some have pointed out that they are difficult to master—just as is anything related to design. A good place to start with CSS is by learning to use *inline styles*. In Chapter 10 you'll learn some better ways to apply styles, but the following examples will enable you to gain some basic experience with CSS and hopefully overcome any intimidation factor.

Add Inline Styles with the style Attribute

Cascading Style Sheets is somewhat of a misnomer for what you are using here. The term "style sheet" implies something separate from the page, and you will learn later why the term "cascading" is used. What you will work with here is called an *inline style*. It works about the same way as what you have learned already with HTML. In Chapter 1 you learned the three most important terms in HTML: elements, attributes, and values. An attribute goes inside an element and describes what you want to modify. A value is attached to the attribute and gives the details of how you are going to modify the element. Thus, to apply an inline style to any element, you simply use the *style* attribute to modify that element's style.

For example, suppose you want to set the text color of a particular paragraph to red instead of black. All you need to do is make a slight addition to the opening paragraph tag, like this:

```
<p style="color: red">
```

Try this in any of the pages you have created thus far. It will work with virtually any element. For example, if you put this attribute inside the <body> element, it will set the font color to red throughout the entire document. However, if you just put it in one paragraph element, only that paragraph will be affected.

In the preceding example, you used the style attribute in combination with the color *property*. You also added a value (red) to the property. Property is a term you will become very familiar with as you learn to work with CSS. It tells a browser what specific characteristic of an element you are modifying. For example, some properties you might use to adjust a font are *font-family*, *font-size*, *text-indent*, *font-style*, *color*, and so forth. Later, you will see that you have a much larger selection of properties to work with in CSS, and you can do many more things with them.

How to ... **Remember Key CSS Terms**

One reason that newcomers to HTML find CSS confusing is that they introduce a whole new array of terms to learn. After all, you've spent a fair amount of time learning the meaning of elements, attributes, and values. Now you encounter terms like *selectors, properties,* and *values*. Don't let the new terms confuse you. Just remember that a selector is like an element. In fact, a selector is used to "select" an element for styling. Likewise, a property is like an attribute; it describes what characteristic of a selector is going to be modified. Finally, value corresponds to value. A value describes the style that will be applied in the page. Returning to our hair color analogy from Chapter 1, if you were going to use CSS to apply a hair color style you would do it this way:

```
hair {color: red}
```

If you are applying the style *inline*, as in this chapter, you would write it like this:

```
<hair style="color: red">
```

For more on Cascading Style Sheets, refer to Chapter 10.

Using inline styles is similar to using any other attribute inside an element. However, there are a few important differences in syntax that you need to remember:

- Property-value combinations must be enclosed in the quotation marks that follow the style attribute:

  ```
  <p style="All properties and values go between the quotes.">
  ```

- Properties and values must be separated by a colon:

  ```
  <p style="property: value">
  ```

- Multiple property-value combinations must be separated by semicolons:

  ```
  <p style="property: value; property: value; property: value">
  ```

CAUTION *In CSS you must put a hyphen (-) between related words. For example, if you use a font that has more than one word in its name, you must hyphenate it. Times New Roman should be Times-New-Roman. If you leave out the hyphens, browsers will not recognize the font name. The same holds true with property names that have more than one word, such as font-size.*

Control Fonts with CSS

Formerly, you would have used the <font> element to adjust the color, size, style, and position of your text. However, with CSS you have a much greater degree of flexibility. For example, the <font> element only allowed you to use seven different font sizes. With CSS, you can not only specify virtually any font size you want, but you can choose from quite a few different measurements, such as points, picas, percentages, ems, and more. Consider the following font controls you have with style sheets.

Adjust Font Size with the font-size Property

You can set the size of your fonts by using the *font-size* property. Insert the style attribute into the opening <p> tag and add the font-size property, along with a description of the size you want to display. For example, to instruct the browser to display text with a 36 point font, you would write your opening tag like this:

```
<p style="font-size: 36pt">This is 36pt text.</p>
```

As the following illustration shows, your text will display in the size you have specified.

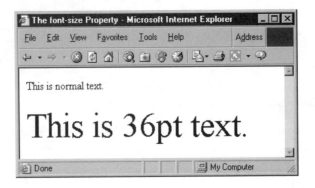

 *To set the font size for an entire page, insert the style attribute into the opening <body> tag.*

Select Fonts with the font-family Property

To select different fonts for your page, use the *font-family* property along with the name of the font you wish to display on the page, as in the following code:

```
<p style="font-family: Times-New-Roman">Times font</p>
```

You can specify any font you wish, but if you choose an exotic or unusual font, keep in mind that not all visitors to your Web site will have that particular font installed on their computers. If that happens, the browser will choose a substitute font—and you may not be pleased with the results. An alternative is to use one of the five *generic* fonts that are specified for CSS. These are *serif* (as in Times New Roman), *sans-serif* (as in Arial), *monospace* (as in Courier), *cursive,* and *fantasy.* You can use these generic fonts by themselves, and the browser will display the font closest in appearance to the generic. You can also use generic fonts in combination with specific fonts. To do this, you simply list your font choices in order of preference, separated by commas, as in the following code listing:

```
<p style="font-family: Arial, sans-serif">Arial font</p>
```

If you list multiple font choices this way, the browser will try to load the first choice. Then, if it doesn't find that font it will move on to the next, and so on. However, if you choose the cursive or fantasy generics, beware. The results vary widely between browsers and computer systems. Try creating an html page and typing in the following code. Save it as *generic-fonts.htm* and then display it on your browser and see how it compares to the illustration that follows:

```
<html>
    <head>
        <title>The Generic Fonts</title>
    </head>
    <body style="font-size: 16pt">
        <p style="font-family: serif">Serif.</p>
        <p style="font-family: sans-serif">Sans-serif.</p>
        <p style="font-family: monospace">Monospace.</p>
        <p style="font-family: cursive">Cursive.</p>
        <p style="font-family: fantasy">Fantasy.</p>
    </body>
</html>
```

NOTE *The text in this example and those that follow has been set to display at 16 points.*

Create Italics with the font-style Property

How do you cause text to display in italics? In the past you would have used the presentational element <i> </i>. With CSS, you do it by using the *font-style* property. By adding this property to a text element, as in the following code and illustration, you will generate italicized text:

```
<p>Normal text</p>
<p style="font-style: italic">Italicized Text</p>
```

Specify Font Colors with the color Property

Earlier in this chapter you saw how to use the color property to specify font colors with the color property. There are many different ways to specify color, and these will be covered in Chapter 4. However, you may wish to experiment with color by using the 16 Windows colors. Browsers recognize these colors by the following names: black, silver, gray, white, maroon, red, purple, fuchsia, green, lime, olive, yellow, navy, blue, teal, and aqua. Try typing the following code, then saving it as *font-colors.htm* and displaying it in your browser to see a sampling of these basic colors, and to get some practice working with the color property as well.

TIP *On the last color (white), you will also need to use the* background-color *property, set to black or another dark color. Otherwise, your white text will disappear against the page's white background. To learn more about the background-color property, check out Chapter 4.*

```
<html>
    <head>
        <title>The color Property</title>
    </head>
    <body style="font-size: 16pt">
        <p>Black</p>
        <p style="color: silver">Silver</p>
        <p style="color: gray">Gray</p>
        <p style="color: maroon">Maroon</p>
```

```
        <p style="color: red">Red</p>
        <p style="color: purple">Purple</p>
        <p style="color: fuchsia">Fuchsia</p>
        <p style="color: green">Green</p>
        <p style="color: lime">Lime</p>
        <p style="color: olive">Olive</p>
        <p style="color: yellow">Yellow</p>
        <p style="color: navy">Navy</p>
        <p style="color: blue">Blue</p>
        <p style="color: teal">Teal</p>
        <p style="color: aqua">Aqua</p>
        <p style="color: white;
            background-color: black">White</p>
    </body>
</html>
```

Create Bold Text with the font-weight Property

One other property you might want to learn early on is the *font-weight* property. This property enables you to create boldface text with CSS, instead of with the deprecated bold <b> element. In fact, as you'll learn in Chapter 10, this property can actually give you more control than simply toggling boldness on and off. On a system that has fonts capable of supporting it fully, the font-weight property enables you to control the degree of boldness. However, to keep things simple, just experiment by using this property to turn boldness on, as in the following code and illustration:

```
<html>
    <head>
        <title>The font-weight Property</title>
    </head>
    <body style="font-size: 16pt">
        <p>This is normal text.</p>
        <p style="font-weight: bold">This is bold text.</p>
    </body>
</html>
```

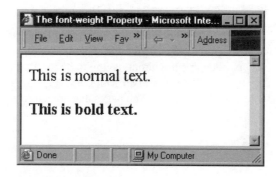

Project 5: Add Style to a Page

To demonstrate the versatility of CSS, take the document you created in Project 4 and use CSS to add style. To simplify the design, remove the <br /> and <blockquote> tags from the page before you add the style information. That way, you'll be working with three identical paragraphs.

1. Insert the *style* attribute within the opening <h1> tag and each opening <p> tag. This tells the browser that you are using an inline style:

   ```
   <p style=" ">
   ```

2. Now, change the color of your heading to red by using the color property:

   ```
   <h1 style="color: red">
   ```

3. Make your heading display in italics by adding the font-style property:

   ```
   <h1 style="color: red; font-style: italic">
   ```

4. Set the font in each of the paragraphs with the font-family property:

   ```
   <p style="font-family: ">
   ```

5. Now specify the font style you want to display:

   ```
   <p style="font-family: arial">
   ```

6. Tell the browser to display a 12pt font. Be sure to separate the new property-value combination from the first one by a semicolon:

   ```
   <p style="font-family: arial; font-size: 12pt;">
   ```

7. Now set the font-weight to bold:

   ```
   <p style="font-family: arial; font-size: 12pt; font-weight: bold; ">
   ```

8. Set the font color to navy:

   ```
   <p style="font-family: arial; font-size: 12pt; font-weight: bold; color:
   navy;">
   ```

9. Save your newly-styled page and display it in your browser. It should look something like Figure 3-2. Quite a difference!

You may have noticed that this process becomes quite tedious, particularly if you are adding a lot of different styles. Take heart. In Chapter 10 you will learn how to create style sheets that will control styles throughout your document without having to be inserted in each individual element. This was only a sampling of what you can do with CSS. As you work your way through this book, you will learn how to use CSS to create Web pages that are attractive and of high quality.

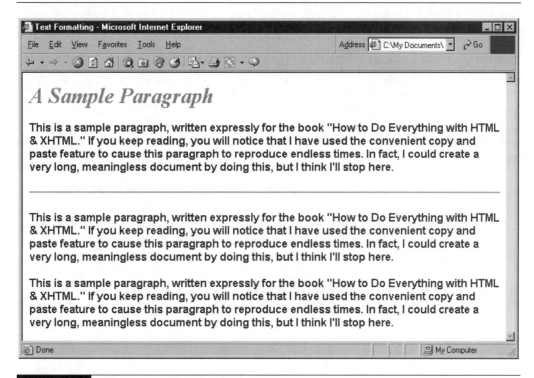

FIGURE 3-2 Text page with style added

Indent Text with CSS

When you want to indent text in a word processor, you just press the TAB key or SPACE bar. In HTML, it's not that simple. For example, if you try to indent text in a paragraph by merely adding spaces after the opening <p> tag, you'll find that those spaces disappear when the page displays. That's because Web browsers are designed to ignore extra *white space*. However, CSS provide a simple solution with the *text-indent* property. To add an indent to a paragraph, you would add the following inline style to its opening tag, as in the following:

```
<p style="text-indent: 5%">
```

If you add this style instruction to one of the paragraphs that you have already created, you'll discover that it indents the text a distance that is equal to 5% of the size of the browser window. In Chapter 10 you'll learn other ways to specify measurements, but percentages are handy because they automatically adjust up or down with the size of the window. You may be wondering how Web authors added indents or extra spaces before style sheets came along. The examples that follow are examples of "workarounds," that is, solving design problems by using HTML markup in ways other than it was intended for. Thus, these workarounds are discouraged.

The   Entity Creates Indents (Discouraged)

The *nonbreaking space* entity   will instruct a browser to add spaces wherever you want them. However, most commonly it is used to create an indent at the beginning of a paragraph. To use it, you type the characters ** ** where you want the spaces inserted. If you want to have a five-space indent at the beginning of a paragraph, type five nonbreaking space entities at the beginning of the line you want to indent. (For more on entities and how to use them, see Chapter 2.)

The Definition Description Element <dd> Indents Text (Discouraged)

Another way to indent is to borrow from the list elements covered in Chapter 2. You'll remember that the dictionary list included a dictionary term <dt></dt> element and a dictionary definition element <dd></dd>. The definition description element automatically indents. So, by enclosing the top line of your text in this element, you can force an indent without typing all those entities.

The <blockquote> Element Indents a Large Block (Discouraged)

If you want to increase the left margin, the old way of doing it was with the <blockquote> element. By nesting one blockquote inside another, as in the following code, it is possible to move the left margin in a considerable distance:

```
<blockquote><blockquote>Big margin</blockquote></blockquote>
```

Although this may seem an easy way to move in the left margin, you will find the *margin-left* and *margin-right* properties give you greater control than you have with <blockquote>. Try increasing the margins of the paragraphs in Project 5 by adding the following style instruction:

```
<p style="margin-left: 5%; margin-right: 5%">
```

With these properties, you can control both margins, something not possible with <blockquote>.

Position and Align Text with CSS

What do you do if you want to center your text or right-justify a block of text? By using the *text-align* property, you can position your text easily. Simply add the style attribute in the element which you wish to align, like this:

```
<p style="text-align: center">This center-aligns text.</p>
<p style="text-align: right">This right-aligns text.</p>
<p style="text-align: justify">This justifies text.</p>
<p style="text-align: left">This left-aligns text.</p>
```

Because left alignment is the default (automatic) setting, you don't normally need to use the text-align: left setting very often. Usually, you would use this when you need to override another alignment setting. In the days before CSS, the align attribute and <center> element accomplished these tasks.

The align Attribute Positions Elements (Deprecated)

The align attribute positions text (or images) at the left, center, or right of a page. For example, to center-align a single paragraph, add the align attribute to the <p> tag at the beginning of the paragraph. The tag will look like this:

```
<p align="center">Center-aligned Text</p>
```

The <center> Element Centers Objects and Text (Deprecated)

By enclosing content (text or images) inside the <center> element, you can center-align large blocks of material, even an entire page if you want to. This element is another example of presentation-related markup that the W3C is phasing out.

```
<center>This content is centered.</center>
```

By now you may be wondering what the W3C hopes to accomplish by deprecating these elements. To understand the answer to that question, you must spend a little time investigating the language that is the future of the Web: XML.

Understand XML and XHTML

As you have seen thus far, Cascading Style Sheets go a long way toward addressing the problems caused by HTML's limitations. However, some problems remain that CSS cannot deal with. The explosive growth and development of the World Wide Web has stretched HTML far beyond its capacity. After all, HTML was not created with the intent of enabling designers to craft attractive Web pages, nor was it developed to address the many new technologies that are coming on the scene. People can now access the Internet in many ways other than through Web browsers and telephone lines. Now, you can use a PDA or even access the Internet through your cell phone. This has created a need for a language that is more flexible than HTML, a language that can be extended and developed as technology changes. That language is XML, the Extensible Markup Language.

XML Is Extensible

HTML is a "fixed" language. That is, you can't modify it to suit your own purposes or needs. HTML has a set structure that you must follow if you want your pages to work. With HTML you have a certain collection of elements and attributes with which to work, and you cannot customize it by adding your own elements. XML, on the other hand, is an *extensible* language. With XML, you can create your own elements, tags, attributes, and values. That's where the term "extensible" comes in. You *extend* XML by creating other markup languages with it.

XML Is a "Meta" Language

XML is not just another markup language; it's a *meta language*. In programming terminology, the word "meta" refers to description. Well, a meta language is a language that can describe other languages. For example, SGML (Standard Generalized Markup Language) is the meta language that was used to create HTML. If you go to the W3C's site and read the current specification for HTML, you can actually read the SGML code (known as a Document Type Description or DTD) that was used to define and describe HTML. XML is also a "child" language of SGML, but it has one important distinction from its sibling, HTML. XML is *extensible*. In other words, it was designed to enable its users to create their own customized markup languages. Does that mean you will have to use XML to create your own markup languages for your Web pages in the future? No, that's where XHTML comes in.

XHTML: The Bridge between HTML and XML

The current recommendation (standard) of the W3C for Web pages is no longer HTML, but XHTML, the Extensible Hypertext Markup Language. XHTML is simply HTML rewritten in XML. You still use the familiar HTML elements, attributes, and values, but in reality you are working with a much more flexible and powerful language: XML. Thus, with XHTML you have a combination of HTML's familiarity and ease of use with XML's flexibility.

So, how do you write XHTML pages? For the most part, you have been learning how to do it throughout these three chapters. However, in case you're still fuzzy on the subject, keep the following principles in mind. There are some more advanced rules for writing XHTML pages, which we'll cover later, but for the present these are all you need:

- **Always include closing tags.** No exceptions. If an element takes an opening tag and a closing tag, always use both. Gone are the good old days of HTML when you could just put a <p> tag at the beginning of every new paragraph and ignore the </p>.

- **Empty elements must always have a closing slash.** If you use an *empty element* (an element that does not enclose content), always make sure that you include a space and a closing slash in the tag, like this: <img />.

- **Always include a value with an attribute.** There were some instances in HTML where it wasn't necessary to include a value with an attribute. Usually this was because the attribute was self-explanatory. For example, when creating a form in HTML, you could sometimes specify an option as preselected by adding the word "checked" inside the tag. Checked was an attribute, but it didn't require a value. Now, even in these cases you *must* include a value, as in: checked="checked". Yes, it's redundant, but that's the way it goes sometimes.

- **Enclose all attribute values in quotation marks.** In the past, you could get away with leaving the quotation marks out, but not anymore. When you enter a value in an attribute, put it in quotes, like this: attribute="value". No exceptions.

■ **Write your code in lowercase.**   You will often find HTML pages that are a mixture of upper and lowercase. Since HTML was not case sensitive, it didn't really matter. However, XHTML *is* case sensitive. By getting in the habit of writing all your code lowercase, you'll be a long way down the road toward compatibility with the new standard.

■ **Make sure your tags are all correctly nested.**   No overlapping tags, period. Sometimes HTML will let you get away with this. XHTML is not so forgiving. Double-check your markup to eliminate any overlapping elements.

If you make these practices part of your regular coding routine, you will have little or no trouble making the transition to the future of the Web, XHTML.

Check Your Markup

Earlier in this chapter, you had the opportunity to experiment with structure and presentation by creating a page with simple text elements, then modifying it with CSS. Hopefully you were able to complete the projects successfully; however, if you need a little help you'll find the code for the projects in the following paragraphs.

HTML for Project 4

The HTML markup that follows might not look exactly like what you came up with, and that's perfectly acceptable. It is included here to provide you with a reference to check on your own code-writing abilities. The following code was used to create Figure 3-1:

```
<html>
    <head>
        <title>Text Formatting</title>
    </head>
    <body>
        <h1>A Sample Paragraph</h1>
<p>This is a sample paragraph, written expressly
for the book &quot;How to Do Everything with
HTML &amp; XHTML.&quot; <br />
If you keep reading,
you will notice that I have used the convenient
copy and paste feature to cause this paragraph
to reproduce endless times. In fact, I could
create a very long, meaningless document by doing
this, but I think I'll stop here.</p>
<hr />
<p>This is a sample paragraph, written expressly
for the book &quot;How to Do Everything with
HTML &amp; XHTML.&quot;
```

```
<blockquote>If you keep reading,
you will notice that I have used the convenient
copy and paste feature to cause this paragraph
to reproduce endless times.</blockquote>In fact, I could
create a very long, meaningless document by doing
this, but I think I'll stop here.</p>
<p>This is a sample paragraph, written expressly
for the book &quot;How to Do Everything with
HTML &amp; XHTML.&quot; <br />
If you keep reading,
you will notice that I have used the convenient
copy and paste feature to cause this paragraph
to reproduce endless times. In fact, I could
create a very long, meaningless document by doing
this, but I think I'll stop here.</p>
    </body>
</html>
```

HTML for Project 5

The following code was used to create Figure 3-2. It is the same as what was written for Project 4, but has inline styles added. Check your code and compare it with this markup:

```
<html>
    <head>
        <title>Text Formatting</title>
    </head>
    <body>
        <h1 style="color: red; font-style: italic;">
            A Sample Paragraph</h1>
        <p style="font-family: arial; font-weight: bold;
            font-size: 12pt; color: navy">
This is a sample paragraph, written expressly
for the book &quot;How to Do Everything with
HTML &amp; XHTML.&quot; If you keep reading,
you will notice that I have used the convenient
copy and paste feature to cause this paragraph
to reproduce endless times. In fact, I could
create a very long, meaningless document by doing
this, but I think I'll stop here.</p>
<hr />
```

```
            <p style="font-family: arial; font-weight: bold;
                font-size: 12pt; color: navy;">
This is a sample paragraph, written expressly
for the book &quot;How to Do Everything with
HTML &amp; XHTML.&quot; If you keep reading,
you will notice that I have used the convenient
copy and paste feature to cause this paragraph
to reproduce endless times. In fact, I could
create a very long, meaningless document by doing
this, but I think I'll stop here.</p>
            <p style="font-family: arial; font-weight: bold;
                font-size: 12pt; color: navy;">
This is a sample paragraph, written expressly
for the book &quot;How to Do Everything with
HTML &amp; XHTML.&quot; If you keep reading,
you will notice that I have used the convenient
copy and paste feature to cause this paragraph
to reproduce endless times. In fact, I could
create a very long, meaningless document by doing
this, but I think I'll stop here.</p>
    </body>
</html>
```

Quick Reference: Paragraphs and Fonts

This chapter has focused on both text elements and font control with inline styles. The following reference chart will help you remember what you have learned. Why not try creating a new page and adding some styles to reinforce what you have learned thus far?

To Do This	Use This
Create a line break	` `
Create a paragraph	`<p> </p>`
Add a horizontal rule	`<hr />`
Identify a short quotation	`<q> </q>` (Not all browsers support this element)
Set off a long quotation	`<blockquote> </blockquote>`
Insert quotation marks	`&quot;`
Apply an inline style	`style="property: value"`
Set font size (inline style)	`style="font-size: value"`

To Do This	Use This
Set font color (inline style)	`style="color: value"`
Select font (inline style)	`style="font-family: value"`
Create italics (inline style)	`style="font-style: italic"`
Create bold text (inline style)	`style="font-weight: bold"`

Chapter 4

Introduce and Control Color

How to…

- Understand color theory
- Use the basic palette
- Mix your own colors
- Understand browser-safe colors
- Choose pleasing colors
- Create an HTML color chart

The Web is a world of color—more than 16 million colors, to be specific. All those choices can be a daunting prospect for a Web designer, making you either throw up your hands in confusion or throw caution to the wind and choose whatever colors seem good to you. This chapter covers the science and art of doing color on the Web. It is a science because you can select from those 16 million colors with mathematical precision. It is an art because a failure to use color wisely can result in a page that is difficult to read, hard on the eyes, or hopelessly gaudy. On the other hand, thoughtfully chosen color combinations can say to the people who visit your site, "This is a class operation."

Understand and Experiment with Color

You might not be an artist, but at some point in your life you've probably used paints, colored pencils, or crayons. When you sat down before a blank sheet of paper you had 10, maybe 12, colors before you. You experimented, mixed colors, and generally had a great time creating a picture that was uniquely your own. Can you imagine what it would have been like if, maybe in school, your teacher plopped down a box of crayons that had more than 16 *million* colors? That's what you have when you work with color in HTML. With that many choices, where do you start? Try starting with the 16 basic colors.

 The figure 16 million (16,777,216, to be exact) derives from the 256 possible "settings" for red, green, and blue—the three colors from which all others are created. If you multiply 256 by 256 by 256, you arrive at 16.7 million.

Experiment with the Basic Palette

You won't need to read many books on Web design before you'll come across the term *palette*. Artists use this term to refer to the colors they have to work with at any given time. Web designers have a number of different palettes available to them, and only a few need to be covered here. The easiest way to begin working with color on the Web is by using the 16-color basic palette. These colors require no special coding for a browser to recognize them; just type in the color's name and the browser does the rest.

The basic palette, sometimes called the HTML or Windows palette, is a range of 16 colors, generally based on the colors that Windows makes available as default colors. The top 16 are white, black, silver, gray, red, maroon, yellow, olive, lime, green, aqua, teal, blue, navy, fuchsia, and purple. Because it's more fun to actually do something with color rather than just read about it, try setting some (or all) of these colors as background colors on a blank Web page. An added benefit is that you can begin to experiment with Cascading Style Sheets as you change the colors on your page.

To specify these colors as a background for your page, use the following:

- The color's name
- The CSS *background-color* property
- The *body* selector

NOTE *A selector, when used with Cascading Style Sheets, frequently is nothing more than an element's name. By using the element's name, you are "selecting" it to be modified. Thus, to apply a color to the entire body of a page, you use the body selector. Selectors can be more complex than just element names, but it's best to start out simple. For more information, read Chapter 10.*

To experiment with the basic palette, open template.htm and save it as colorcompare.htm. In between the <head> tags, add the <style> element. Then add the *background-color* property, with its value set to blue. Your markup should look like this:

```
<html>
   <head>
     <style>
       body {background-color: blue}
     </style>
   </head>
   <body>
   </body>
</html>
```

Save the page and display it in your browser. You'll notice that the screen is a nice shade of blue. Go back into the page and change the color to any of the other color names to see how it displays as a background color.

Mix Your Own Colors

Now that you've had a chance to play with a simple, 16-color palette, you're probably beginning to feel the boredom setting in. After all, the 16 colors that are available in the Windows palette aren't very exciting, and they certainly don't give you a lot of variety. Fortunately, with today's computer systems you have a *lot* of colors to choose from.

Think of the colors on a computer monitor as being made up from three master "tubes" of paint: red, green, and blue (often referred to as *RGB*). In this case, the "pigment" is light rather than paint. Any of the 16.7 million colors referred to earlier in this chapter can be created using a combination of those three colors of light. However, because of differences in equipment (older monitors and computer systems have limited display capabilities), the majority of those 16 million colors will be *dithered* when displayed. Dithering isn't a great problem in itself, but it does tend to make Web pages look sloppy. If you want to avoid it, you must use browser-safe colors.

> TIP
>
> *If you're not sure what dithering is, just set your computer's display properties to show only 256 or 16 colors; then surf the Net for a few minutes. Do you see the "speckling" that shows up in most of the graphics? That's dithering. It's the computer's way of simulating a color that it is not able to display.*

Understand Browser-Safe Colors

Not sure what browser-safe colors are? Well, it doesn't mean that the browser will crash or the computer will explode if you use unsafe colors. It does mean that your Web pages won't look very good on some people's systems. The so-called "browser-safe" palette dates back to the time when most computers could only display a maximum of 256 colors. Out of those 256 colors, about 40 colors were either reserved for the Windows and/or Mac operating systems, or they didn't display consistently on different platforms. That left 216 colors that could be expected to display without dithering.

Browser-safe colors are made up of a very specific mixture of red, green, and blue light. To be browser safe, a color can be made up of combinations of RGB only in the following amounts: 0%, 20%, 40%, 60%, 80%, and 100%. Feeling a bit confused? It's really quite simple.

Say you want to create a browser-safe shade of red. You could try this formula: Red=100%, Green=20%, Blue=20%. Because you're using color in the proper amounts, you won't have any problems with dithering; but what if you decide to create a shade of red with this formula: Red=93%, Green=27%, Blue=14%? The odd percentages mean that the color is not browser safe and is likely to produce dithering when viewed on certain systems.

Now that you understand browser-safe colors, how do you tell a browser to use them? You actually have several different options. You can specify the color using hexadecimal code, RGB percentages, RGB numeric values, or—in the case of the basic palette—the color's name.

Apply Color with Hexadecimal Code

What is hexadecimal code? In simple terms, it is the base-16 numbering system used by computers. Trying to learn hexadecimal could be very confusing, but for color application, all you really need to know is how to specify the browser-safe percentages mentioned above. Table 4-1 lists the percentages and their hexadecimal equivalents.

Specifying a color using hex code really is quite easy. Just remember that the individual colors you will mix are always red, green, and blue and that they are always listed in that order. To mix the shade of red mentioned in the preceding section, the code would be: 100% red = ff,

20% green = 33, and 20% blue = 33. If you're not sure where these codes come from, look at Table 4-1 again. It's important that you understand this.

TIP *In case you're wondering why the code for 100% red is identified by "ff," it's because hexadecimal code is a base-16 numbering system. Since the base-10 system we use every day does not have enough numerals to cover the extra numbers, letters are used to take up the slack. The numerals of the hexadecimal system are 0,1,2,3,4,5,6,7,8,9, a,b,c,d,e,f.*

You build the color code by combining the codes for the individual RGB values and by adding the pound (or number) symbol in front. Your completed code for a browser-safe red is: #ff3333. Try it out. Open your colorcompare.htm and in the style element, use the *background-color* property to set the color to your custom browser-safe code. It will look like this:

```
<head>
    <style>
     body {background-color: #ff3333}
    </style>
</head>
```

Did you know?

Browser-Safe Colors May Not Be All That Safe

Nowadays, the browser-safe palette should probably be referred to as the so-called browser-safe palette. Because computer displays can be configured to various palettes such as "True Color" and "High Color," which are figured differently than the 256 color palette, the possibility of dithering on some systems is all but inevitable—even with browser-safe colors. Ultimately, you have to estimate who will be visiting your Web pages and whether some color dithering will significantly detract from your Web site's presentation.

Some online articles and resources about browser-safe color issues that you might find helpful are as follows:

- *The Web Safe Color Dilemma* by Lynda Weinman at www.lynda.com/hex.html
- *Death of the Web Safe Color Palette* by Dave Lehn and Hadley Stern at http://hotwired.lycos.com/webmonkey/00/37/index2a.html?tw=design
- *All You Need to Know about Web Safe Colors* by Gary W. Priester at www.webdevelopersjournal.com/articles/websafe1/websafe_colors.html
- *Web Safe Color Chart* by VisiBone at http://html-color-codes.com

There are 216 different choices of browser-safe colors, more than enough to give your Web site that distinctive look. Try experimenting with the colors by creating browser-safe combinations from the chart listed in Table 4-1.

The author's Web site, www.jamespence.com, provides a chart of all the browser-safe colors. To see them side by side, go to the site and choose the colorchart.htm file.

Use the Basic Colors by Code

You also can specify the 16 basic colors by their hexadecimal codes. Table 4-2 lists the colors and their codes together. Notice that half of them do not fit the browser-safe description by using the specific percentages listed in the preceding table (80 is equal to 50% in hexadecimal, and c0 is just less than 80%). However, because they are basic system colors, they are still considered safe to use.

Try using one of the basic colors for a background on your colorcompare.htm page. To change your background color to teal, adjust the <body> tag to read this way:

```
<head>
    <style>
     body {background-color: #008080}
    </style>
</head>
```

Now, save the page and view it in your browser. Your background should be teal.

Apply Color with Percentages

Perhaps the easiest way to apply color in your Web pages is by using percentages. In other words, instead of using cryptic hexadecimal code to assign the values of red, green, and blue in your pages and text, you just list the amount of each color you want by percentage. This particular approach can be used only with Cascading Style Sheets, which provides a great incentive for you to learn how to use CSS.

Percentage	Hexadecimal Equivalent	Numeric Value
0%	00	0
20%	33	51
40%	66	102
60%	99	153
80%	cc	204
100%	ff	255

TABLE 4-1 Web-Safe Color Percentages, Hexadecimal Equivalents, and Numeric Values

Color	Hex Code	Color	Hex Code
Black	#000000	White	#ffffff
Aqua	#00ffff	Blue	#0000ff
Navy	#000080	Teal	#008080
Yellow	#ffff00	Lime	#00ff00
Green	#008000	Olive	#808000
Red	#ff0000	Maroon	#800000
Fuchsia	#ff00ff	Purple	#800080
Gray	#808080	Silver	#c0c0c0

TABLE 4-2   The 16 Basic Colors with Hex Codes

To specify colors by using percentages, you simply need to list the letters *rgb*, followed by the percentage values you want for each color, like this: rgb(100%,100%,100%). Be sure to note that the percentages are enclosed inside parentheses, and that commas separate the values. And never forget that the colors are *always* listed in the same order: red, green, and blue—RGB.

To see for yourself how easy it is to assign colors with percentages, try creating a background color that is made up of a mixture of 100% red, 100% green, and 0% blue. You might be thinking what an ugly, muddy color a mixture of red and green would produce. Open the page you have been using to experiment with color backgrounds and change the line in the <style> element to look like this:

```
<head>
    <style>
    body {background-color: rgb(100%,100%,0%)}
    </style>
</head>
```

Now save the page and display it in your browser. Are you surprised? Instead of a muddy mixture of red and green, your page displays a bright yellow background. This is because you are mixing colors with light rather than with pigment.

The primary colors for pigment (paints, crayons, chalk, and so on) are red, yellow, and blue. If you mix them all together, you wind up with black. This is known as *additive* color mixing because all the colors "add" together as you mix them. However, if you mix the primary colors of light (red, green, and blue), you end up with white. This is *subtractive* color mixing. The more color you add, the brighter it gets. Thus, if you mix equal amounts of red and green pigment together, you get mud. Mix red and green light and you wind up with yellow! This is a good principle to remember as you experiment with color.

TIP   *For dark colors, use lower percentages; for bright colors, use higher percentages.*

Did you know?

How Monitor and Display Screen Colors Work

Do all of these different color combinations confuse you? Osborne technical editor George Semerenko suggests you just think of your TV set. Semerenko comments, "The colors displayed on a computer monitor work in the same way a large projection color TV set deals with color. Large projection-screen TVs have three color electron guns—red, green, and blue—that pulse a stream of electrons against exact spots on the back side of a tube. The pulses intensify to brighten the colors that appear on our TV screens in the same way colors are determined by the HTML code."

Apply Color by Using Numeric Values

Another alternative for applying color is using the numeric value of the color. If you recall from earlier in the chapter, red, green, and blue each have 256 possible values or "settings." These numeric values begin at 0 (0%) and go through 255 (100%). If you're having problems visualizing this, imagine that you have a red, green, and blue light, each wired to a dimmer switch that has 256 "notches." A setting of 0 means the light is off. A setting of 255 means the light is as bright as it can be.

To assign colors using numeric values, you write your style rule the same way you do for percentages—with one very significant change. When using numeric values, you drop the percent symbol after each color value. If you wrote the preceding example with numeric values, the markup would look like the following listing:

```
<head>
    <style>
     body {background-color: rgb(255,255,0)}
    </style>
</head>
```

TIP   *If you want to use Web-safe numeric values for colors, Table 4-1 lists these for you.*

Use Cascading Style Sheets to Specify Color

If you are working through this book chapter by chapter, you have undoubtedly noticed the emphasis on structure versus presentation in XHTML. Although it is possible to use HTML elements and attributes to specify colors for your page, you are much better off if you learn to use Cascading Style Sheets right from the beginning. By using CSS for style and HTML for structure, you will already be a long way down the path to writing "standards-compliant" XHTML.

An added benefit is that, when it comes to applying color, CSS are much more versatile than HTML. After all, style are what CSS are all about.

TIP   *For an explanation of what "standards-compliant" XHTML means, check out Chapter 7.*

Set Page Colors with the Color Property

In straight HTML, your ability to set page colors is limited to the <font> and <basefont> elements and the text, color, and bgcolor attributes. CSS allow you to set page colors with a freedom you could only dream of before. You'll learn in detail what you can do with CSS in Chapter 10, but the following are some samples.

Embed a Style Sheet with the <style> </style> Element

If you have been working the examples in this chapter, you have already been creating embedded style sheets, although you might not have realized it. You learned in the previous chapter how to do an inline style sheet by using the *style* attribute. However, if you're going to do very much with CSS, you need to learn to use embedded style sheets. With inline styles, you must use the style attribute in every element you wish to modify. An embedded style sheet is contained between the <head> tags on your page, and its styles affect all the elements to which they are applied. For example, suppose you want all of your <h1> elements to be blue. If you are using inline styles, you must insert the *style* attribute every time an <h1> occurs on your page. With an embedded style sheet, you need to add the style rule only once, and it will be applied to every <h1> on your page.

To add an embedded style sheet to a page, open template.htm and save it as csscolor.htm. Then, in between the <head> </head> tags, insert the following lines:

```
<html>
<head>
<title>CSS Color Samples</title>
<style type="text/css">
</style>
</head>
<body>
</body>
</html>
```

Set Background Colors with CSS

As you have seen in the preceding examples, setting background colors with CSS is a simple and straightforward process. You simply place a *rule* inside the <style> element. A rule is a CSS style instruction. It is made up of three parts: a selector, a property, and a value. Don't let the terms confuse you, as they are very similar to what you have already learned with HTML: elements, attributes, and values. In CSS terminology, *selector* corresponds to *element*, *property* to *attribute*, and (of course) *value* to *value*. Still confused? Look at the next listing.

To use CSS to embed a style sheet on your page and set an aqua background for the page, insert the following line between the <style> tags:

```
<head>                                      ————— Selector
    <style type="text/css">
        body {background-color: aqua}
    </style>                                 ————— Value
</head>                                       ————— Property
<style type="text/css">
    body {background-color: aqua;}
</style>
```

Save the page and display it in your browser. The background will be aqua.

Recalling what you covered in the previous chapter, you used a property (background-color) and combined it with a value (aqua). But in this case, you've added another item: a *selector* (body). The selector is the HTML element you wish to be affected by your style rule. Because you want to set the background for the entire page, you chose *body* as your selector. You could just as easily have chosen another element—h1, for example—and specified a particular background color for that element. To see this work, try creating some level-one headings with their own background colors.

Create Style Classes

One of the most exciting things about embedded style sheets is that you can apply your styles to any element. You can even create different *classes* of styles. For example, say you want to define not one, but four different styles for <h1> elements, giving a different style and background color to each. With straight HTML or inline styles, you can do it using some of the techniques you learned in the last two chapters, but you would have to insert the control elements every single time you wanted to modify <h1>. With style sheets, you do it just one time, by creating classes.

To create a class, just add a period after the selector and follow it up with a class name. In the example that follows, we create a class for the <h1> element that is named "red." There's nothing special about the name. You could name it "Toledo" if you wanted to, but a descriptive name generally works better. To create a special "red" style class, you just modify the h1 selector to look like this: h1.red. To apply your class selector on a Web page you just add the *class* attribute, like this: <h1 class="red">. Then the styles that you set for that particular class will be applied to that <h1> element.

To see how this works, try adding the following lines in between the <style> </style> tags on your page:

```
h1 {font-family: arial;  color: blue;}
h1.red {font-family: times-new-roman; color: red;
```

```
                       background-color: white;}
h1.white {font-family: times-new-roman; color: white;
          background-color: blue;}
h1.bluered {font-family: arial; font-style: italic;
                color: blue; background-color: red;}
```

After you've included the style lines, add the lines that follow in the <body> </body> portion of your page to see how they display. To apply the special style classes you created, remember to include the *class* attribute inside each opening <h1> element tag. The value should be set to the class name you assigned your style. That's the portion of the selector that follows the period.

```
<h1>Blue text on white background</h1>
<h1 class="red">Red text on white background</h1>
<h1 class="white">White text on blue background</h1>
<h1 class="bluered">Blue text on red background</h1>
```

Save and display the page in your browser. Your results should resemble this:

Blue text on white background

Red text on white background

White text on blue background

Blue text on red background

Anywhere you specify one of those four classes you created, the display takes on the characteristics of that class. You can see that using style sheets can save you a great deal of time, not to mention open up many creative options. Style sheets can also help you develop a consistent look for your Web site that spans all of your pages.

Remember, when using embedded style sheets, always enclose properties and values inside curly braces {}.

NOTE
For inline style sheets, properties and values are enclosed in quotation marks (see Chapter 3).

Properties should be separated from their values by a colon (:) and from other properties by a semicolon (;). Selectors (the elements you wish to set a style for) should be outside and to the left of the curly braces. Proper style sheet syntax is reflected in the following line:

```
selector  {property: value;  property: value;  property: value;}
```

It also can be written this way:

```
selector  {
        property: value;
```

```
property: value;
property: value;
}
```

Set Font Colors and Paragraph Styles with CSS

Suppose you want to include several different font colors on a page, each with a distinctive look and background. With CSS it's a breeze. Just remember that the *background-color* property controls an element's background, and the *color* property controls the *foreground* (in this case, the font). Thus, to set font colors for any element, you simply write your style rule like this: selector {color: value}. Try creating three paragraph styles for your csscolors.htm page, with different font and background colors. Insert the following lines of code between the <style> </style> tags:

```
p.blackback    {font-family: arial; font-style: italic;
                font-weight: bold; color: aqua;
                background-color: rgb(0,0,0);}
p.yellowbk     {background-color: rgb(100%,100%,0%); font-size: 16pt}
p.red          {font-weight: light; color: #ff0000;
                text-align: center; font-size: 32pt;}
```

 To set the background color for an element, use the background-color *property. To set font colors, use the* color *property.*

You have defined three paragraph classes:

- **Blackback** An Arial italic font, displaying in aqua with a black background
- **Yellowbk** A 16-point font with a yellow background
- **Red** A light, 32-point font that will be centered and displayed in red

These are in addition to the undefined <p> element, which will display as it normally does. To see these new paragraph styles in action, insert the following lines of code into the <body> </body> portion of your page:

```
<p class="blackback">This is a sample of the blackback style.</p>
<p class="yellowbk">Here is how yellowbk looks.</p>
<p class="red">I enjoy this red, centered font.</p>
<p>An unmodified paragraph looks like this.</p>
```

When you have saved the page, display it in your browser. It should look something like the following illustration. Are you beginning to see the possibilities?

This is a sample of the blackback style.

Here is how yellowbk looks.

I enjoy this red, centered font.

An unmodified paragraph looks like this.

Set Link Colors

You can use CSS to set link colors, too, using what is called a *pseudo-class*. A pseudo-class is used to define a "class" that doesn't actually exist in a page's HTML code but exists because it fulfills certain conditions. For example, a visited link is defined by a pseudo-class because there is no specific HTML element for visited links. Instead, your visitor's browser "remembers" whether a link has been visited. You need not worry too much about what that means right now, as it will be covered in Chapter 10. To use CSS to set link colors:

- **a:link {color: navy}**   Sets link colors to navy
- **a:visited {color: #0000ff}**   Sets visited link colors to blue
- **a:active {color: rgb(0, 255, 0)}**   Sets active link colors to bright green
- **a:hover {color: rgb(100%,0%,0%)}**   Turns a link red when a cursor moves over it

Setting Colors with HTML

Thus far, you have been learning how to specify colors with CSS. However, it is possible to add color to Web pages directly in your HTML code, without the use of style sheets. You'll find this method a bit more limiting, because you can only use hexadecimal code or color names with HTML. Also, the methods for adding color in the sections that follow have been *deprecated* in favor of CSS. Nevertheless, you'll find it helpful to at least be familiar with these elements and attributes, even if you decide not to use them.

Specify Background Color with the bgcolor Attribute (Deprecated)

To specify the background color of a page, use the bgcolor= " " attribute inside the <body> tag. The value that goes inside bgcolor can be one of the recognized color names or a color's hexadecimal code. To select a red background for a page, you could write:

```
<body bgcolor="red">
```

However, you could just as easily use the hex code for red, in which case your code would look like this:

```
<body bgcolor="#ff0000">
```

Either way, you wind up with the same result—a Web page with a red background. To do a black background, you can use either the name "black" or the hex code "#000000"; for a yellow background, use "yellow" or "#ffff00". . . you get the idea.

The bgcolor attribute is useful for more than just setting a page's background color. As you already discovered, it can be used in a table to set the individual background color for cells. It also can be used to set the background color for table headings.

> **NOTE** *The bgcolor attribute has not been deprecated for use with tables. Thus, at least for now, you can use it without worrying about future compatibility.*

Set Text Colors with the text Attribute (Deprecated)

You can set the color for all the text in your page by using the text=" " attribute inside the opening <body> tag. Again, using a color's name or hex code will cause all the text in a page to display in that color. For example, if you want all the text on a page to be maroon, write your <body> tag this way:

```
<body text="maroon">
```

To have a page with a yellow background and maroon text, construct your tag like this:

```
<body bgcolor="yellow" text="maroon">
```

Set Text Colors with <basefont /> (Deprecated)

As you learned in Chapter 3, you also can specify text characteristics with the <basefont /> element. If you include the following instruction in the body of your page:

```
<basefont color="purple" />
```

all the text will display in purple.

Set Link Colors with link, vlink, and alink (Deprecated)

Just as you can modify link colors with CSS, you also have this capability with HTML, although in a more limited way. For example, if you want to set the link to red, the active link to yellow, and the visited link to blue, write the opening <body> tag this way:

```
<body link="red" vlink="yellow" alink="white">
```

Try typing out the following code, even if you don't understand it all. It will create a small table on your page and a sample link below the table. If you try this out, you will see that the link on the page displays in the colors you have chosen rather than the default colors.

```
<html>
   <head>
      <title>Color Comparison Table</title>
```

```
   </head>
   <body bgcolor="teal" link="red" vlink="yellow" alink="white">
      <table border="0" cellpadding="100">
         <tr>
           <td bgcolor="aqua">Sample Color</td>
         </tr>
      </table>
      <a href="http://www.osborne.com"><h2>Sample Link
         to Osborne's Web Site</h2></a>
   </body>
</html>
```

Before you change the colors of your links, keep in mind that many Web surfers have gotten used to the blue/red/purple color scheme for links. Be careful that you don't make your page difficult to navigate by making your links difficult to identify.

Use the color Attribute and <font> Element to Change Font Color (Deprecated)

If you want to set a particular portion of text apart by changing its color, but you want the rest of the page to retain its default color, you can do it with the <font> element and the color=" " attribute. To see how it works, add the following line to the page you just created:

```
<p>This line will have one <font color="red">
red</font> word.</p>
```

When you save and display your page now, you will see that the word "red" is displayed in bright red text. Remember, you also can use the hex code for red. Substitute the hex code #ff0000 for the word "red" in the <font> tag. Save and display it. You still get the same result.

Use the color Attribute with Horizontal Rules (Deprecated)

Remember the horizontal rule <hr />? You can specify colors for it by including the color attribute inside the tag. Try adding this line to your page:

```
<hr color="yellow" width="50%" size="7" />
```

When you save and view the page, you will find a bright yellow horizontal rule has been inserted wherever you put the <hr /> element.

Use bgcolor=" " to Set Colors for Table Cells

You have already experimented a bit with tables in this chapter. When you get to Chapter 8, you will learn that tables are used for much more than displaying columns and rows of data on a Web page. Tables are one of the most frequently used means of establishing a page's layout. The bgcolor attribute enhances this by enabling you to set different colors for individual table cells, which allows you to create very pleasing layouts for your pages. To see how this works, try adding the following lines to the table you already created:

```
<html>
   <head>
      <title>Color Comparison Table</title>
   </head>
   <body bgcolor="teal" link="red" vlink="yellow" alink="white">
     <table border="0" cellpadding="25">
       <tr>
         <td bgcolor="aqua">Sample Color</td>
       </tr>
       <tr>
         <td bgcolor="#0000ff">
           <font color="white">
             <h1>Sample Two</h1>
           </font>
         </td>
       </tr>
     </table>
     <a href="http://www.osborne.com"><h2>Sample Link</h2></a>
   </body>
</html>
```

When you save and view this file in your browser, you'll see that another "cell" has been added just below the first one. This time the cell has a blue background and the text displays in white. Perhaps by now you're thinking, "There's got to be an easier way!" After all, to get some text to have a special background color, its own color, and a large size, you have to write this:

```
<tr><td bgcolor="#0000ff"><font color="white"><h1>Sample
Two</h1></font></td></tr>
```

What's worse is that you have to do that every time you want to produce those results! Is there a better way? You bet! You can do all this and more with Cascading Style Sheets. That's why the W3C is phasing out (deprecating) these older methods of formatting.

Understand Appealing Use of Color

Have you ever driven down the road and seen a house painted bright yellow with hot pink trim? Do you shudder when you think about it? Good color combinations can enhance your Web site. At best, poor use of color makes your page difficult to read and hard on the eyes. At worst, it's like the screech of fingernails on a blackboard. It will send people away from your site in droves.

When you begin to plan your Web site, choose your colors carefully. Don't just grab them at random as if you were taking a handful of crayons out of a box. Put some thought into your colors, keeping in mind that you should

- Put at least as much thought into your color scheme as you do your site's layout.

- Compare colors side by side before you construct your page.

- Choose soft colors rather than deep, bright, or garish shades.

- Make your color scheme consistent throughout your site.

- Keep in mind the possible equipment limitations of visitors to your site.

- Never forget that visitors can set their browsers to override your designs and styles. (What will your page look like if your styles are not used?)

- Remember that some of your visitors might suffer from color blindness. Take steps to ensure your color choices do not make your pages less accessible to them.

TIP *A great site for information on Web color in general—and color blindness in particular—is www.visibone.com. It's worth checking out.*

Project 6: Create a Color Chart

Using color in Web pages is fun and tricky at the same time. If you will take the time to experiment with different color combinations, you can develop a way to reinforce some of the things you have learned about color and how to use it. For a challenging exercise, try creating a file named 16colors.htm and then type this code. It will create a chart of the basic color palette you began this chapter with. You'll be using HTML to create a table to structure the color chart. If you want to learn about tables before you try this, read Chapter 8 first. Otherwise, just be careful to type the code in *exactly* as written in the following code listing. After you've finished, save your page and display it in your browser. It should resemble the following illustration:

The 16 Basic Colors

White	Black	Gray	Silver
Navy	Blue	Teal	Aqua
Lime	Green	Olive	Yellow
Fuchsia	Red	Maroon	Purple

```
<html>
   <head>
     <title>The 16 Basic Colors</title>
     <style> td {font-family: arial; font-weight:
                 bold; font-size: 18pt}
     </style>
   </head>
   <body>
     <h1>The 16 Basic Colors</h1>
       <!-- Table starts -->
       <table border="1" width="50%" cellpadding="50">
         <tr>  <!-- Row 1 -->
<td bgcolor="white">White</td> <!-- TD tags define table cells -->
<td bgcolor="black" style="color: white;">Black</td>
<td bgcolor="gray">Gray</td>
<td bgcolor="silver">Silver</td>
         </tr> <!-- End of row 1 -->
         <tr> <!-- Row 2 -->
<td bgcolor="navy" style="color: white;">Navy</td>
<td bgcolor="blue" style="color: white;">Blue</td>
<td bgcolor="teal">Teal</td>
<td bgcolor="aqua">Aqua</td>
         </tr> <!-- End of row 2 -->
         <tr> <!-- Row 3 -->
<td bgcolor="lime">Lime</td>
<td bgcolor="green">Green</td>
<td bgcolor="olive">Olive</td>
<td bgcolor="yellow">Yellow</td>
         </tr> <!-- End of row 3 -->
         <tr> <!-- Row 4 -->
<td bgcolor="fuchsia">Fuchsia</td>
<td bgcolor="red">Red</td>
<td bgcolor="maroon" style"color: white;">Maroon</td>
<td bgcolor="purple" style"color: white;">Purple</td>
         </tr>  <!-- End of row 4 -->
       </table> <!-- End of table -->
     </body>
</html>
```

In this chapter, you have learned only a small sample of what you can do with color in your Web pages. You are limited only by your imagination and your visitors' equipment. Keep the equipment limitation in mind, as it is one of the unfortunate (and continual) frustrations of a Web designer. Designing Web pages will bring out the artist in you, but don't stray too far from the scientist. Test your pages to make sure they work for everyone, not just for you.

Quick Reference: Applying Color

Learning to control and apply color in Web pages is easy and fun. Remembering all the different methods for adding color can become confusing, however. The following chart lists the different ways you can use Cascading Style Sheets to apply color to the different elements on your pages:

4

To Do This	Use This
Control background color (CSS)	`selector {background-color: value}` example: `body {background-color: red}`
Control foreground (font) color (CSS)	`selector {color: value}` example: `h1 {color: red}`

Specify colors by hex code (HTML or CSS)	`#ffffff`
	CSS example: `td {background-color:`
	`#ff0000}`
	HTML example: `<td bgcolor="#ff0000">`

Specify colors by rgb percentages (CSS only)	`rgb(#%,#%,#%)` example: `body {color: rgb(100%,0%,0%)}`
Specify colors by rgb numeric values (CSS only)	`rgb(#,#,#)` example: `body {color: rgb(255,0,0)`
Create a special class selector (CSS)	`selector.className` example: `h1.red`
Apply a class to an element	`<element class="className">` example: `<h1 class="red">`

Chapter 5

All About Links

How to...

- Link to another page
- Link to a different Web site
- Link to precise locations on a page
- Open linked pages in a new window
- Create e-mail, FTP, and news links
- Adjust the appearance of links

The Web wouldn't be the Web without hyperlinks. No matter how much material is available on the World Wide Web, without a way to tie all that information together, it is little more than a gigantic library without a cataloging system. Prior to the development of the Web in 1990, other means of accessing information dominated the Internet. You might have heard terms like *gopher, archie, veronica,* and *jughead* and wondered what they meant. No, they're not comic book characters, at least not in this case. They are terms that describe some of the ways to search the Internet in its early days. Although they're still around, the development of the World Wide Web and its use of *hypertext* has eclipsed gopher and company, pushing them into the background in favor of a system that radically changed the way we access information online.

Understand Hypertext and Links

Why did the arrival of hypertext links make such a difference? You can understand it better by comparing the Internet to a vast library. What if you went into a library and discovered that the only way you could find anything was by going through multiple lists of items, each one becoming a little more specific, until you narrowed your search down to the information you were looking for? Then, when you found the book you wanted, you had to access the information in it, page by page, until you found what you needed? Thankfully, libraries don't work that way. But, if you've ever used a *gopher* server, that's about what it's like.

The development of HTML and the creation of the World Wide Web made it possible to go right to the document you want—and a lot more. Because pages are linked together, it is possible to go to the specific page you want. Even better, assuming a link is provided, it is possible to go to a precise location on the page you are looking for. And with all those pages linked together around the world...well, you see where the term *web* comes from. And it's all possible because of *hypertext*.

Understand URLs

What is hypertext? Even if you've never been on the Web, you've probably used hypertext before. Often the help files of computer programs use hypertext to help you quickly find the answer to your question. Computerized encyclopedias are another place you've probably encountered hypertext. The articles in such encyclopedias and dictionaries generally have related subjects listed at the bottom. If you click on the subject, you are instantly transported to another article for more information. That's hypertext at work. To understand how to use it on the Web, you must learn a little about *uniform resource locators* (URLs). URLs are more commonly known as Web addresses, Internet addresses, and even "dot.coms." But simplistic names won't give you an idea of how a URL works.

A URL is made up of several parts, each of which helps identify a specific location where a *resource* can be found (or sent). For example, if you want to visit Osborne's Web site, the address would be http://www.osborne.com/. The first part of the address is the *protocol,* usually *http://.* This stands for *Hypertext Transfer Protocol,* the specification for transferring documents using hypertext links or *hyperlinks.* As you'll see in the following, there are other protocols, depending on what you are trying to do on the Net, but the primary one for the Web is http://. When an Internet server sees http:// at the beginning of an address, it knows to expect an HTML document.

The next portion of a URL identifies the *host* (also called a *server*). In the case of Osborne's address, the host portion is www.osborne.com. The host is the system where the file or document you are looking for can be found or where it is to be sent. You probably are more familiar with the term *domain name*, as in www.domainname.com. When you type in a domain name, it is translated into what is known as an *IP address,* which numerically describes the exact location of the server that hosts that particular Web site (see Chapter 7 for more information on IP addresses).

The last part of a URL locates the *file* on the server. You generally don't have to type in this part because the browser supplies it for you. If it is displayed, the file location might look something like this:

```
http://www.mysite.com/index.htm
```

No directory is listed in this address because the index page is usually located in a site's main, or *root,* directory. If you are accessing a page that is in a different directory on a Web site, the address might display this way:

```
http://www.mysite.com/vacations/pictures.htm
```

In the case of this address, the file is pictures.htm; it resides in the vacations directory.

SHORTCUT   *If you know the filename and directory of the page you are looking for, you can go straight to it without having to visit the site's home page. Just type in the complete address, including directory and filename, and you'll take a shortcut to the page.*

A complete URL points to a specific resource on the Internet by identifying the *protocol://host/directory/filename.ext.*

NOTE   *Because you normally go to the first, or root, directory when you visit a Web site, you might not always see a directory listed in the URL.*

Table 5-1 shows how URLs change to reflect the action you are requesting.

5

Action	URL Format
To access a Web site	http://www.domainName.com/index.htm
To access a secure Web site	https://www.domainName.com/index.htm
To use File Transfer Protocol	ftp://domainName.com/directory/file.txt
To use the Mailto Protocol	mailto:emailAddress@domainName.com
To access a newsgroup	news://newsServer.com/directory/filename
To use a Gopher server	gopher://server.address/directory/file
To access a local file (on your computer)	file:///c:\myDocuments\myfile.htm

TABLE 5-1   URL Formats for the Most Commonly Used Protocols

Link to Another Web Site with the Anchor Element <a> </a>

Hypertext points to a precise location on the Internet by using a URL to identify where information is and what should be done with it. But how do you create the link? That's where HTML comes in. *HTML* stands for Hypertext Markup Language. You can create hypertext links or *hyperlinks* using an element specially designed for that purpose: the anchor element, <a> </a>.

A link is simply a connection between one hypertext document and another created by enclosing text or an image inside two anchor tags. However, the link must point somewhere, so you also must include the href attribute. Href stands for *hypertext reference* and is the place where you put the URL or pointer so your link has a destination. A link that doesn't point anywhere will look like this:

```
<a href=" ">This link doesn't go anywhere</a>.
```

If you type this link into a Web page, it will appear as the default blue underlined text that characterizes links, but it won't take you anywhere because it doesn't have an address. To give the link somewhere to take you, insert a URL between the quotation marks beside the href attribute. To make the link take a visitor to Osborne's site, change the link to read:

```
<a href="http://www.osborne.com">Go to Osborne's Web site.</a>
```

Create an HTML file from your template and try typing these lines in. You should see a pair of links that looks like this:

<u>This link doesn't go anywhere</u> <u>Go to Osborne's Web site.</u>

That's all there is to creating a simple link to another Web site. Oh, but there's so much more you can do with them.

Help People Navigate Your Site with Internal Links

One of the most common uses for hyperlinks on a Web site is for *site navigation*. Site navigation is just a fancy term for helping people find their way around. It's good to keep that in mind as you develop your site. As you develop links to other pages on your Web site, remember that you want to make things as easy for your visitors as possible. The larger and more complex your site becomes, the more links you will find yourself using. If your links are complicated, confusing, or non-functional, visitors will become frustrated and probably will leave.

Link to Pages on Your Own Site

Linking to another page on your own site is even simpler than linking to a different Web site; all you need to include is the name of the file you're linking to and the directory where it is located. If the file happens to be in the same directory, you need only the filename.

Link to Another Page in the Same Directory

To link to another page in the same directory, simply include the filename in the href attribute of the opening anchor tag. For example, to add a link to your index.htm page that will open up headings.htm, type

```
<a href="headings.htm">Headings Page</a>.
```

This creates a link that looks like this:

Headings Page

This kind of link will work as long as the file is stored in the same directory. However, if you have a large site, you might find it easier to organize your files in different directories, much as you do on your computer. If you do this, you will have to provide the *path* to your file. You can do this by using either *absolute* or *relative* URLs.

Link to Another Page in a Different Directory with Absolute and Relative URLs

You have two options when linking to a file in another directory: *absolute* or *relative* URLs.

Use Absolute URLs for Simplicity   The least complicated option is to use an *absolute* URL. Although that term might sound intimidating, it simply refers to the exact path to the file's location, including all directories and subdirectories you have to go through to get there. It is called *absolute* because it specifies a precise address. For example, suppose you have a site devoted to facts about famous people. One of your subdirectories might be named Biographies. In that directory, you might have several other directories; for example, Actors, Musicians, or Presidents. If you want to link to a file named washington.htm and that file is located in the Presidents directory, you would write the URL in your link this way:

```
<a href="/biographies/presidents/washington.htm">Washington</a>
```

This tells the browser to go to the Biographies directory, then to go to the Presidents directory, and finally to load the washington.htm file.

> **TIP** *Remember that directories should be separated by a forward slash, and the filename comes last.*

If you want to create a link on the washington.htm page that will take a visitor back to the home page, you can use an absolute pathname that goes in the opposite direction:

```
<a href="presidents/biographies/index.htm">Home</a>
```

Absolute URLs work fine, provided you never move your pages to different locations. If you do, you'll have to go back into each page and rewrite the links to reflect the new paths. If you have a small site, that might not be a problem. However, if you have a large site with lots of files, you can plan on spending quite a few hours just rewriting links. To avoid this problem, use *relative* URLs.

> **NOTE** *How many directories you decide to use on your site is entirely up to you. If you plan on a small and relatively uncomplicated site, or you will be your own Webmaster, you might choose to keep your files all in a single directory, thus eliminating the need for complicated pathnames in your URLs. However, if you plan on a large, difficult-to-maintain site or if more than one person is accessing the files, you probably will want to organize similar files in directories with descriptive titles; for example, Images, Personnel, Statistics, Reports, and so forth. This will make working on your site much easier.*

Use Relative URLs for Flexibility If you want your site to have maximum flexibility and you definitely don't want to waste your time rewriting links, relative URLs are your solution. Whereas an absolute URL contains the exact address of the file you want the browser to load, a relative URL uses a kind of shorthand to tell the browser to go backward one or more directories. If you want to write the link from washington.htm-to-index.htm using a relative URL, it will look like this:

```
<a href="../../index.htm">Home</a>
```

The two dots followed by a slash are the code that instructs the browser to move backward (or up) one directory level. Because you must go up two levels to get to the main (or root) directory and index.htm, you must use the code twice. What makes relative URLs advantageous is that the link will work even if you move the file to another directory.

What if you want to link to a file in a parallel directory; that is, go sideways rather than backward? On our famous persons' Web site, to link to Mozart's biography, you'd send the browser to the Musicians directory. You would write a link to tell the browser to go up one directory (to

Biographies), to go forward one directory (to Musicians), and to load the file mozart.htm. How would it look?

```
<a href="../musicians/mozart.htm">Mozart Biography</a>
```

Confusing? It can be if you let your Web site structure get complicated. A good rule is to keep the structure of your Web site as simple as you can and still accomplish what you need to accomplish. In the meantime, remember that two dots followed by a slash (../) take you backward or up one directory. To go forward, give the directory name followed by a slash, *directory/*.

TIP *If you're struggling with the whole idea of relative URLs and how to use them, try creating several practice directories on your computer. Name your root directory* home *and create a subdirectory named* sub-a. *Make another directory inside sub-a and name it* sub-b. *Just for fun, create another subdirectory of home and call it* sub-c. *Then create an HTML page in home, naming it* index.htm. *Put a page in each of the other directories and practice linking them together until you are confident using relative URLs.*

5

Link to Precise Spots on a Page

Another practical use of links is to help visitors navigate a single, long page. Have you ever visited a site where most of the content was contained on a single page? You could scroll down through the entire page, but you might be interested in only one particular topic covered there. If the page's author included links to location markers with *ids* or *named anchors,* you'd find it much easier to get around.

Create a Place Marker with the id Attribute

The most versatile way to create a place marker is with the *id* attribute. With this attribute, you can assign a specific name to virtually any element on your page. For example, suppose you have divided your page into four major sections, each beginning with an <h1> element. You can identify each individual heading by assigning it its own id, as in the following markup:

```
<h1 id="heading1">First Heading</h1>
<h1 id="heading2">Second Heading</h1>
<h1 id="heading3">Third Heading</h1>
<h1 id="heading4">Fourth Heading</h1>
```

TIP *If you try this out, be sure to make your page long enough for the links to actually take you somewhere. Your content needs to exceed the length of your browser window.*

To create a link to one of your newly created ids, you use the anchor <a> element and href attribute but apply a slightly different URL. In this case, you use the crosshatch symbol (pound sign) # along with the id you wish to link to, as in the following:

```
<a href="#heading2">Go to Second Heading</a>
```

When visitors click this link, they will be taken to the second heading on your page without having to scroll through the rest of the content. You can use the id attribute with almost any element, but there are some important rules to keep in mind when applying it:

- ID names must be unique. If you use id to create your place markers, you must choose a unique name for each one you make.
- IDs can be anything you choose, but they *must* begin with either a letter or an underline.
- IDs may not begin with a number.
- An ID may be used only one time (as an anchor) in a single document. In other words, you can't have several different elements all using the same ID.
- ID names must go inside an element's opening tag.

Create an Anchor with the name Attribute (Deprecated)

Another way to create a place marker and link is by using the *name* attribute along with the anchor <a> element. Because it works with the anchor element, this is sometimes called a *named anchor.* To use a named anchor to place a link at the bottom of a page that will take visitors back to the top without using the scroll bar:

1. Place an anchor at the top of the page by typing **<a name="top"> </a>**. Notice that even though there is no content between the two anchor tags, both are still required.

2. At the bottom of the page make a link to your anchor by typing the following:

```
<a href="#top">Top of Page</a>
```

 Be sure to include the pound sign (#) at the front of the name when you use it as a URL in the link.

3. Your markup might look like this:

```
<html>
<head><title>Named Anchors</title></head>
<body>
<a name="top"> </a>
<h1>This is the text of your page</h1>
<a href="#top">Top of Page</a>.
</body>
</html>
```

NOTE *It is not necessary to put your named anchor around an actual line of text or image. The browser will go to the spot where the anchor is located, whether or not it is attached to something visible on the page. However, the longer and more complicated your page is, the more desirable it is to have your anchor actually tied to something you can see. Plus, some browsers will ignore the anchor element if it doesn't contain some content.*

The W3C has deprecated the name attribute in favor of id. However, because some older browsers will not recognize the id attribute when used as a place marker for links, it is still helpful to be familiar with the procedure for using named anchors.

Whether you use id, name, or both, you can see how links to place markers can be useful for enabling people to navigate a long page, for example, a glossary of terms. You could create place markers at each new letter of the alphabet with links at the top of the page. Each term could include links that would take the visitor back to the alphabetical directory or just to the beginning of the particular section in which the term was found.

Use Place Markers to Link to Precise Locations on Different Pages

Suppose you are designing a site for a university and you want to create links that will direct online visitors to a brief paragraph describing a certain course but you want to include all course descriptions in a single document. One way to do it would be to create a place marker for each course and create a link to each course's description. It might look something like the following code:

- Anchor (on a courses.htm page):

```
<p id="biology103">Biology 103</p>
```

- Link (perhaps on a degree program page, listing required courses):

```
<a href="courses.htm#biology103">Click for a description
 of BI-103</a>
```

NOTE   *You also can link to other pages using the name attribute. Instead of putting the name in an element, as with id, write it as <a name="biology103"> </a>.*

The preceding link will take visitors to the courses page where they will find a description of the Introduction to Biology course. The advantage of linking this way is that you can reference a single pool of information from any number of different pages. When using an anchor to link to a different page, you should not separate the filename and anchor name or ID with spaces or any other characters.

Use Named Anchors to Link to a Different Web Site

This same approach will work, even if you want to link to an entirely different site. All you need to know is the anchor name or the id name and the site's URL to link to a specific portion of that site.

Suppose the preceding imaginary university has several satellite campuses, each with its own site. They could access the information on the main site's servers simply by linking to the site's anchors, like this:

```
<a href="http://www.imaginaryu.edu/catalog/courses.htm#biology103">BI-103</a>.
```

Note that you need to use the complete URL when you are trying to link to another site.

 *Although it is possible to link to any site this way, keep in mind that not everyone will be delighted by the idea of you linking to their sites; copyright issues also can come into play. Always get the permission of the Webmaster if you plan to link to another site.*

Open Links in a New Window

If you are reluctant to include links to other Web sites because you don't want your visitors to leave your site too quickly, there are several steps you can take to encourage them to stay. One of the easiest is to set up your links so that they open a new browser window. That way, visitors can visit the site you're linked to and remain at your site. You can configure a link to open in a new window by using the *target* attribute.

Use the target Attribute to Open New Browser Windows

When a visitor clicks a link with the target attribute, the content will open in a new browser window. To indicate a new window with the target attribute, add the target attribute with a value of "_blank" between the quotation marks as in the following code sample:

```
<a href="www.newSite.com" target="_blank">
This link opens a new window.</a>
```

NOTE   *The value "_blank" must have the underscore character before the letter b.*

Use Special Types of Links

Using links for site navigation and to connect with other sites only scratches the surface of what you can do with links. Remember the different protocols mentioned earlier in this chapter? The following describes how some of them are used.

Use mailto: to Create E-mail Links

One of the more challenging aspects of Web authoring is designing systems for your visitors to respond to your site. Many of these require venturing outside the secure world of HTML into more complex programming languages. One easy way to enable people to contact you from your site is by including an e-mail link with the mailto: protocol.

To put an e-mail link in a page you can type something like this:

```
<a href="mailto:myEmail@server.com">Email Me!</a>
```

When someone clicks this link, it opens the browser's e-mail program with an e-mail window already addressed to you. All they have to do is write a note and click Send.

Use ftp:// to Link to Download Sites

FTP stands for *File Transfer Protocol*. You will become very familiar with the ftp:// protocol when you are ready to publish your Web site to a server because that's how you get your files from your computer to your host's. What you might not know is that there are many public FTP sites called *anonymous ftp sites*. These allow you to log in, usually with the username "anonymous," and download information. You might want to provide a link to a site that offers information related to your site's topic. For example the following code listing contains a link that will take your visitors to Microsoft's FTP site. The illustration that follows shows you what your visitors will see if they follow that link.

```
Find Microsoft downloads at the: <a href="ftp://ftp.microsoft.com">
Microsoft FTP Site</a>.
```

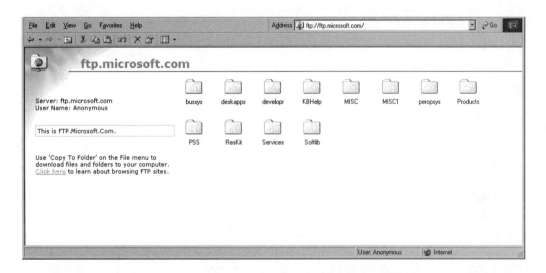

A visitor who clicks this link will be transferred to Microsoft's anonymous FTP site, where they will be able to find a wealth of downloads and information. As always, be sure you have the right to link to information on the Internet before you do so. With most public sites such as this, there will be no problem. However, if you're in doubt, be sure and contact the site administrator before creating the link.

Link to Usenet Newsgroups with news:

The news:// protocol enables you to link your visitors to Usenet newsgroups. *Newsgroups* are veterans of the Internet's early days and work something like huge e-mail groups. Groups organized around common interests abound and can be a great source of information. Perhaps you might like to put visitors in touch with a link to an amateur astronomy newsgroup. You could add a link such as this:

```
<a href="news:sci.astro.amateur">
Amateur Astronomers' Newsgroup</a>
```

Assuming your visitors have their browsers configured for newsgroups, this link opens up their news reader and enables them to tie into the group. As you read in the "Understand URLs" section, there are other protocols, but these are the ones you are likely to use most often.

 To find newsgroups to link to, try doing a search on Usenet in any search engine.

Until now, you have been working with plain text links—nothing fancy and definitely not pretty. Not many years ago, that's what you would have been limited to when adding links to your page. Fortunately, things have changed. It is now possible for you to have useful links and good-looking ones, too.

 *Another way to write the newsgroup protocol is nntp://.*

Dress Up Your Links

Links can be modified several different ways to affect their appearance and function. They can even be modified to give your visitors feedback. Unfortunately, not all of these work with every browser, so keep in mind that these are bells and whistles; they are nice to use, but don't make your site dependent on them.

Give Link Details with the title Attribute

The title attribute is a nice little addition that unfortunately has limited browser support. By adding the title attribute to your anchor tag, you can add an explanatory comment to your link. When a visitor's mouse passes over the link, a small text box will appear with your comment. For example, the Webmaster of the imaginary university referred to earlier could add the title attribute to the biology course link explaining what the link leads to:

```
<a href="courses.htm#biology103" title="Introductory Biology">
BI-103</a>
```

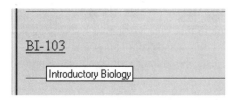

TIP *The title attribute is a very useful universal attribute. You can put it inside any element and get the same explanatory box (called a ToolTip) in IE4 and above.*

Modify Link Appearance with CSS

If you've read Chapter 4, you've already covered much of what can be done with links through Cascading Style Sheets. There are a few other things you can do to modify your links, both with inline and embedded style sheets.

Remove Underlines with text-decoration: none

You might decide you'd rather not have the links in your page underlined. You can turn off underlining on a link-by-link basis by using the style attribute with the "text-decoration: none" property, as in the following code listing:

```
<a href="anypage.htm" style="text-decoration: none">
This link has no underlining.</a>
```

This link has no underlining.

This particular style affects only the link with which it has been included. To turn off underlining as the default setting for a page, embed a style in the <head> </head> portion of the page:

```
<style> a:link {text-decoration: none}</style>
```

CAUTION *Link underlines are an easy way to identify the links on your page. Many authorities on Web design discourage Web authors from removing these underlines. However, if you choose to remove the underlining, be sure that you make your links easily identifiable by some other means. After all, the purpose of links is to help visitors navigate your site. If they can't find the links, they can't navigate.*

Change Link Colors Dynamically with a:hover

If you've done much Web surfing, you certainly have encountered *mouseover* effects, in which an image (usually a navigation tool) changes appearance when the cursor moves over it. With Cascading Style Sheets you can easily create that effect in links by using the pseudo-class a:hover (see Chapter 10 for more on pseudo classes). The downside of this effect is that it is not recognized by older versions of Netscape. Your links will still work; they simply won't be affected by this style. The following code, inserted in the head portion of any page, will alter the links so that they have no underline and change to red when a cursor moves over them:

```
<style type"text/css">
    a:link {text-decoration: none}
    a:active {text-decoration: none}
    a:visited {text-decoration: none}
```

```
        a:hover {color: red}
</style>
```

There are many more things you can do with inline and embedded style sheets. If you want to learn more, skip ahead to Chapter 10.

Modify Link Appearance with Text Elements (Discouraged)

Although the W3C discourages this, another way to change the appearance of your links is by using text elements. As always, the preferred method of controlling presentation is through Cascading Style Sheets. However, virtually any of the text elements covered in Chapter 2 can be applied to a link. You are not limited to lines of default, which is basic blue text for links. You can change the size, color, and even the font. Experiment with some of the following possibilities:

```
<h1><a href="anypage.htm">This is a link inside a heading element.</a></h1>

<a href="anypage.htm"><font face="arial" color="red" size="5">This is
a size 5, Arial link.</font></a><br /><br />

<small><a href="anypage.htm">Links in small text are great
for page bottom navigation bars.</a></small>

<center><a href="anypage.htm">You can center links, too.</a></center>
```

This is a link inside a heading element.

This is a size 5, Arial link.

<u>Links in small text are great for page bottom navigation bars.</u>

<u>You can center links, too.</u>

Check out the text elements in Chapter 2 and create some modified links of your own. The only limitation is that you can't put a *block level* element inside the <a> </a> element. You can use most of the block level elements with links, but they must go on the outside of the <a> tags. For example, because <h1> is a block level element, it must go outside the <a> tags. See the following note for more block level elements:

```
<a href="anypage.htm"><h1>This won't work.</h1></a>
<h1><a href="anypage.htm">This will.</a><h1>
```

Block level elements generally (but not always) insert a line break and space after the element. They are <address>, <blockquote>, <div>, <form>, <h#>, <hr>, <p>, <pre>, <table>, and the list elements.

Project 7: Link Your Pages

If you've been working with all the examples thus far in the book, you've created quite a few HTML files. In this project you're going to use what you have learned about hyperlinks to link all of your files together. You will create a simple navigation system that lists all the files you have created and also provides links to them. Additionally, you will create a simple return link that you can insert in each of the pages to bring you back to your home page. As you continue to work through this book, you will take this simple group of files and mold them into a model Web site. So roll up your sleeves and prepare to become a Webmaster.

Select the Files You Want to Link

5

You may not want to use every file that you have created, but in case you do, Table 5-2 provides a listing of all the files created for the first four chapters of this book. The column on the left is a suggested name for the link you will create; the column on the right is the filename you will use to create the link. Of course, if you used different filenames when you made your own pages, you'll need to substitute those when you design your links.

Page Description or Link Name	File Name
Home Page	index.htm
Headings	headings.htm
Text Elements	text.htm
Superscript & Subscript	sup.htm
Deleted Text	del.htm
Preformatted Text	pre.htm
Unordered List	ulist.htm
Multi-Level Unordered List	ulist2.htm
Ordered List	olist.htm
Ordered List with Start Attribute	olist2.htm
Outline List	olist3.htm
Definition List	dlist.htm
Text Formatting	text-format.htm
Generic Fonts	generic-fonts.htm
The Color Property	font-colors.htm
The Sixteen Basic Colors	16colors.htm
CSS Color	css-color.htm

TABLE 5-2   Files Created in Chapters 1–4

Write the HTML to Link Your Pages

When you have identified the files you want to link, all you need to do is to write the HTML markup that will link your index.htm page to these files. Although there are any number of different ways you can do this, for this project you are going to create a simple unordered list, with each list item providing a link to a page. Each list item will also have a short descriptive term that identifies the content of the file you're going to link to. To create your list of links, follow these steps:

1. Open index.htm.

2. Delete the existing sentences between the <body> </body> tags.

3. Change the <title> to **My HTML Reference Guide**.

4. In the <body> of the page, add an **<h1>** heading that reads **Pages I've Created**.

5. Below your heading, type an opening unordered list **<ul>** tag.

6. On the next line, type an opening list item **<li>** tag.

7. Beside the <li> type your opening anchor tag like this: **<a href="headings.htm">**.

8. Next, add your link text: **Headings**, followed by the closing anchor tag **</a>**.

9. Finally, add a closing list item **</li>** tag.

10. Your completed link should look like the following markup:

    ```
    <li><a href="headings.htm">Headings</li>
    ```

11. Create a similar link for each of the remaining files listed in Table 5-2.

12. When your list is complete, don't forget to add the closing unordered list tag **</ul>**.

13. Add a final link that directs visitors back to **Home** (your home page). This link should point to index.htm, as in the following code:

    ```
    <a href="index.htm">Home</a>
    ```

14. Save *index.htm*.

15. If you want to, insert the Home link at the top or bottom of each of the pages you linked to. This will enable visitors to click the link to return to the home page, rather than having to use the Back button on their browsers.

If you created a link for each of the files listed in Table 5-2, then your home page should look something like Figure 5-1 when displayed in a browser.

Congratulations! You've taken a big step toward creating your own Web site. If you had some problems with this project, the code is provided for you in the "Quick Reference" section of this chapter, coming up next.

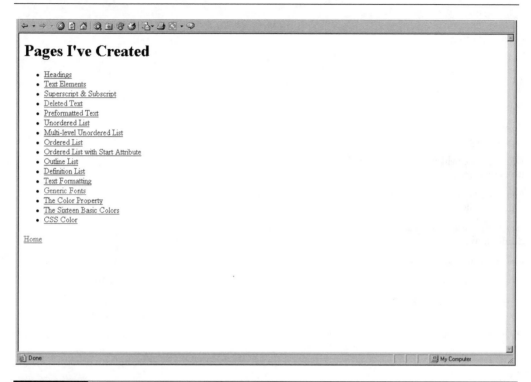

FIGURE 5-1   Sample "Pages I've Created" Page

Quick Reference: Hyperlinks and Projects

In this chapter you have learned how to create hyperlinks to weave your Web site into a cohesive whole. You have also learned how to link to specific locations on a different page as well as linking to other Web sites. This quick reference section will remind you of what you have learned as you begin to create and link together the pages of your own Web site.

Create Hyperlinks

Hyperlinks are what make the Web a web. You can create links from text, photos, clip art, and so on, by enclosing them inside the anchor element. You also can link to a particular spot on the same page and even a certain spot on a different page. The elements and attributes in the next table will help you remember how to create and style your own links.

To Do This	Use This
Create a hyperlink	`<a href=" "> </a>`
Link to a different page	`<a href="webpage.htm">Link</a>`
Set a place marker that you can link to (used for linking to a specific spot on the same page or on another page)	`<element id="spot"> </element>`
Create a named anchor using the name attribute (deprecated)	`<a name="spot"> </a>`
Link to a place marker or named anchor on the same page	`<a href="#spot">Link</a>`
Link to a place marker or named anchor on a different page on the same Web site	`<a href="Webpage.htm#spot">Link</a>`
Link to a place marker or named anchor on a different Web site	`<a href="http://www.newSite.com/ webpage.htm#spot">Link</a>`
Open a link in a new window	`<a href="webpage.htm" target="_blank">Link</a>`
Create an e-mail link	`<a href="mailto:email@server.com">Link</a>`
Cause links on a page to change to red when a cursor passes over them	`<style> a:hover {color: red} </style>` Note: This must be nested in between the <head> tags.
Remove link underlines	`<a href="webpage.htm" style="text-decoration: none">Link</a>`

Code for Project 7

If you had problems getting your Project 7 page to match up with the picture in Figure 5-1, the HTML markup for creating that page is provided here. Compare your code to that which follows, and try to find the solution to your problem. If you're really adventuresome, try modifying this code by creating some place marker links to other pages or changing the color or appearance of your links:

```
<html>
    <head>
      <title>My HTML Reference Guide</title>
    </head>
    <body>
      <h1>Pages I've Created</h1>
        <ul>
          <li><a href="headings.htm">Headings</a></li>
          <li><a href="text.htm">Text Elements</a></li>
          <li><a href="sup.htm">Superscript &amp;
                Subscript</a></li>
          <li><a href="del.htm">Deleted Text</a></li>
```

```
      <li><a href="pre.htm">Preformatted Text</a></li>
      <li><a href="ulist.htm">Unordered List</a></li>
      <li><a href="ulist2.htm">Multi-level
          Unordered List</a></li>
      <li><a href="olist.htm">Ordered List</a></li>
      <li><a href="olist2.htm">Ordered List
          with Start Attribute</a></li>
      <li><a href="olist3.htm">Outline List</a></li>
      <li><a href="dlist.htm">Definition List</a></li>
      <li><a href="text-format.htm">Text
          Formatting</a></li>
      <li><a href="generic-fonts.htm">Generic
          Fonts</a></li>
      <li><a href="font-colors.htm">The Color
          Property</a></li>
      <li><a href="16colors.htm">The Sixteen
          Basic Colors</a></li>
      <li><a href="css-color.htm">CSS Color</a></li>
    </ul>
    <a href="index.htm">Home</a>
  </body>
</html>
```

5

Chapter 6

Enhance Your Presentation with Graphics

How to...

- Understand graphics formats
- Find graphics
- Insert an image on your page
- Control image placement and appearance
- Create image links
- Use CSS with images

Web pages without pictures can be pretty dull places. The content might be great, but today's world is visually oriented. People who visit your site expect to see more than straight text. But how do you give it to them without having to invest in (and learn how to use) a lot of expensive software? The good news is that there are more resources available than you'll ever have time to check out, and many of them are free. But before you begin working with graphics, you must absorb a little background information about how graphics work on the Web.

Understand Web Graphics

There are scores of different ways to create, save, store, and send graphics over the Internet. Fortunately, you don't need to be concerned with most of them. To put images on your Web sites, you need only to have a working familiarity with two or three different formats.

Learn the Differences in Graphics Formats

Although the sheer number of different graphics formats out there is enough to give you a headache, the three that are best suited for use on the Web are GIF, JPEG, and PNG. Each has its own unique qualities and is best used for a particular type of image. A key difference among these three formats lies in how images are *compressed;* that is, how the images are made smaller when they are saved and sent over the Web.

Use the GIF Format for Art

If you are doing navigation buttons, using clip art, or creating banners, drawings, or anything that has large blocks of the same color, you want to use *GIF* (*Graphics Interchange Format,* pronounced *jiff,* like the peanut butter). GIF's particular compression format makes it ideal for these purposes.

When an image is saved, it is compressed to save space and transfer faster. Each of these formats compresses images in a different way. GIF uses something called *LZW* (named after its inventors, Lempel-Ziv and Welch) compression. When an image is saved, LZW takes rows of pixels with the same color and reduces them, in effect, by taking inventory of the number of pixels with that color. For instance, it is easy to compress an image of a button that is solid red and 10×72 pixels; you would merely make a computerized notation that there are 10 rows of red pixels with 72 in each row.

Use JPEG for Photos

If you are planning to use photos on your Web page, GIF is not your best option. The reason, again, is compression. A photograph generally has a much broader range of color varieties and shades, which makes it unsuitable for GIF's method of compression. Instead, you need to use the *JPEG (Joint Photographic Experts Group,* pronounced *jay-peg)* format. Instead of inventorying pixels, as GIF does, JPEG uses a more complicated process that compresses an image by removing colors from parts of the photo where they are least likely to be missed.

Look to the Future with PNG

PNG (pronounced *ping*), stands for Portable Network Graphics. It was developed in response to the controversy over the licensing fee being charged for the GIF compression program and looks to be a very promising format for the future. PNG combines some of the best qualities of both GIF and JPEG; however, older browsers don't support it. Thus, if you are concerned about your images being available to *everyone* who visits your site, you might want to stick with GIF and JPEG for a while.

NOTE   *If you use a scanner, you can also capture your images as bitmaps (BMP). Although Internet Explorer will display bitmaps, there are two good reasons to avoid them on your Web pages. First, Netscape does not support them, so your images will not display on Netscape browsers. An even better reason to avoid them is that bitmap files are larger and will slow down your page loading time. Always convert bitmaps to GIF, JPEG, or PNG files.*

Learn Key Terms

Whenever you are dealing with images and image-editing programs, you will encounter certain terms that come up repeatedly—such as *bit depth, transparency, compression,* and so forth—which can be intimidating but are important to understand; they will influence which kind of format you choose for any given image on your page.

Color Depth

The *color depth* or *bit depth* of an image refers to how much "computing power" is packed into the processing of an image. The greater the bit depth, the more colors the image can contain, and the larger the size of the file. GIF images allow a maximum of 8 bits for every pixel. Because there are three basic colors used in video and graphics displays (red, green, and blue), each gets 8 bits. A little quick arithmetic (2^8) will give you 256 possible color combinations; thus, GIF images can display a maximum of 256 colors. JPEG and PNG both will allow as many as 24 bits per image. With these formats you can have as many as 16.7 million colors in an image file ($256\times256\times256$). That is why JPEG and PNG images work better for photographs and images, both of which require a lot of color definition. The downside of the higher color depth is that it requires a larger file and a longer loading time.

6

 *If you are creating or editing your own graphics, you can choose even smaller color depths. This is a great way to make image files load faster, as long as you don't need as high an image quality.*

Transparency

When it is said that an image supports *transparency*, it means that it is possible to cause one or more of the colors in the image to act as if it were transparent, thus matching the background color of the Web page. This makes your graphics look much cleaner as you use them on different pages, allowing you to create a "cut out" effect and making the borders of the picture invisible. GIF and PNG support transparency; JPEG does not. If you are creating a logo for your page, you probably will want to use GIF or PNG.

Lossless or Lossy Compression

Image compression is said to be *lossless* when the graphic can be compressed or saved without any loss of information. In other words, the image is exactly the same before and after the compression process. On the other hand, *lossy* compression involves a loss of data when the image is saved. GIF and PNG are lossless compression formats. JPEG is lossy, but the loss of quality generally is small.

Interlacing

Have you ever loaded a Web page and noticed that the images start out fuzzy or looking like they were made with blocks, then after a few seconds they sharpen into focus? These images are *interlaced*. Interlacing is a means of saving an image so that when it loads, it gradually progresses from a low resolution to a high resolution. This gives the visitors to your Web site something to look at while the image is loading. The image itself begins "out of focus" and gradually sharpens. JPEG does not support interlacing; GIF and PNG do.

Grayscale

Some formats support images in *grayscale*, that is, a large range of shades from white to black. If you want to put a black-and-white photograph on your site, or display a color picture as black and white, you will want to use a format that supports grayscale. JPEG and PNG support grayscale; GIF does not.

Table 6-1 compares the main characteristics of the different kinds of graphic files that are best suited for Web use. A good rule of thumb is to use GIF for logos, lettering, or any image

	GIF	JPEG	PNG
Color Depth	256	16.7 million	16.7 million
Compression	Lossless	Lossy	Lossless
Transparency	Yes	No	Yes
Interlacing	Yes	No	Yes
Grayscale	No	Yes	Yes

TABLE 6-1   Comparison of Web Graphics Formats

that has large blocks of color; for photographs or detailed images, use JPEG. Support for PNG is growing. If you prefer its versatility to GIF and JPEG, go ahead and use it. However, remember that a small percentage of your visitors (those not using IE6+, Netscape 6+, or Opera 6+) will not be able to view your PNG images.

Obtain Graphics for Use on Your Site

You will find that you have several options as you search for images to use on your site. You can capture images right off the Web as you surf various sites, or you can hit one of the many free and paid clip art and image sites. If you're ambitious and want to create your own graphics, you can find a number of low-cost (and sometimes free) graphics editors to help you get the job done.

Capture Images from the Web

The easiest way to find graphics and art is to capture them directly from the Web. You might be surprised to learn that you can save virtually any image that appears on your screen when you visit a site. It is as simple as a right-click with your mouse. To see how easy it is, follow these steps:

1. Go online and find a picture, logo, or graphic that you like.
2. Put the mouse cursor somewhere on the image and right-click.
3. A dialog box will pop up, giving you several options.
4. Choose Save Picture As.

5. Either accept the image name as supplied or type in your own. You also should specify which directory you want to save the image in.

6. Click OK.

That's all there is to it. You now will be able to insert that image into your own Web pages.

CAUTION   *Whenever you use an image or a photo someone else has created, copyright issues become involved. Even though you can easily capture any image from the Web, that does not mean you have the right to use it without its creator's permission. If you plan to use other people's graphics, be sure to contact them to ask for permission. Generally you can find an e-mail link to the Webmaster of a site at the bottom of the main page.*

Find Royalty-Free Clip Art

Fortunately, there are so many royalty-free sources for clip art, buttons, backgrounds, and pictures on the Web, there's no need to "borrow" someone else's without permission. A quick search on Yahoo or any other search engine generally will bring you more sites offering free images than you have the time or desire to visit. Some helpful sites to check out are in Table 6-2.

Site	URLs
Art Web Site Directories—Online directories of Web sites offering different types of art, organized by subject	www.webplaces.com/html/clipart.htm www.clip-art.com
Clip Art—Some nice sources for free art. The subscription services charge a fee for access to the site, but the content is otherwise free	www.1clipart.com (free) www.free-clip-art.com (free) www.clipart.com (subscription service—$7.95/week or $50/3 months) www.GifArt.com (subscription service—$24.95/month or $49.95/year)
Buttons, Banners, and Backgrounds—Sites that offer free navigation buttons, Web page templates, and background wallpaper	www.freewebtemplates.com www.buttonland.com
Photos—Sites that provide royalty-free photographs for your use	www.stockphotowarehouse.com www.freestockphotos.com www.freeimages.co.uk

TABLE 6-2   Resources for Locating Images

NOTE *Although free, www.freestockphotos.com requires that you mention the source of each of their pictures you use in your Web pages.*

Use Pictures from Your Digital Camera

If you have access to a digital camera, you already have a great way of creating images for your Web site. Most digital cameras come with software that enables you to manipulate and "doctor" your photos. Thus, if you feel so inclined, you can exercise your creativity and easily develop images that can give your Web site a distinctly unique look.

Create Your Own Graphics with an Image Editor

If you're really artistic, you might want to consider creating your own images and graphics from scratch with image-editing software. It's not that difficult, and you might even find yourself having fun in the process. Playing with an image editor is sort of like using finger paints without getting messy or having to clean up. Once you try it, you might find it hard to stop.

If you're interested in purchasing a graphics editor, they are available in a wide range of prices. Table 6-3 lists a few of the programs currently available.

TIP *If you want to put your company logo or letterhead on your site, try using a scanner. A scanner comes in handy when you have hard copies of graphics (logos and so forth) that you need to convert to digital format. You can also use a scanner to convert hard copies of your own photographs, too. While it is possible to scan art you find in print sources, remember the copyright issue. Just because you can scan an image doesn't mean you have the right to use it on your site. Always ask for permission.*

Editor	Approximate Price
Adobe Photoshop	$500
Corel Draw	$300
Macromedia Fireworks	$150
Adobe Photoshop Elements	$80
Corel Draw Essentials	$70
PaintShop Pro 8	$100
AceDesign Pro	$70
Microsoft Imaging and Microsoft Paint	Included with Windows

TABLE 6-3   Image Editors' Price Comparison

Insert Graphics on Your Page

HTML provides a number of ways to insert images and control their placement and appearance on a page. Although many of these have been deprecated in favor of Cascading Style Sheets, they still are the easiest tools to use for simple image placement and positioning. However, as you use them, keep in mind that you ultimately need to move in the direction of CSS. When you have learned how to insert images with HTML, you can expand your design control with Cascading Style Sheets. See Chapter 10 for more information on CSS.

Project: 8 Embed an Image with <img />

When you have found or created some images to work with, you're ready to place them on a page. Inserting an image is easy. You simply use the image element <img /> to insert the image, along with the *src* attribute to tell the browser where to find the image. When you add a graphic to your page this way, it is known as an *embedded* image. To embed an image, follow these steps:

 *If you want an easy way to locate image files to experiment with, try searching your system's hard drive for files that end in .gif or .jpg. In Windows 95 or above, you can do this by simply clicking Start and then selecting the Find or Search option. From there, select the Files or Folders option and type ***.gif** or ***.jpg**. The computer will then search your hard drive and provide a list of files in these formats.*

1. Create a blank html document.

2. Between the <body> tags insert the image element: **<img />**.

   <img /> is an empty element and has no closing tag. Don't forget to put the slash at the end of the <img /> tag.

3. Identify the image's location with the *source* attribute: src=" ". The source attribute tells the browser where to find the image. If the graphic is in the same directory as the Web page, you need to include only the file name, as shown here:

   ```
   <img src="image.gif" />
   ```

4. However, if you have placed your pictures in a different directory, you will need to at least include the directory where the graphic file is located:

   ```
   <img src="images/image.gif" />
   ```

   For more on relative and absolute file addressing, see Chapter 5.

5. Add a description for nonvisual browsers with *alt*. The alt (alternate text) attribute provides a place for you to include a text description of the image. Similar to the title attribute covered in Chapter 5, alt creates a pop-up text box with your description in it when the cursor moves over it. But one of alt's most important uses is to provide content for those who might have images turned off on their browsers or those few who might

still be using text-only browsers. Wherever you have placed an image, visitors will see a display that tells them an image is present, and your description will be included. The same description appears when someone passes the mouse cursor over the image, as in the following illustration:

```
<img src="boo.jpg" alt="My cat, Boo" />
```

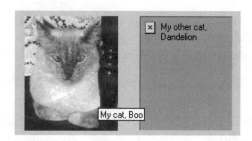

TIP *Although graphics, pictures, and images provide necessary visual interaction for your visitors, never forget that they make your page take longer to load. It's simple mathematics. The more images you have, and the bigger they are, the longer your pages will take to load. To speed up your pages, keep graphics files small and limit the number you use per page. Imagine each of your Web pages as a small container that can hold only about 60K of material; then try to keep the sum of all your content on each page within that limit. Another alternative is to include a small thumbnail-size picture that links to a larger image. Many catalog or photo gallery sites use this technique. It can greatly reduce your page's loading time.*

Specify Graphic Size with the height and width Attributes

The height and width attributes enable you to specify the amount of space your image takes up on the page. With these attributes, you can scale an image up or down, depending your needs. However, it's important to keep in mind that the height and width attributes do not change the image file's actual size. A 1MB image still takes up a full meg of space, even if you scale it down to a thumbnail size. So why should you bother using these attributes?

If you use the height and width attributes with each of your images, it enables a browser to load your pages much faster. As the browser scans through the code, it reads these attributes and then reserves the appropriate amount of space for the image as it lays out your page structure. Thus, it is able to skip over the images and display the text portions of your page first, leaving "place holders" for your pictures. After the text is displayed, it goes back and loads the graphics. This way, your visitors are able to read your content while they're waiting for your images to download. If you don't use the height and width attributes, the browser must load each picture as it comes to it, making the page-loading process much slower.

- **height=" "**   The height attribute specifies the height of the image in pixels.
- **width=" "**   The width attribute specifies the image's width in pixels.

```
<img src="image.jpg" alt="My Favorite Picture" height="100" width="150" />
```

The smaller image is set to 100 X 150; the larger is set to 200 x 250.

Wrap Text and Align Images with align (Deprecated)

Suppose you want to have an image right aligned with the text wrapping around to the left. You can do this with HTML by using the *align* attribute. Although align has been deprecated in favor of style sheets, it is by far easiest to use when you are learning. However, if it is your goal to write "standards-compliant" Web pages with XHTML, you will eventually need to move away from the this method of positioning your images and develop your layouts using style sheets.

NOTE *If you want to learn more about image placement using CSS, check out Chapter 11.*

Use align with "left" and "right" Values for Text Wrapping

To control text wrapping, use the align attribute with left or right as the value. The picture will appear on one side of the page, with the text on the other. If you choose align="left", any text will be wrapped around the right side of your image. Align="right" wraps the text around the left side of your graphic.

```
<img src="pansy1.jpg" align="left" />
<img src="pansy2.jpg" align="right" />
```

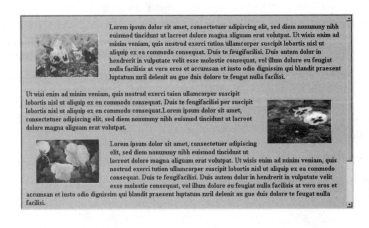

Use align with "top," "middle," and "bottom" Values for Vertical Positioning

To control the vertical alignment of an image relative to text, another image, or anything else on the page, specify the value as top, middle, or bottom, like this:

```
<img src="image.gif" align="top" />
<img src="image.gif" align="middle" />
<img src="image.gif" align="bottom" />
```

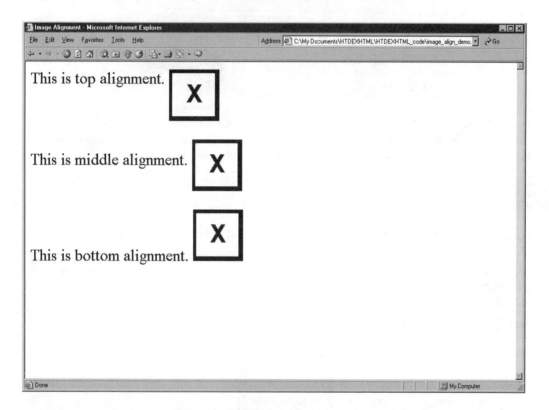

Add White Space with hspace and vspace (Deprecated)

If you want to create a buffer zone of white space around your image, you can do it with the hspace and vspace attributes. *hspace* stands for horizontal space; *vspace* stands for vertical space. Adding hspace inserts space along the horizontal axis, and vspace inserts space along the vertical axis. In the following illustration, the image in the lower right corner has space added, while the image in the upper left corner does not.

```
<img src="pansy3.jpg" hspace="50" vspace="50">
```

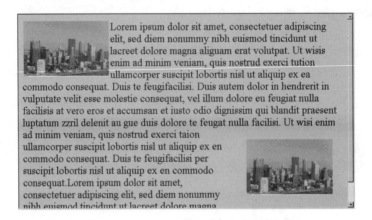

The values for hspace and vspace are specified in pixels; thus, in the preceding case, the browser adds a buffer zone of 50 pixels around the entire image. If you want to add space on only the sides or only above and below the image, simply use one of the attributes rather than both.

 The hspace and vspace attributes have both been deprecated. As you will learn in Chapter 10, you can accomplish the same effects with the CSS padding property.

Add a Border with the border Attribute (Deprecated)

To add a border around your image, you can include the deprecated border=" " attribute. You specify the size (thickness) of the border in pixels. So, border="5" will insert a border 5 pixels in width. Adding a border to an image is a nice way to give a picture a "large image" feel with a "small image" performance.

```
<img src="boo.jpg" border="5" alt="My cat Boo" height="100" width="50" />
```

6

> **TIP**
>
> *The border attribute enables you to create only one kind of border. Style sheets are the better choice because they enable you to assign borders in as many as eight different styles, including dotted, dashed, solid, double, groove, ridge, inset, and outset. Also, different border styles may be used in combination with one another and can be placed around any element—not just images.*

Practical Uses for Images

You can use images purely for decoration, but they also have many practical uses on a Web page. Images can serve as links, backgrounds, buttons, watermarks, and much more.

Use an Image as a Link

You can use an image as a link by placing the <img /> element between a set of anchor <a> tags. This will create a link in much the same way that text becomes a link when placed inside this element.

```
<a href="http://www.linksite.com">
<img src="image.gif" /></a>
```

Those who come to your site through a nongraphical, nonvisual browser will need some other way to navigate. You can make things easier for them by including a text link with the image. Inserting the text between the <a> tags accomplishes this, as shown in the following illustration:

```
<a href="flowerpage.htm".>
<img src="image.gif"alt="Link to flower site" />
  Click to go to my flower page.</a>.
```

Click to go to my flower page.

Link to flower site

> **NOTE**
>
> *If your image is a link, a border is automatically drawn around it. If you do not want a border around a linked image, you must specify border="0".*

Insert a Background Image with background (Deprecated)

You can insert a background image on your page by using the background=" " attribute inside the opening <body> tag. The browser will then "tile" the image to fill up the page. To use the background created earlier in this chapter as the wallpaper for a page, the opening body tag would look like this:

```
<body background="image.gif">
```

A page with a seamless tile background

 TIP   *Don't choose garish or harsh-looking images or patterns for backgrounds. You might think they look really good, but unless your content is incredibly compelling (and sometimes not even then), your visitors will not be back for a second visit. Remember, your* content *is the most important part of your Web site, not your background.*

The image, whatever it is, will fill the page and scroll right along with the page's content. But what if you would like to have your company's logo remain stationary on the page, where your visitors can always see it? For that you need to create a watermark.

Create a Watermark Effect with bgproperties (Deprecated)

If you would like to create a *watermark* effect, you use an additional attribute in the <body> tag, called bgproperties. This attribute allows the background to remain stationary while the page's content scrolls. To create this effect, make the following change to your <body> tag:

```
<body background="image.gif" bgproperties="fixed">
```

NOTE   *Until recently, this attribute was supported only in Internet Explorer and Opera; Netscape 6 now supports the watermark effect. However, older Netscape browsers still ignore this attribute and scroll the background.*

Use Cascading Style Sheets with Graphics

If you have been working through this book chapter by chapter, hopefully you have already begun to appreciate the value and versatility of Cascading Style Sheets (CSS). By combining style sheets with graphics, you can create some wonderful effects for your Web pages. As always, you need to make sure that your pages are not dependent upon any of the effects you create, so that a person with a browser that does not fully support CSS can still enjoy your site.

Project 9: Add a Watermark with CSS

Cascading Style Sheets enable you to control background images and do all the same things covered earlier in the chapter. However, CSS throw in some extras that are not available in

HTML. As you have already read in this chapter, HTML allows you to specify a background image, which will be tiled to fill up the page. The style rules for CSS background images give you a much greater range of choices. For example:

- To specify an image as a background image:

  ```
  background-image: (url)picture.jpg
  ```

- To tile an image to fill up the page:

  ```
  background-repeat: repeat
  ```

- To make an image repeat across the top of the page:

  ```
  background-repeat: repeat-x
  ```

- To make an image repeat straight down the page:

  ```
  background-repeat: repeat-y
  ```

- To cause an image to be used only once:

  ```
  background-repeat: no-repeat
  ```

- To allow an image to scroll with the page:

  ```
  background-attachment: scroll
  ```

- To fix the image in place, such as a watermark:

  ```
  background-attachment: fixed
  ```

- To position the background image on the page:

  ```
  background-position: top (or center, bottom, left, right)
  ```

Thus far, you have primarily applied styles *inline*—that is, right inside the various element tags of your pages. However, you will find it much less cumbersome to add your styles as an embedded style sheet inside your page's <head> element. The only difference is that because you are not placing the style inside the element itself, you have to specify the name of the element you want to modify. In CSS terminology this is called a *selector*, but don't let the term confuse you. For now, just think in terms of the element's name. For example, if you want to set styles that will affect all the other elements on the page, use the "body" selector. If you only want to affect first level headings, use the "h1" selector. A page with styles embedded in the <head> will look something like the following markup:

```
<html>
  <head>
  <title>Page Title</title>
  <style type="text/css">
```

```
elementName { cssProperty: value;
              cssProperty: value;
              cssProperty: value;}
elementName { cssProperty: value;
              cssProperty: value;}
</style>
</head>
<body>
</body>
</html>
```

TIP *For a quick reference on how to create CSS style rules, download Appendix B from www.jamespence.com or www.osborne.com.*

I might have positioned the CSS watermark section ahead of the deprecated watermark methods in the text. To use the <style> element to create an embedded style sheet that creates a background image down the left side of the page and allows it to remain fixed, copy the following HTML code and display it in your browser. (Don't forget to replace image.gif with your own image.) It should resemble the illustration that follows:

```
<html>
  <head>
    <title>CSS Watermark Effect</title>
    <style type="text/css">
body      {     background-image: url(image.gif);
                background-position: left;
                background-repeat: repeat-y;
                background-attachment: fixed; }
    </style>
  </head>
  <body>
(Cut and paste some text here)
  </body>
</html>
```

Lorem ipsum dolor sit amet, consectetuer adipiscing elit, sed diem nonummy nibh euismod tincidunt ut lacreet dolore magna aliguam erat volutpat. Ut wisis enim ad minim veniam, quis nostrud exerci tution ullamcorper suscipit lobortis nisl ut aliguip ex

Project 10: Place a Decorative Border Around an Image

Maybe you would like to put an attractive border around your images. HTML allows you to specify a border, its width, and sometimes its color. However, with CSS, there are many more available options. A sample style rule that will give a decorative red border, with something of a 3-D effect, would look like this:

```
img      {border-color: red;
          border-style: inset;
          border-width: thick;}
```

To see how this looks, choose any image on your system and then copy the code here, putting the image filename in the <img /> element, and your own values in the height and width attributes:

```
<html>
  <head>
    <title>CSS Image Border</title>
    <style type="text/css">
body     {margin-left: .50in; margin-top: .50in}
img       {border-color: red;
            border-style: inset;
            border-width: thick;}
    </style>
  </head>
  <body>
    <img src="image.jpg" alt="A sample image and border"
      height="200" width="300" />
  </body>
</html>
```

This code creates a red "picture frame"–type border around any image that is placed on the page. It also specifies a 1/2" margin on the top and left sides of the page.

Try experimenting with some of the other CSS properties and see what varieties you can come up with. The best way to learn CSS (or HTML, for that matter) is to play with it. Go have some fun and see what you can do.

6

Quick Reference: Adding Images

In this chapter, you have learned the basics of adding images to your Web pages. Although there is more to learn, this will give you enough to practice with as you become comfortable with HTML. The following table lists some of the markup required to embed and position images on your Web page:

To Do This	Use This
Embed an image	`<img src="image.gif" />`
Make an image a link	`<a href="webpage.htm"><img src="image.gif" />`
Make a combined image link and text link	`<a href="webpage.htm"><img src="image.gif" />Place Text Here</a>`
Provide alternate text	`<img src="image.gif" alt="alternate text" />`
Specify an image's height and width	`<img src="image.gif" height="#" width="#" />` (# in pixels)
Align an image to the left or right, with text wrapping (Deprecated)	`<img src="image.gif" align="left" />` or `"right"`
Position an image relative to text or another image (Deprecated)	`<img src="image.gif" align="top">` or `"middle,"` or `"bottom"`
Add white space on the sides of an image (Deprecated)	`<img src="image.gif" hspace="#">` (# in pixels)
Add white space on an image's top and bottom	`<img src="image.gif" vspace="#" />` (# in pixels)
Use CSS to add a background image (tiled)	`<style> body {background-image: (url)image.gif} </style>`
Use CSS to add a background watermark	`<style> body {background-image: (url)image.gif; background-attachment: fixed}</style>`
Use CSS to add a background image down the left side of your page	`<style> body {background-image: (url)image.gif; background-repeat: repeat-y; background-position: left}</style>`
Use CSS to add a red inset border around your images	`<style> img {border-style: inset; border-width: thick; border-color: red} </style>`

Chapter 7

Enter the World of XHTML

How to...

- Understand XHTML
- Create an XHTML document
- Validate your XHTML
- Plan, publish, and promote your Web site

In Chapters 1 through 6, you learned enough HTML basics to construct a simple Web site. You have also been introduced to XHTML and its somewhat stricter rules. By now you may be wondering if all you have to do to write in XHTML is to write your HTML markup more carefully. Well, that's a good start, but there's a bit more to writing XHTML than that. In this chapter, you will enter the world of XHTML. You will also learn how to plan, publish, and promote your XHTML Web site.

Understand XHTML

As you recall, XHTML was developed because of HTML's inability to grow and change with the ever-expanding technology of our day. After all, when HTML was first developed, the concept of accessing the Internet by means of your cellular phone was more the stuff of science fiction than science. Because HTML markup is, as it were, set in stone, it does not have the capacity for being adapted on the fly to new, ever-changing technologies. XHTML, on the other hand, can be adapted and changed. As you'll learn in Chapter 16, even *you* can adapt XHTML and design your own markup. How is this possible? It is possible because of XHTML's powerful "parent" language, XML.

XML Means Extensibility

The acronym XML stands for the *Extensible Markup Language,* a powerful *meta*-language that is a subset of an even more powerful meta-language called the *Standard Generalized Markup Language (SGML).* Just in case you're wondering, a meta-language is a language that is used to develop or describe other languages. For example, HTML is actually a daughter language (or *subset*) of SGML. XML is also a daughter language of SGML, but there's one big difference between XML and its older sibling HTML: extensibility. HTML was not designed with adaptability in mind. XML, on the other hand, was designed to be a meta-language in its own right. In other words, XML was developed to make it possible for you to create your own markup languages. With XML, instead of being restricted to a fixed set of elements, attributes, and values, *you define your own.* You'll learn how to do this in Chapter 16, but for now, it's important to understand that your personalized markup is defined by means of a *Document Type Description (DTD).*

Understand DTDs

If you were working in XML and wanted to use it to develop your own markup language, you would create a *DTD (Document Type Description)*. This is essentially a "blueprint" that lists all the possible elements, attributes, and values for your new markup language. For example, say you developed several different markup languages with XML. Each language would have its own DTD. Then, when you want to use one of your new languages, you simply include a statement at the top of your document that identifies which language the document conforms to and where to find your "blueprint" (DTD). This enables a browser to properly interpret your "homemade" elements, attributes, and values. This identifying statement is known as a *document type declaration* or DOCTYPE declaration.

Understand Document Type Declarations

A document type declaration is found at the very beginning of an XML document and functions as a pointer, directing a browser (or other software) to the location of that document's DTD. That way, the browser can look up the "blueprint," compare your document to it, and then display your document properly. For example, the document type declaration for an HTML 4.01 document looks like this: <!DOCTYPE html PUBLIC "-//W3C//DTD HTML 4.01//EN">. You don't often see the HTML Doctype declaration used because Web browsers don't need it for interpreting HTML pages. However, when a document type declaration *is* used, it is placed before the opening HTML tag, as in the following code listing:

```
<!DOCTYPE html PUBLIC "-//W3C//DTD HTML 4.01//EN">
<html>
    <head> (and so on)
```

Although this strange line might appear to be an element (because of the "less than" and "greater than" symbols enclosing it), it is actually an SGML command. It identifies for a Web browser the DTD that should be used in displaying that particular Web page. Although document type declarations are not often used for conventional HTML pages, if you plan on working with XHTML, you had better get used to them. As you'll soon see, they are very important.

Sort Out XHTML's Relationship to HTML and XML

So how do you sort out the differences between SGML, HTML, XHTML, and XML without getting a headache? It's really quite simple. SGML is the "source" language for HTML, XHTML, and XML. As for XHTML, it is simply HTML 4.0 reformulated as an XML application. Remember that XML can be used for creating markup languages? What the W3C did was to use XML to "recreate" HTML. This is reflected in a new name XHTML, or *Extensible Hypertext Markup Language*. On the one hand, XHTML will bring to the Web designer's arsenal a greatly increased flexibility; on the other hand, it requires a bit more discipline in its use.

XHTML Documents Must Conform to a DTD

The current specification is XHTML 1.1, and it will be covered in Chapter 16. However, the original version of XHTML (and the one still most commonly used) is XHTML 1.0. This specification actually uses *three* different DTDs: Transitional, Strict, and Frameset.

- The *Transitional DTD* still allows for the use of HTML's deprecated elements and attributes.

- The *Strict DTD* does not permit the use of any presentational (deprecated) elements or attributes. In other words, you may not use HTML elements and attributes to control the appearance (color, font size, layout, and so on) of your document. You must use CSS to add "style" to your document.

- The *Frameset DTD* is for use when you are designing frame-based pages.

When you write an XHTML 1.0 page, you need to identify which of the preceding DTDs the document will conform to. You do this by adding the appropriate <!DOCTYPE> command at the beginning of the document. The <!DOCTYPE> declarations for each of the DTDs are as follows:

- **Transitional** <!DOCTYPE html PUBLIC "-//W3C//DTD XHTML 1.0 Transitional//EN" "http://www.w3.org/TR/xhtml1/DTD/xhtml1-transitional.dtd">

- **Strict** <!DOCTYPE html PUBLIC "-//W3C//DTD XHTML 1.0 Strict//EN" "http://www.w3.org/TR/xhtml1/DTD/xhtml1-strict.dtd">

- **Frameset** <!DOCTYPE html PUBLIC "-//W3C//DTD XHTML 1.0 Frameset//EN" "http://www.w3.org/TR/xhtml1/DTD/xhtml1-frameset.dtd">

 *The <!DOCTYPE> command is case sensitive. Make sure that you type the commands in* exactly *as you see them here, or your page will not validate. See Chapter 16 for the XHTML 1.1 <!DOCTYPE> command.*

XHTML Documents Should Use the XHTML Namespace

Another small change in how an XHTML document is written is found in the opening <html> tag. Although you still use <html> as your root element, you must add a reference that points to the XHTML *namespace*. If you're confused about what this term means, think of a namespace as sort of a glossary of names associated with an XML application. That's a bit of an oversimplification, but it's all you need to be concerned with at the moment. Because your document is an XHTML document, it must point to the XHTML namespace. You do this by adding an attribute to the opening <html> tag, as in the following code listing:

```
<!DOCTYPE HTML PUBLIC "-//W3C//DTD XHTML 1.0 Transitional//EN"
"http://www.w3.org/TR/xhtml1/DTD/xhtml1-transitional.dtd">

<html xmlns="http://www.w3.org/1999/xhtml">
```

As you'll see in Chapter 16, it is this ability to identify with a namespace that enables you as a Web designer to extend XHTML by adding your own markup. For now, just remember to add the namespace attribute to your opening <html> tags.

XHTML Documents Must Be Well Formed

Another requirement for writing XHTML documents is that they must be *well formed*. This is in contrast to HTML, which can be (and often is) written rather haphazardly. Browsers sometimes ignore mistakes in HTML code. You don't have this luxury with XHTML. Your document must be well formed, which simply means it must contain no errors in syntax. A simple guideline for writing well-formed XHTML is as follows:

■ All elements (except empty elements) must have opening and closing tags:

```
<element> </element>
```

■ All elements must be properly nested:

```
<a> <b> </b> </a>
```

■ Empty elements must be properly closed:

```
<empty-element />
```

■ All attribute values must be quoted:

```
<element attribute="value">
```

■ Attributes must always have values:

```
<input checked="checked">
```

■ Elements and attributes must be written in lowercase:

```
Incorrect: <HTML>, <Html>  Correct: <html>
```

XHTML Documents Must Be Valid

An XHTML document must not only be well formed, but must also be *valid*. What's the difference? The term "well formed" applies to the document's grammar or syntax. If an XHTML document is written correctly, according to the rules mentioned in the preceding section, then it is well formed. However, in order to be "valid," the document must be checked or *validated* against a DTD. Think of it this way: Suppose you were a counterfeiter and had access to a high quality color printer. You would be able to reproduce $20 bills with a high degree of accuracy. In fact, you could produce bills of such quality that most people could not tell them from the real thing. Those bills would be "well formed." However, for the bills to have any monetary value, they would also have to be valid. In other words, they would have to pass the test of genuineness. In the case of a $20 bill, it would be validated by the security watermark and other built-in features. Thus, a counterfeit $20 bill can be well formed but not valid. Likewise, an XHTML document can be well formed (syntactically correct), but not valid.

How do you validate your pages? The first step is by including the proper <!DOCTYPE> declaration for the version of XHTML you are using. The second step is to write your pages according to the rules that apply for that DTD. For example, if you decide to use the Strict DTD, be sure that you don't use any of the deprecated elements or attributes. Otherwise, your document will not validate. This is because those elements and attributes are not recognized in the Strict DTD.

Finally, you will be wise to validate (compare) your page against that DTD. How do you do this? Many HTML editors have built-in validation programs that will point out where your pages need to be changed if you want them to be valid. The W3C has a validation service (http://validator.w3.org/) that checks your pages free of charge. You simply go to the site, enter the URL of the page you want validated into the form, and in a few seconds you will have a generated report showing where your page measures up against the DTD you've chosen. Some programs, such the *HTML Tidy* program, actually make the changes for you. HTML Tidy is freeware and can be downloaded from the W3C's site at www.w3.org. It is also bundled with the freeware HTML editor *HTML-Kit*, available at www.chami.com.

 You are not required to validate your pages against a DTD in order to write XHTML. In fact, even if they are not valid, your XHTML pages will still display correctly—for now. However, there are at least two good reasons to take the time to validate your pages. First, it will speed up your learning process. These sites help you find mistakes in your code and learn why your pages are not doing what you want them to. Second, in the future as browsers begin to follow the stricter standards, invalid pages may fail to display at all. That is why it's a good practice to validate all of your XHTML pages. It's more work now, but you will save yourself a lot of work in the future.

Project 11: Create and Validate an XHTML Document

Although the idea of well-formed and valid XHTML documents is simple once you've had time to think about it, there still can be a rather large intimidation factor. This project is designed to walk you through the process of creating and validating a simple XHTML document. To complete the project, you need Internet access so that you can use the W3C's free validation service. An alternative is to download HTML Kit from www.chami.com and use HTML Tidy to validate your document. When you are ready, complete the following steps:

1. Open the first page of your sample Web site, index.htm, and save it as *xhtml1.htm*.

2. Add the <!DOCTYPE> declaration for the XHTML Transitional DTD. This should be inserted just before the opening <html> tag.

3. Modify the opening <html> tag to include the XHTML namespace:

```
<html xmlns="http://www.w3.org/1999/xhtml">
```

4. Because the W3C's validator requires that your document provide character encoding (or Unicode) information, add the following <meta> element between the <head> tags:

```
<meta http-equiv="Content-Type"
      content="text/html; charset=iso-8859-7" />
```

TIP *Because of the explosive growth of the Internet, it's a good idea to always provide character-encoding information in your pages. This lets browsers know what character set they need to use in displaying your text. In the preceding code, this is done by using the <meta /> (descriptive) element.*

5. Now save your document and go online to http://validator.w3.org.

6. Under the Validate Files heading, select the Local File option by entering into the input window the location of the page you just saved, as shown here:

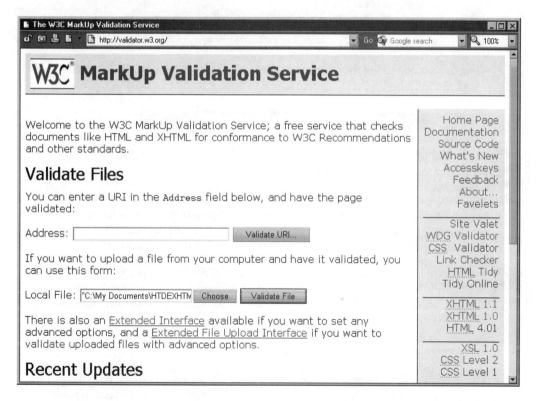

7. If you don't want to type the information, click Choose. The Open dialog box pops up, and you can navigate to the proper file folder and click the file you want to validate, as in the illustration that follows:

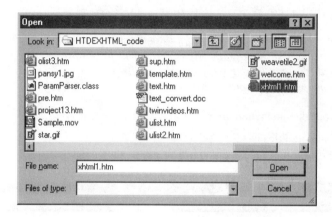

8. When the location of the file has been entered into the input window, click Validate File. If your xhtml1.htm file is valid, you will see a window that looks like this:

> This Page Is Valid <u>XHTML 1.0</u> Transitional!

> **NOTE** *If your page validates, the W3C provides you with a nice little icon that you can display on that page, identifying it as valid XHTML.*

9. But what if your page is not valid? Then you will see a different window, informing you that the page has not validated and giving you the reasons why. To see what this looks like (assuming your page validated on the first try), try changing the <!DOCTYPE> declaration for your xhtml1.htm page from the Transitional to the Strict DTD.

> **NOTE** *You'll discover that the page does not validate according to the Strict DTD. Why? Because the home page link near the bottom of the page is not nested inside another element. According to the Strict DTD, the <a> element cannot stand on its own. It must be nested in another element (such as <p>, <h1>, and so on). To bring the page into conformance, just enclose the <a> element inside a set of <p> tags, as in the following:* ***<p><a href="index.htm">Home</a></p>***.

If you are having difficulty getting the page to validate, try working from the code listing that follows. It validated against the XHTML 1.0 Transitional DTD and, with the correction made in the above Note, against the XHTML 1.0 Strict DTD.

```
<!DOCTYPE html PUBLIC "-//W3C//DTD XHTML 1.0 Transitional//EN"
"http://www.w3.org/TR/xhtml1/DTD/xhtml1-transitional.dtd">
```

```
<html xmlns="http://www.w3.org/1999/xhtml">
  <head>
    <title>My HTML Reference Guide</title>
    <meta http-equiv="Content-Type"
          content="text/html; charset=iso-8859-7" />
  </head>
  <body>
    <h1>Pages I've Created</h1>
    <ul>
      <li><a href="headings.htm">Headings</a></li>
      <li><a href="text.htm">Text Elements</a></li>
      <li><a href="sup.htm">Superscript &amp;
           Subscript</a></li>
      <li><a href="del.htm">Deleted Text</a></li>
      <li><a href="pre.htm">Preformatted Text</a></li>
      <li><a href="ulist.htm">Unordered List</a></li>
      <li><a href="ulist2.htm">Multi-level
           Unordered List</a></li>
      <li><a href="olist.htm">Ordered List</a></li>
      <li><a href="olist2.htm">Ordered List with
           Start Attribute</a></li>
      <li><a href="olist3.htm">Outline List</a></li>
      <li><a href="dlist.htm">Definition List</a></li>
      <li><a href="text-format.htm">Text
           Formatting</a></li>
      <li><a href="generic-fonts.htm">Generic Fonts</a></li>
      <li><a href="font-colors.htm">The Color Property</a></li>
      <li><a href="16colors.htm">The Sixteen
           Basic Colors</a></li>
      <li><a href="css-color.htm">CSS Color</a></li>
    </ul>
    <a href="index.htm">Home</a>
  </body>
</html>
```

7

Plan Your Site Effectively

Now that you have learned how to validate your XHTML pages, you are equipped to put up
your own Web site. It doesn't take a lot of expensive software or programming knowledge. All
it takes is your time and planning. Yet it is in the planning stage that most would-be Web authors
fall short. Web authoring software has made creating a site so easy that it is commonplace

for beginning authors to throw together Web sites in an afternoon, publish them, and sit back, confident that the world is going to rush to behold their creations.

If all you want to do is have a site online, this approach works fine. If you actually want an effective site, you'd better reject the haphazard approach. An effective Web site not only reflects care in the design of the pages, it also reflects careful thought in its overall layout.

Just as a building contractor would never think of beginning construction on a building without a good set of blueprints, you shouldn't begin developing your site without planning it well. A good Web site "blueprint" will take into consideration your site's layout, your choice of hosts, and an idea of how you are going to promote the site.

Identify Your Site's Purpose

The first step in creating your site is to identify its purpose. Depending on whether your site is personal, informational, or for business, you will want (and need) to add different things. The more clearly you define a purpose for your site, the easier it will be to decide what needs to go into it. For example, your site could be

- A personal family album–type site
- An informational or resource site
- An entertainment-oriented site
- A brochure site, advertising a business or organization
- An online business

By developing a concrete idea of your Web site's reason for existence, you will find it much easier to decide what—and what not—to include. For example, if you are planning to set up an online business, you'll probably need to have a page that contains an order form and a catalog for your products. A brochure-type site isn't likely to need these, but you'll probably want to include an e-mail link and response form so potential customers can contact you. A family album site won't need much in the way of bells and whistles, but if you're putting together an informational site about your model rocketry hobby, you might want to consider a page with a streaming video of a model rocket launch.

A good rule is to put in everything you *need*; leave out anything that won't contribute to your site's goal. The only way to know what those things are is if you have clearly defined that goal.

Identify Your Target Audience

In addition to defining your site's purpose, you should give some thought to your target audience. Who do you want to attract to your site? How do you plan to get them there? Whether your audience is made up of friends and relatives, people with a shared interest, or potential customers, your site design, layout, and content depend on your having a clear idea of that audience.

Another question about your target audience has to do with the kind of equipment they will be using to view your site. If you're designing for a corporate network and you know exactly what types of browsers and monitors will be used to display your site, you'll have a great deal of freedom in design. Likewise, if you're designing for family and friends, and you don't really care whether anyone else can see your site, you are free to set things up the way you want. However, if you are trying to reach a broad audience, you must decide whether or not to design your pages with cutting-edge effects, possibly excluding those whose equipment can't display your pages properly.

As you plan your site, keep the following questions in mind:

- Who do you want to come to your site? (Family? Friends? People with a shared interest? Potential customers?)

- What kind of equipment (browsers, monitors, computers, and so on) will your visitors be using?

- Based on the age and background of your intended audience, what types of graphics and design will they find most appealing?

- Do you want to design your site so that older browsers will be able to display it, thus increasing your potential audience (but limiting your design options)?

- If your site is business related, what is its mission or goal? Is it intended for commerce, information, research, leisure, or some other purpose?

Storyboard Your Site

After you have identified your site's purpose and audience, you can begin drawing up a blueprint. In Web design, this is called *storyboarding*. If you've ever watched a documentary on how Disney produces one of its animated movies, you're familiar with the idea of storyboarding. For a movie, the writers sketch out various scenes so that they can visualize the overall content of the film. In a similar way, you visualize a Web site's layout and organization by storyboarding the individual pages that will make up the site.

You can storyboard a site by sketching it out on a piece of paper or by using sticky notes to represent each page—you can even use three-by-five cards. You can get really fancy and draw the layout with a graphics or flow chart program. Most important is that you are able to easily rearrange your layout so you can try out different approaches to structuring your site.

To create a storyboard for your site, follow these steps:

1. Decide what pages you want to start with. You will need a home or an index page, of course, but you also need to plan your other pages. For example, if you are constructing a family album site, you might decide on a page that focuses on each member of the family. Each of those pages could have its own series of subpages such as hobbies, favorite music, pictures, and favorite books.

2. Decide on your layout. Is your site going to be linear? Pyramid? This is partly determined by your site's content and purpose. If you want visitors to move progressively through your material, you might choose a linear site. If you want them to be able to take different paths, depending on their interests, a site organized like a pyramid might be more suitable. You would have a single "entry" page that leads to several more pages, each of which leads to several more pages related to the topics.

3. Use a 3×5 card to represent each page, and write the page's main title on the blank side. Obviously, if you're planning to have hundreds of pages on your site, this could be cumbersome. At this point, you need to storyboard only your main pages.

4. Rearrange the cards, trying different layouts, until you find one you like.

5. Copy the layout onto a sheet of paper.

6. Revise the site design until you are satisfied.

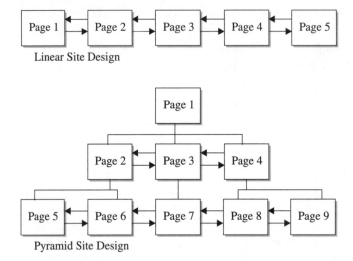

Linear Site Design

Pyramid Site Design

Gather Your Content

In the final step of site organization, you will plan and gather your content. When it comes to planning, don't skimp here. Your content will determine whether people keep coming back to your site. To find content for your site, you can

- **Write your own.** The first and most obvious place to go looking for content is right at home. Whatever your site's subject matter, if you are going to the trouble of building a Web site, you probably have enough interest or expertise to produce a large portion of the content. If you're putting up a site dedicated to Monarch butterfly migration patterns, chances are you know enough about the subject to be your own resource for at least a portion of the site.

- **Invite others to contribute.** If you are constructing a large site or one that will provide a lot of information, you'll find it difficult to keep up with the content all by yourself. However, if you make your content needs known to others who share your interest, you might find that your only problem is finding time to put all the offerings onto your site.

- **Use a content supplier.** A great way to provide fresh content for your site is by taking advantage of free Web content suppliers. These Web sites provide up-to-date news, financial, weather, and general interest content for your site, and generally they are free of charge. Simply visit the site and choose what content you would like to add to your page. They will send you (generally by e-mail) some code to paste into your HTML document. That's all there is to it. To find sources, just do a search with the keywords "free Web content" or "syndicated Web content." You'll find plenty of resources. The downside of these content suppliers is that a Web browser must contact their site and download the content as your page loads, thus slowing down the loading time. However, it's hard to beat them for providing fresh content on a consistent basis. You can find a list of free content providers in Table 7-1.

TIP *Don't forget to update your content regularly. If your site never updates or provides new information, your visitors have little reason to return.*

Develop Your Web Site

When you're done with your planning, it's time to begin the process of creating, testing, and previewing your pages. By the time you get to this point, you might be in a hurry to get your site uploaded. Resist the temptation to rush, and take the time to develop your pages carefully. You want your Web presence to be perfectly functional when you finally put it online. Among other things, taking your time here helps make sure that none of your visitors sees a "404 Not Found" message when they try to access one of your pages.

7

Write Your Pages

It might seem like stating the obvious, but you have to write your pages before you publish them. And with all the options available to would-be Webmasters, that might not be as simple as you think. If you've been working through the book and doing the exercises in Notepad or some other text editor, you might have wondered about the different Web authoring tools that are available and which—if any—you should use. Here they are:

- **WYSIWYG programs (Microsoft FrontPage, Macromedia Dreamweaver, Net Objects Fusion, and so forth)** WYSIWYG (pronounced *wizzy wig*) is an acronym for "What you see is what you get." These programs enable you to construct your

Web Content Provider	URL
IT News	www.it-news.com/freecontent.htm
Click for Content	www.clickforcontent.com
Free Sticky	www.freesticky.com/stickyweb
Free Content	www.certificate.net/wwio
IdeaMarketers	www.ideamarketers.com
4Free Content	www.4freecontent.com

TABLE 7-1   Sources for Free or Syndicated Web Content

pages visually, just as you might lay out a brochure or poster with a desktop publishing program. WYSIWYGs are helpful tools in that they enable you to create pages much more quickly than you can by writing the HTML code yourself. Also, many of them double as site management tools, alerting you to broken links and displaying the structure of your site. Although WYSIWYGs are helpful, they do have some disadvantages. First, they can become crutches that keep you from learning HTML yourself. Even with these programs, you'll often need to go in and tweak your HTML code. If you don't know HTML, you're at the mercy of the program. So, even if you decide to use a WYSIWYG, take the time to learn to work with HTML first.

■ **Word processors (Word, WordPerfect, and so forth)**   Most word processing programs can save pages in HTML format and many of the newest ones will even work like a WYSIWYG editor. Unfortunately, word processors are not known for writing very good code, and you might find it necessary go in and clean it up.

■ **Web browsers (Netscape Composer, Microsoft FrontPage Express)**   Some Web browsers also incorporate their own Web page editing programs. These aren't bad, although their capabilities are somewhat limited compared to the WYSIWYG programs. They also tend to suffer from the same limitations as the full-featured WYSIWYGs.

■ **HTML editors (Amaya, HTML Kit, Coffee Cup HTML Editor, Allaire Homesite, and so forth)**   HTML editors combine the best of both worlds. They function much like simple text editors, but also include special features for writing HTML. In preview mode, many will give you a WYSIWYG-like display (although you can't edit in preview mode), so you can keep tabs on what your page actually will look like. What's more, the best HTML editors are available as freeware—just download them and go to work! Table 7-2 lists some shareware and freeware HTML editors you might want to check out.

HTML Editor	URL	Approximate Cost
HTML Kit	http://chami.com/html-kit	Freeware
First Page	www.evrsoft.com	Freeware
Arachnophilia	www.arachnoid.com/arachnophilia	Freeware
Amaya	www.w3.org	Freeware
Cute HTML	www.globalscape.com	$20
CoolPage	www.coolpage.com	$30
CoffeeCup HTML Editor	www.coffeecup.com	$50
Hot Dog PageWiz	www.sausagetools.com	$70
Hot Dog Professional	www.sausagetools.com	$100
Macromedia Homesite	www.macromedia.com/software	$100

TABLE 7-2   HTML Editing Software

Test Your Links and Site Navigation

When writing your pages, or when you are done writing them, the next important step is to test your links. The larger the site you are constructing, the more tempting it will be to let this part slide. However, there's nothing more frustrating to your visitors than clicking on a dead link. So bite the bullet and test those links. It's good practice to begin testing as you add each new page, but whether you do it all at once or page by page, make sure every link works.

You'll also want to make sure your site navigation is straightforward and easy to follow. Don't leave your visitors guessing about how they should navigate your site. At the very minimum, you should provide a link to the main page and a link to a site map on every page. As its name implies, a *site map* is a page that functions as a directory, containing direct links to all of your pages. If your visitors want to get a bird's-eye view of your site rather than following your navigational links, they can go to this page. A site map can be very simple, such as a plain text page of links, or it can be done with graphics and images and made as attractive as the rest of your site. How much time you invest in creating your site map is up to you. But by all means include one so that your visitors can quickly find their way to a particular page.

Preview Your Pages

If your visitors are frustrated by broken and nonfunctional links, you will be equally upset if you discover that the design that looks great on your system looks awful when displayed on a different system. One of the realities of designing for the Web is that your page design is affected by the user's equipment. There are many variables that can affect the look of your Web site and, as much as possible, you must take them into account:

- **Test your pages in different browsers.**   You should at least check your pages out in Netscape and Internet Explorer, and it's not a bad idea to find some older versions of each browser. Although Opera is still a minor player in the browser world, you should try your pages in it, too.

- **See what your pages look like in browsers with the graphics turned off.**   Some users with slow connections turn off the graphics to speed up page loading. Make sure your Web pages make sense, even with the pictures turned off.

- **See what your pages look like when you set your monitor to different resolutions.** Depending on the capabilities of your own monitor, you can preview your pages in different resolutions by right-clicking anywhere on the Windows desktop and selecting Properties from the pop-up dialog box. When the Display Properties window comes up, click the Settings tab. This should give you the different display resolutions your monitor is capable of handling.

After you have tested your links and previewed your pages and are satisfied with any corrections you have made, you are ready to put your site online.

7

Publish Your Site

For a beginner, perhaps the most perplexing part of the whole process of setting up a Web site is actually trying to put it online. When you are ready to publish your site, you must venture outside of the comfortable world of HTML and into the mysterious world of FTP, domain names, IP numbers, Web servers, and more. However, if you're willing to just take things step by step, you'll find it's not nearly as confusing as you imagined.

Find a Host

The first hurdle you must jump in getting your site online is finding a host or a Web server. Actually, the only thing that makes this difficult is the sheer number of choices you now have in this area. How do you decide which server is right for you and your Web site? Primarily your budget and your needs will influence your decision. Consider some of the possible choices:

- **Your own Internet service provider** If you're putting together a small personal Web site, you probably already have an account with an Internet service provider (ISP). Most providers give you several megabytes of disk space for your own home page. Three to ten megabytes go a long way, and if you're not planning to construct a large site, you might find them sufficient for your needs. If so, look no further—you've found your host.

- **Free hosts** If you plan to put together a medium-sized site and you know you'll need around 15–25 megabytes of space, but you're on a budget, try one of the free servers. These advertiser-supported hosts give you lots of room to work with and generally provide quite a few resources that actually make it easier for you to set up your site. So, what's the catch? To get the free space, you will either have to consent to rotating banner ads placed conspicuously on your pages (usually at the top) or to a pop-up window that opens when someone loads your site. If the advertising does not put you off, it's a great way to put a site online at virtually no cost to you. Some of the most popular of the free hosts are www.fortunecity.com, www.geocities.com, and www.tripod.com.

- **Paid hosts** If you need space and really don't want someone else's banner ads cluttering up your page, you will need to find a paid host. A Web server works much the same way as an Internet service provider does (in fact, many of them function as both). This is one area where it pays to shop around, as you will find a wide fluctuation in prices and what you get for your money. You can find hosts that offer 750 megabytes of space for as little as seven dollars a month—but don't be influenced by price alone. Check them out to see if they provide:

  - **Space** A *minimum* of 100 megs of disk space.

  - **Data transfer or bandwidth** This is a measure of how much traffic your site will be allowed to handle in a given month. Even the free hosts offer up to 3 gigabytes of bandwidth. If you expect a lot of traffic, make sure that this number is sufficiently high to accommodate your needs. The last thing you want is to have a wildly successful site that goes offline for a while because you have exceeded your maximum bandwidth.

- **CGI bin**   You'll need this if you plan to use forms, guestbooks, or other things on your site that require a user response. See Chapter 14 for more about CGI.

- **FrontPage Extensions support**   If you plan to develop pages with Microsoft's FrontPage, your server will need to be equipped with FrontPage Extensions.

- **POP3 e-mail accounts**   If you want people to contact you, it's nice to have an e-mail account that works directly through your Web site and bears your domain name.

- **Web traffic statistics**   You'll want to know how much attention your site is getting. A good server will provide a means for you to track your site's hits. If it doesn't, you can always use the advertiser-supported tracking info provided through hitbox.com.

- **Good customer service**   If you have a problem, it's nice to know you have someone you can contact.

- **Support for e-commerce**   Will your server permit you to do business on your site and use a transaction processor? Or do they provide their own transaction processing services?

- **Downloads**   Will the server allow you to provide downloads?

TIP   *A transaction processor allows you to accept payments and process transactions online. If you're planning to operate an e-business or just extend your current business to the Web, you should check out what's available. Some good sources are Signio (www.signio.com/products/payment.html) and Visa (www.visa.com/nt/ecomm/ merchant/main.html).*

To begin researching the market, just go to any search engine and type **Web hosting**—you'll have enough possibilities to keep you busy for quite a while.

Register a Domain Name

Do you really need to have a domain name? It all depends. Your domain name is your Internet identity. It is the means by which people will find—and hopefully remember—you. Although it's not mandatory that you spend the money to register your own "dot.com," it's a pretty good idea, and it's a great value.

Domain name registration used to be heavily regulated, not to mention expensive. However, when the United States Congress deregulated it, domain name registration opened up to competition. As a result, the price dropped to the point where it's reasonable to have not just one, but several domain names. Often, your Web server will be able to handle registering your name for you, but if they don't provide that service, it's easy enough to find someone who will. Just do a search on the words "domain name registrars" and you'll find more than enough options. Table 7-3 lists just a few of the many domain name registrars who can help you obtain your own domain name. Keep in mind that when you register a name you are, in effect, leasing that name. You have the rights to it only as long as you keep the registration current.

Domain Name Registrar	URL
Network Solutions	www.networksolutions.com
GoDaddy	www.godaddy.com
Powweb	www.powweb.com
Register.com	www.register.com
Domain Direct (TuCows)	www.domaindirect.com
Signature Domains	www.signaturedomains.com
Domain Bank	www.domainbank.net
Low Cost Domains	www.lowcostdomains.com
BudgetNIC.Com	www.newbudgetregister.com
123 Domain Name Registration	www.123-domain-name-registration.com
Ampira Hosting	www.ireg.com

TABLE 7-3   Domain Name Registrars

When you decide to get your own domain name, be sure to shop around. Prices range from about $35 a year for a name registered through Network Solutions to under $10 a year with most other registrars. Also, certain extensions may have added fees. For example, the .tv extension is owned by a small island country in the Pacific named Tuvulu, which charges an added fee for the use of its extension.

TIP   *With the boom in domain name registrations, a lot of the most popular .com, .net, and .org names have already been taken. If the name you want has been taken, don't despair— new extensions, such as .biz, .tv, .us, and many more, are being approved all the time.*

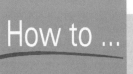

How to ... Find Out if the Name You Want Is Available

One way to see if the name you want is available is to just open your browser and type in the domain name, just as if you were trying to visit a Web site. If a Web site comes up, you know it's been registered. You might find a "place holder" page in the case of a name that has been registered but has not yet posted a Web site. If you get a response that says something like "Page Not Found," chances are good that the name has not been registered. To be absolutely sure, you'll want to find a site where you can do a search on a *whois* search engine. This is an engine that specifically searches through a database of registered names. It will tell you whether or not someone has already registered the name you want. You can do a whois search at Network Solutions' Web site. The URL is www.networksolutions.com.

Upload Your Site

The final hurdle in getting a site online is in actually uploading the site to your server. To upload your site, you'll need to use *File Transfer Protocol (FTP)*, and for that you'll need some special software. If you are using one of the free hosting services, generally it will provide FTP capability through its server. Otherwise, you'll need to obtain a program such as CuteFTP, CoffeeCup Direct FTP, WS_FTP, or one of many others.

NOTE *WS_FTP LE is available free of charge to educational and home (nonbusiness) users at www.ftpplanet.com/download.htm. Also, all Windows operating systems include an FTP program that is available from the DOS prompt. For Macs, Fetch is a popular FTP program. Fetch is free to educational and nonprofit groups and is a $25 shareware program, available at http://fetchsoftworks.com/. Also, a number of other free FTP programs can be found at www.allfreespot.com/freeFTP.html.*

To upload your site with CuteFTP, follow these steps. If you're using a different FTP program, the steps will be very similar. Generally the key information that an FTP program needs is your FTP host address, your user name, and your password. Your Web host or Internet service provider (if you are building your Web site on the free space they provide you) can provide you with this information:

7

1. Open your FTP program and make sure you are connected to the Internet. In CuteFTP, a dialog box will open, requesting some basic information about your site.

2. Label for Site—This is the top window in the dialog box. Because it is for your own reference purposes, it can be any name you choose.

3. FTP Host Address—This second box is the address where the program will be uploading your files. You put your domain name in this box. For example, www.mywebsite.com.

4. FTP Site User Name—You would have been given a user name by your host. Type that in the User Name box.

5. FTP Site Password—The next input line is for your password. Again, your host would have assigned you a password; that goes here.

6. FTP Site Connection Port—The next line is for the connection port. This generally is filled out automatically so you don't need to worry about it.

7. Login Type—Next, you have three options from which to select under Login type: Normal, Anonymous, and Double. Check Normal.

8. After you have filled in the necessary information, click Connect. (If your computer does not dial in to your server automatically, you'll need to make sure you're online when you do this.) After you have logged in to your host, simply transfer files as you would between two disks on your own computer. The left window generally displays the *local* files (the files on your system). The window on the right will display the *remote* files (the files on the server). To upload your site, simply select the files on your system that you want to transfer; then make sure you have opened the proper directory on the server.

If you're not sure which is the proper directory, check with your host to be certain you have the correct one.

9. Click the Upload button after you have selected the files you want to transfer; the program will do the rest.

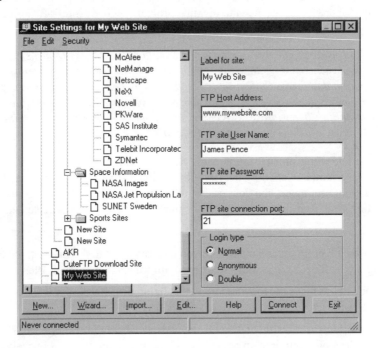

NOTE *Usually, you put your site in the root directory or a directory named www.*

Promote Your Site

When you have your site online, the next logical question is how to get people to visit it. Considering that you are competing with millions of other Web sites, that can be more challenging than you might think. Even if the focus of your site is narrow enough that you are competing with only hundreds of other sites, you still have a daunting task ahead of you. Because most people don't go past the first 10 or 20 sites that a search engine brings up, your job is to get your site listed in that top group. How do you do it?

Design Your Pages with Strategic Keywords

The first thing to understand about search engines is that they look for keywords on your site and categorize your site based on those word. If you know where to place your keywords, you can dramatically increase your chances of being in the upper echelon of search engine hits.

- **Choose several keywords.** What's important to remember here is that your potential visitors don't necessarily know that they are searching for *your* page. Thus, you have to think in terms of how your visitors will conduct their search. Usually they are searching on a broad topic, planning to visit whatever pages come up high on the list. For example, suppose you have a site devoted to the Monarch butterfly, and you want to attract Monarch enthusiasts. Take some time to think through what words you would use in a search engine if you were looking for a page like yours. Perhaps you would choose *butterfly, Monarch butterfly, butterfly migration, insects: butterfly,* among others. Make sure that those words occur in the headlines and text of your pages.

- **Put keywords in the <title> element.** Search engines also look at the page title. Which title is more likely to attract butterfly enthusiasts: Fran's Home Page or Monarch Butterfly World? Choose your titles strategically.

- **Strategically place keywords in the top part of your document.** The higher up in your document your keywords occur, the better. Search engines look toward the top of the file for keywords to categorize your site. If in constructing Monarch Butterfly World, the Web designer puts a half page of biographical information before ever getting around to his or her subject, chances are the site won't score very high in the search engine rankings.

Submit Your Site to Search Engines and Directories

After you have optimized your site for search engines, you are ready to submit it. Although most search engines are automated and will find your site sooner or later, directories such as Yahoo! are not automated. The directory's staff reviews every site that is submitted. If you want to be considered by these sites, then you need to submit your site to them. Submission also speeds up the process with automated search engines, drawing their "spiders" to your pages much sooner. You can do this yourself by accessing each search engine site and manually submitting your URL or by using site submission software or a submission service to do the job for you.

NOTE *A "spider," or "crawler," is an automated program that visits and indexes Web sites and then makes the results available to search engines.*

To submit your site manually, follow these steps:

1. Go to a search engine site; for example, altavista.com.

2. Somewhere on the page (usually near the top or bottom) there will be a link that reads Submit a Site or Add URL. Click that link.

3. You will go to another page that has a window where you can add the URL for your site. Just type in the URL and click the submit button. Within a few days, the engine's *spider* will crawl through your site and index it.

There are hundreds of possible search engines you could submit to. If you want to speed up the process, consider using site submission service or software. Table 7-4 lists some options you might want to explore.

Search Engine Submission Service or Software	URL
Submit Express	www.submitexpress.com
Add Me	www.addme.com
Launch	www.nnh.co.uk/launch
GNet	gnet.dhs.org/sess
Submission Pro!	www.submissionpro.com
Search Engine Monkeys	www.searchenginemonkeys.com
World Wide Data Link	www.wwpromote.com

TABLE 7-4 Search Engine Submission Services and Software

If you prefer a faster way, try a site submission service or software to automate the process. Many of the services charge a small fee but some offer limited submissions free of charge. With the software (which is usually shareware) you'll have to pay a registration fee, but you'll have the advantage of using the software as frequently as you want to without added fees. To locate a service, do a search on the keywords "site submission services."

If you are promoting an online business, you can even pay a fee to search engines to feature your site along with search engine results for certain keywords. For example, if you've ever noticed the small advertising boxes that come up beside Google search results, those are paid ads which have been linked to the keywords you have searched on.

What Happened to <meta keyword=" " />?

A few years back, Web authors used the <meta /> element and keyword attribute to help search engines index their sites. This element would be placed between the <head> tags of a document and would contain comma-separated lists of keywords that supposedly described a page's content. These keywords would be invisible to a page's visitors, but search engine spiders could make use of them for indexing and ranking a site. Unfortunately, many unscrupulous page authors began "spamming" the search engines by including long lists of keywords (for example, "xxx" or "sex") that were unrelated to the page's content but would cause the page to come up frequently in search results. Because of this abuse, most search engines began ignoring the <meta /> element altogether. Although there are attempts to "resurrect" the <meta /> element in progress, none are broadly supported at this writing. For more information on the current state of the <meta /> element, visit the following URL: http://hotwired.lycos.com/webmonkey/03/24/index0a.html.

Promote Your Site Online and Offline

Don't depend only on search engines to direct traffic to your site. There are many other ways to get visitors, and a savvy Web author will take advantage of all of them:

- **Promote your site through newsgroups and forums.**   You have to be careful how you do this, lest you be accused of *spamming* (sending unwanted solicitations to) the group. However, if you want your site to get noticed, try participating in one or two newsgroup discussions about your subject. If you add a short signature line with your URL, people might visit your site just out of curiosity. Also, as people get to know you and appreciate your expertise, they might ask you questions. You then can refer them to your site without spamming them. Check out Yahoo! Groups (http://groups.yahoo.com) for some possible starting places.

- **Include your URL in your e-mail signature.**   Add a signature line to your e-mails that gives your Web site, its name, and the URL.

- **Join a Web ring.**   A Web ring is a group of related sites that are interlinked. Someone who visits one site might follow the ring to your site. Yahoo! is a good place to start looking for a Web ring to join.

- **Check out banner exchanges.**   Banner exchanges often are free and a great way to get some publicity for your site. You permit someone else's banner to be displayed on your site; in return you get to display your banner on their site.

- **Try paid banner advertising.**   This option isn't great if you're on a budget, but if you have the funds (for example, if you have an online business) you might experiment with some paid advertising.

- **Try reciprocal linking.**   This is when you agree with another Webmaster whose site is similar to yours to link your sites together. If you cultivate and choose reciprocal links properly, you can dramatically improve your rankings in search engine results.

- **Check with your local Chamber of Commerce.**   If you have a business, church, civic, or charitable Web site, your local Chamber of Commerce may be willing to post a link to your site on their own Web site.

- **Put your URL on your stationery and business cards.**   Get your URL out in whatever way you can. This includes putting it on stationery, business cards, and any other advertising you do.

- **Remember good old "word of mouth."**   Be sure to tell everyone you know about your site.

It's incredibly rewarding to see your site online for the first time. It's even better when you begin to hear from people who have visited. Getting your site online might seem like a daunting process, but it's really not that difficult. But don't take the trouble to publish your site without promoting it. Publishing a site without promoting it is as silly as writing a book and then not telling anyone that you've written it. Tell people about your site. They'll come. And if you've got a good site with quality content, they'll come back!

7

Quick Reference: XHTML Documents

In this chapter you have been learning how to write well-formed and valid XHTML documents. The <!DOCTYPE> declarations for XHTML 1.0 are difficult to remember, not to mention case sensitive. Thus, it's a good idea to create several different templates, one for each of the three different DTDs. After you have validated those templates against the DTDs, you will be able to save yourself a lot of time and grief by simply reusing them every time you want to create an XHTML document. For reference, the <!DOCTYPE> declarations are listed in the following table, along with some other important XHTML information:

To Do This	Use This
Add an XHTML 1.0 Transitional <!DOCTYPE> declaration	`<!DOCTYPE html PUBLIC "-//W3C//DTD XHTML 1.0 Transitional//EN" "http://www.w3.org/TR/xhtml1/DTD/xhtml1-transitional.dtd">`
Add an XHTML 1.0 Strict <!DOCTYPE> declaration	`<!DOCTYPE html PUBLIC "-//W3C//DTD XHTML 1.0 Strict//EN" "http://www.w3.org/TR/xhtml1/DTD/xhtml1-strict.dtd">`
Add an XHTML 1.0 Frameset <!DOCTYPE> declaration	`<!DOCTYPE html PUBLIC "-//W3C//DTD XHTML 1.0 Frameset//EN" "http://www.w3.org/TR/xhtml1/DTD/xhtml1-frameset.dtd">`
Add the XHTML namespace to a document	`<html xmlns="http://www.w3.org/1999/xhtml">`
Add character encoding information to a document	`<meta http-equiv="Content-Type" content="text/html; charset=iso-8859-7" />`
Validate an XHTML document	`http://validator.w3.org`

Part II Structuring Your Site

Chapter 8

Organize Data with Tables

How to...

- Understand the table controversy
- Create a simple table
- Modify your table's appearance
- Create page layouts with tables
- Design a table of links for site navigation

Chapters 1–7 focus on equipping you with the raw materials for creating your own Web site and acquainting you with XHTML and "standards-compliant" Web design. With what you learned in those chapters, you could easily put together a series of Web pages that you would be proud of. However, if you have been working with some of the exercises, you also have become aware of some of HTML's limitations. The chief limitations Web designers wrestle with are presentation and layout. How do you learn to position the various parts of your page so that your content is presented in a pleasing manner? Chapters 8–10 cover the issues of structure and style, and how best to control them on your Web pages. In this chapter, you will be introduced to perhaps the easiest (and likely the most controversial) method of influencing the layout and design of a page: tables.

Understand the Table Controversy

Have you ever used a spreadsheet program? If so, you have a rough idea of what tables are and how they normally look. Tables were developed and added to the HTML standard in the early 1990s to provide a way to display structured information, such as in a spreadsheet. Before that time there was no good way to display columns of data in an HTML document; because HTML originally was devised for scientific and academic material, this presented a problem. The introduction of tables not only solved this problem, but also provided a solution to another, as yet undiscovered, problem.

The Origins of the Table Controversy

When the Internet was in its infancy, presentation and design weren't very problematic, but graphical browsers changed all that. However, basic HTML did not provide the tools for control that designers were used to. In fact, a Web designer was completely at the mercy of browser, system, and HTML limitations when it came to doing Web page layouts. Placement and appearance of text and graphics were not absolute, but static. A layout that looked good on a designer's machine might be totally transformed on someone else's system.

Then Web authors discovered tables. By putting text, graphics, and other content inside table cells, designers could take advantage of a table's structure to "force" a browser to stay within a particular layout. Tables certainly did not solve all the difficulties Web developers faced, but they represented a great improvement. However, tables were not designed with layout in mind.

They were created to organize "tabular" data. In other words, when Web designers use tables to create a layout, they are applying HTML markup in a way that was never intended. The issue isn't merely that the leaders in the Web community are zealous to keep HTML pure. Rather, it is because using tables this way creates accessibility problems for people who must use alternative or nonvisual browsers.

The Accessibility Issue

If a visually impaired person tries to access your site using an aural (audio) browser and you have used tables to create your visual layout, the browser will probably have difficulty deciphering your code. Nonvisual browsers depend on HTML code being applied according to standard, not in whatever manner a designer finds useful. That is why there is such a strong emphasis on learning to write standards-compliant code in the Web community. It's about making your pages available to everybody. However, even though the overall trend in the Web is toward using Cascading Style Sheets (CSS)—and ultimately XSL or Extensible Stylesheet Language—tables still are the layout tool of choice for most Web authors. If you're not convinced, just go to virtually any major Web site and view the source code. More often than not, you will find that tables figure significantly in the design. Despite accessibility issues, clearly many Webmasters are reluctant to abandon tables. Why?

8

The Browser Support Issue

Tables remain the design tool of choice largely because they enable designers to maintain a certain degree of control and consistency in their Web layouts. Because the browsers are inconsistent in their support of Cascading Style Sheets, layout and page design can vary radically between different browsers, and even between different versions of the same browser. This necessitates the creation of multiple style sheets that are custom designed for the quirks of all the different browsers and versions. Unfortunately, the CSS positioning (layout) properties are among the most poorly supported. Thus, a design that depends solely on CSS is likely to be very unstable. On the other hand, tables provide a stable and consistent means of structuring a page. Therefore, they remain popular and probably will continue to be so until browser manufacturers offer more consistent support for CSS.

Create a Simple Table

Tables are not difficult to understand or build. They *can* become quite complex, but the basic concept is easy. If you just keep in mind the idea of a spreadsheet, most of the structure of a table will be demystified. Tables are merely structures in which information (or parts of a Web page) is presented in rows and columns. Each individual segment of a table is called a *cell;* for example, row one, column one represents one cell; row two, column one is another; and so on. Thinking in terms of rows and columns might be confusing, though. The best way to understand how tables work is to create one.

Open template.htm and save it as tables.htm; then copy this code to construct a simple 3×3 cell table:

```
<table>
    <tr> <td>X</td> <td>X</td> <td>X</td> </tr>
    <tr> <td>X</td> <td>X</td> <td>X</td> </tr>
    <tr> <td>X</td> <td>X</td> <td>X</td> </tr>
</table>
```

After you've typed in the code, save your page and open it in your browser. Your table should look like this illustration.

Now that you've created an uncomplicated table, take a look back through the HTML you've written to learn about each of the elements you used. You created that table with only three elements: <table>, <tr>, and <td>.

- **<table> </table>**   The *table* element creates the table. Use this element for each table you wish to create on a page.

- **<tr> </tr>**   The *table row* element establishes, as you would expect, a row. If your table is to have ten rows, you will use this element ten times.

- **<td> </td>**   TD stands for *table data*. This element creates individual cells in a row (and, by default, the table's columns). Whatever content you want to place in the table goes between the <td> tags.

As you look at the preceding code, you'll see that <tr> is used to create three rows. The <td> element occurs three times in each row; so in that particular table, you end up with three rows and three columns. These are the only elements you need to create a table. As you will see, by adding attributes and some extra elements, you can do just about anything with this little table.

TIP   *The letter X has been placed between each of the sets of <td> tags because browsers will not display empty table cells. When you are designing a table, always remember to put something in each cell, even if it is not your final content. The nonbreaking space entity ( ) is another good choice for temporary cell content.*

Modify a Table's Appearance

Although you need only the three basic table elements, your HTML toolbox includes additional elements and attributes that can be used to modify a table's appearance. In addition, the content you choose to put in each cell will affect how your table looks on a Web page. As you work through this chapter, try modifying the simple table you created earlier by adding the lines in the following section (or sometimes modifying existing tags) and watch how your table develops.

Add Headings and Captions

In keeping with a table's original purpose for displaying structured information, HTML provides some elements that allow you to add headings, captions, and footers to your table.

TIP
Sometimes existing code will be displayed to make it easier to understand where you need to add or modify code. In these cases, type in only the code that appears in boldface.

Use the <th> </th> Element to Add Headings to Your Table

To add a heading, you use <th> </th> instead of the <td> element. <th> creates cells the same way <td> does, but also displays the text inside the cells as centered and boldface. Try adding a heading to the table by adding this line of code above the first row:

```
<tr> <th>Col 1</th> <th>Col 2</th> <th>Col 3</th> </tr>
<tr> <td>X</td> <td>X</td> <td>X</td> </tr>
<tr> <td>X</td> <td>X</td> <td>X</td> </tr>
<tr> <td>X</td> <td>X</td> <td>X</td> </tr>
```

Col 1	Col 2	Col 3
X	X	X
X	X	X
X	X	X

8

Add Captions with the <caption> </caption> Element

A caption can be used to display a title for your table. Use the <caption> </caption> element just above the first row of cells. To add a caption to the sample table, add this line: **<caption>How to Use Tables</caption>**. The following code shows where that line should be placed in your table:

```
<table>
<caption>How to Use Tables</caption>
<tr> <th>Col 1</th> <th>Col 2</th> <th>Col 3</th> </tr>
<tr> <td>X</td> <td>X</td> <td>X</td> </tr>
```

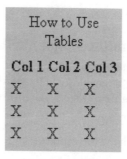

Display a Border

By now you probably are thinking that your table would be easier to work with if it had borders and lines defining the separate cells. To tell the browser to display a border, simply add the border=" " attribute to the opening <table> tag. To add a border that is three pixels wide, go back

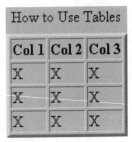

to your code and modify the table tag to read like this: <table **border="3">**. Now look at how your table has changed. It should resemble the illustration at the left.

You can change the thickness of your border by altering the number in the quotation marks. Thus, border="10" produces a 10-pixel–wide border, and border="20" makes it 20 pixels wide. Try experimenting with some different border sizes to see what you like best.

TIP   *Although it is easier to work with tables that have borders, you might prefer to have borderless tables for your final layout. In this case specify border="0", or simply remove the border attribute altogether.*

Position Your Content

As soon as the border appears, you will notice that all the Xs in your table are aligned to the left sides of their cells. That's because the default alignment in tables is to the left. If you want the content to be centered or right justified, there are a couple of options for controlling its position.

Position Content Horizontally with the align Attribute

Although the align attribute has been deprecated for most other purposes in XHTML, it has not been deprecated for use in table cells. To use align to position cell content, you must include the align attribute in each cell where you want to specify the position. For example, to center text you would modify a <td> tag to read <td align="center">. The align attribute will take several different values:

- **Left**   Aligns cell contents to the left. This is the default alignment.
- **Right**   Aligns cell contents to the right.
- **Center**   Aligns cell contents to the center.
- **Justify**   Also aligns the cell's contents to the left.

Control Vertical Alignment with the valign Attribute

You can determine whether your content aligns at the top, middle, or bottom of a cell by using the valign attribute. valign (vertical align) enables you to specify the vertical positioning for individual cells (<td valign="top">), entire rows (<tr valign="middle">), or a complete table (<tbody valign="bottom">). The values you can supply with the valign attribute are as follows:

- **Top**   Aligns cell contents with the top of the cell.
- **Middle**   Aligns cell contents with the middle of the cell; middle is the default value.
- **Bottom**   Aligns cell contents with the bottom of the cell.
- **Baseline**   Aligns with a baseline shared by all the cells in a given row.

The following code and illustration demonstrate how the align and valign attributes affect cell contents:

```
<table border"3" height"200" width"200">
<tr> <td align="left">Left</td> <td align="center">Cent.</td>
    <td align="right">Right</td>
</tr>
<tr> <td valign="top">Top</td> <td valign="middle">Mid.</td>
    <td valign="bottom">Bottom</td>
</tr>
<tr> <td valign="baseline">Baseline</td>
    <td align="justify">Justify</td>
    <td>Default</td>
</tr>
</table>
```

8

How to Use Tables		
Col 1	Col 2	Col 3
Left	Center	Right
Top	Middle	Bottom
Baseline	Justify	Default

Setting the characteristics of each element of a large table can become tedious and time consuming. Fortunately, CSS provide a way to set table properties that control the entire table. Whenever possible, consider using CSS to develop your tables.

Use CSS for Alignment

Cascading Style Sheets give you more options for cell content alignment. By using an inline style sheet, you can align the contents of individual cells, much as you did with the align attribute. However, you also can use CSS to align the text in all of your table cells at once by embedding a style sheet in the head portion of your XHTML page.

CSS use the same four alignment properties: left, center, right, and justify:

- **Center alignment with an inline stylesheet: <td style="text-align: center;">** This controls an individual cell.

- **Center alignment with an embedded stylesheet: <style type="text/css"> td {text-align: center;} </style>** This controls all the cells in your table.

NOTE *The justify property works differently with CSS from the way it works with the align attribute. With CSS it causes text to be justified to both the left and right margins. The align="justify" attribute justifies only to the left.*

Try centering the contents of the sample table by adding these lines inside the <head> portion of your HTML page; then compare your results with the following illustration:

```
<style type"text/css"> td   {text-align: center;} </style>
```

How to Use Tables		
Col 1	Col 2	Col 3
X	X	X
X	X	X
X	X	X

After you've typed in the style element, save your page and display it in your browser. Now the Xs in each cell will be centered, instead of just those in the first row. As you can see, CSS can be quite a timesaver.

Add Background Colors

Setting background colors for your table is easy. The background color attribute, bgcolor=" ", which has been deprecated for use with the <body> element, is still a legitimate attribute for tables. You can set the color for individual cells, for individual rows, or for the whole table. If you would like to set the color for more than one table at once, try using CSS.

Set Table Colors with bgcolor

The bgcolor=" " attribute controls the portion of the table in which it is placed. This attribute, used with a table, is great for creating navigation bars in your Web pages. By setting the colors for individual table cells and putting your links inside the cells, you can create an attractive and quick loading navigational system. To specify colors for your table, use the following:

- Place bgcolor in the <table> element to control the color of the entire table.
- Place bgcolor in the <tr> element to control the color of a row.
- Place bgcolor in <td> or <th> element to control the color of individual cells.

Experiment with the colors of your table by setting the overall table color to magenta, the color of the heading row to yellow, and the color of the center cell to aqua. Compare your results with the following illustration:

```
<html>
  <head>
```

```
    <title>Table Exercise</title>
    <style type"text/css">
      td {text-align: center}
    </style>
  </head>
  <body>
    <table border="3" bgcolor="magenta">
      <caption>How to Use Tables</caption>
        <tr bgcolor="yellow">
            <th>Col 1</th>
            <th>Col 2</th>
            <th>Col 3</th>
        </tr>
        <tr>
            <td>X</td>
            <td>X</td>
            <td>X</td>
        </tr>
        <tr>
            <td>X</td>
            <td bgcolor="aqua">X</td>
            <td>X</td>
        </tr>
        <tr>
            <td>X</td>
            <td>X</td>
            <td>X</td>
        </tr>
    </table>
  </body>
</html>
```

8

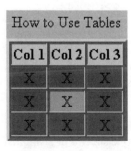

Set Table Colors with CSS

You also can use style sheets to control table colors. The advantage here is that you can set the style for all the tables in a page or even an entire Web site with just one set of commands. You also can control individual cells with CSS.

■ Set cell, row, or table colors with an inline style sheet:

```
<td style="background-color: blue;">
```

NOTE *To set row colors, the style attribute goes in the <tr> tag. To set table colors, put it in the <table> tag.*

■ Set cell, row, or table colors with an embedded style sheet:

```
<style> td {background-color: red;} </style>
```

NOTE *In the preceding examples, an individual cell was set to the color blue, whereas the overall table style was set for red cells. Which one takes precedence? In CSS the inline style has priority over the embedded style.*

Try putting the following style sheet into the head portion of your tables.htm page. It should change your table background to blue, with white text (that's what color: white does). All captions will have a red background with yellow text. The heading cells will be yellow with navy text; the center cell will be white with black text.

CAUTION *In this style sheet, to select the colors for the center cell, a class has been created. In this case it is named td.center. To apply that style to the center cell of your table (or any other cell, for that matter), modify the <td> tag for that cell to read **<td class="center">**. If you do not insert the class attribute into the <td> element, the style will not be applied. For more about classes in style sheets, read Chapter 10.*

```
<style type"text/css">
table   {background-color: blue; color: white;}
caption {background-color: red; color: yellow;}
th {background-color: yellow; color: navy}
td.center {background-color: white; color: black;}
</style>
```

TIP *When you modify your page to add the preceding style, leave the bgcolor attributes alone. You'll see when you display your page that the style sheet overrides any colors you set with HTML attributes.*

To really see how style sheets work, try creating another table of any size in your page. It will take on the characteristics of the style sheet. For a simple example, here's a one-celled table with a header and caption. Copy it into your page just after the closing <table> tag for your first table. Your results should resemble the following illustration. To see it in color, visit the color insert in the center of this book.

```
<br /><table><caption>Table 2</caption>
<tr><th>Heading</th></tr>
<tr><td>Content</td></tr></table>
```

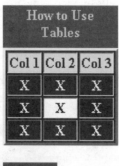

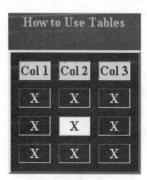

Adjust Space In and Between Cells

So far you have learned how to construct a table and change its colors, but what about controlling the position, size, and spacing of cells? HTML provides attributes to control these aspects of a table's appearance. With cellspacing and cellpadding, you can manipulate the overall size of your tables and cells.

Use cellspacing to Adjust the Space Between Cells

The *cellspacing* attribute allows you to add space between the cells in your table as measured in pixels. This attribute must go inside the <table> tag. To add a 10-pixel–wide space between the cells in your table, modify the opening <table> tag to read:

```
<table border="3" bgcolor="magenta" cellspacing="10">
```

Use cellpadding to Add Space Inside Cells

Just as cellspacing adds space around the outside of your cells, *cellpadding* adds space inside them. It also adds a layer of padding (defined in pixels) around the contents of the cell. Add a 10-pixel "pad" around the content of your table cells by modifying the <table> tag to read as follows:

```
<table border="3" bgcolor="magenta" cellpadding="10"
cellspacing="10">
```

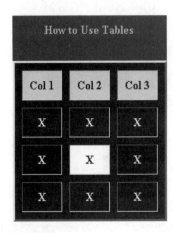

Use CSS for More Padding Options

This is where CSS really shine. With the cellpadding attribute you are able to add padding for the entire cell only; by using CSS' cellpadding properties, you have many more options. CSS enable you to place the padding only where you want it. It also enables you to use measurements other than pixels. For example, if you want a quarter-inch padding added to the bottom of each cell, you can add a style rule in the head portion of the page that reads td {padding-bottom: .25in}.

CSS padding properties include padding, padding-right, padding-left, padding-top, and padding-bottom. CSS measurement units include, among others, inches (#in), percentages (#%), pixels (#), and ems (#em).

SHORTCUT *If you use the padding property (as opposed to padding-right and so forth), you simply put the value to the right of the property. The more values you supply, the greater the difference in how they are applied. For example, padding: 10 adds a 10-pixel pad around the cell contents; padding: 10, 15 puts a 10-pixel pad on top and bottom and a 15-pixel pad on the sides. Three values control the top, left-right, and bottom padding. Four values control the top, right, bottom, and left sides, respectively.*

NOTE   *An em is a unit that is relative to the font size. For example, a padding of 1.5 ems would be one-and-one-half times the size of the font in use in the table cell.*

To apply padding to individual cells, use an inline style sheet. The HTML for the cell you want to modify might look something like this:

```
<td style="padding-right: 15">X</td>
```

To set the default cellpadding for the table with an embedded style sheet, you might write your code this way:

```
<style type="text/css"> td  {padding: 1em, 2em} </style>
```

Make Cells Span Multiple Columns and Rows

Another way to modify the appearance of your table is to make one cell span two or more rows or columns. This is especially useful when you are using tables for layout purposes and wish to have an image in one large cell accompanied by a navigation bar made up of several cells.

To make a cell span multiple rows, insert the rowspan=" " attribute in the cell's opening <td> tag. For example, to make the top left cell in your table span two rows, modify its <td> tag to read <td rowspan="2">. Your modified code will look like this:

```
<tr> <th>Col 1</th> <th>Col 2</th> <th>Col 3</th> </tr>
<tr> <td rowspan="2">X</td> <td>X</td> <td>X</td> </tr>
<tr> <td>X</td> <td>X</td> </tr>
<tr> <td>X</td> <td>X</td> <td>X</td> </tr>
```

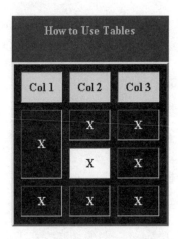

CAUTION   *Don't forget that if you are going to make one cell take the space of two, you must remove the cell it is going to replace. Otherwise, your table will be unbalanced. When you add the rowspan attribute to the code for your table, be sure to remove one of the cells (<td>X</td>) in the second row.*

To make a cell span more than one column, use the colspan=" " attribute. If you remove one of the cells from the bottom row of your table and modify the last cell's opening <td> tag to read <td colspan="2">, it causes the browser to display the cell across two column widths.

The code for the table rows now will resemble this:

```
<tr> <th>Col 1</th> <th>Col 2</th> <th>Col 3</th> </tr>
<tr> <td rowspan="2">X</td> <td>X</td> <td>X</td> </tr>
<tr> <td>X</td> <td>X</td> </tr>
<tr> <td>X</td> <td colspan="2">X</td> </tr>
```

Adjust Height and Width

With HTML you can adjust both the height and the width of your tables and cells. This can be very important when you are using tables for a page's layout, as you can specify how much of a page you want the table to use. By using percentages to describe table dimensions, you can enable a browser to adjust your table to fit a monitor's display, no matter what its resolution.

Set Table Width with Fixed or Dynamic Design

Fixed design involves specifying a table's dimensions in concrete terms. For example, if you want to stretch the sample table horizontally, you could specify that the sample table you've been constructing should be 500 pixels wide by changing the opening table tag to read <table width="500">. When you display the page in a browser now, it will look quite different from the table you originally designed. The disadvantage of this approach is that your table will always be 500 pixels wide, regardless of the size of the browser window. A better approach is dynamic design. Try making the change in tables.htm and compare your results with the following illustration:

TIP   *Both the height and width attributes can be used define the size of individual cells. However, this usage has been deprecated in favor of style sheets.*

8

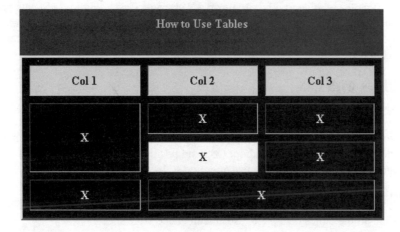

Dynamic design is when you describe a table's dimensions using percentages. Perhaps you want a table to take up a full screen, no matter what screen resolution your visitors' systems are set to. In this case you would describe your table's width with a percentage: <table width="100%">. This creates a table that will adjust dynamically to fill the browser window. Your table will adjust in size, larger or smaller, depending on the size of the browser window.

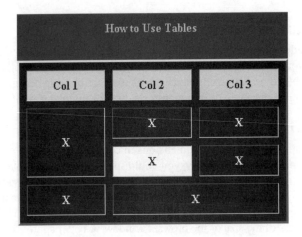

Position Tables on a Page

Until now, the table you have been working on has been aligned to the left margin of the page; this is XHTML's default alignment for tables. However, there are several ways for you to influence the positioning of tables relative to other items on a Web page. Cascading Style Sheets provide an option for table alignment with float and clear properties. Elements such as <div>, and <center> provide a quick and easy solution for alignment. You also can position tables with the deprecated align attribute.

Position Tables with CSS

Cascading Style Sheets use the float property for positioning objects on a page. To use this property you would write **float: right** (other options are left or none). There is no center value for the float property. If you want to center a table with CSS, you'll have to do it with margins or with absolute positioning. (For more about CSS and positioning, see Chapter 10.)

To left-align a single table with CSS, use an inline style sheet:

```
<table style"float: left;">
```

To right-align all the tables on a page, use an embedded style sheet:

```
<style type="text/css"> table {float: left;} </style>
```

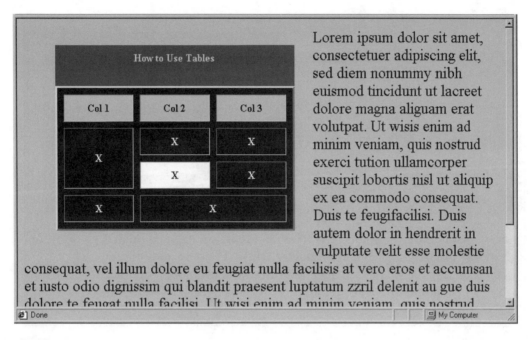

TIP *The difference between the left, right, and none options for float is that text does not wrap with the none option. Any text or other content comes after the table. With left or right, the text wraps on the opposite side of the table.*

Position Tables with Elements (Deprecated)

If you enclose your table inside the <div> element along with the align=" " attribute, you can position the table to the left, center, or right. Any text or page content coming after the table will start immediately below it. For example, to right-align a table using <div>, you would write your code as follows:

```
<div align="right">
<table><tr><td>X</td></tr></table>
</div>
```

8

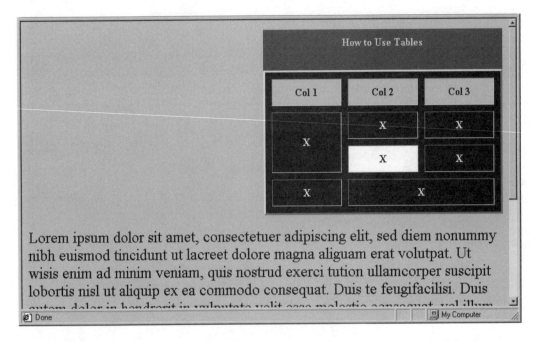

If you want to center your table, you can bypass the align attribute by using the <center> element instead. The center element is the basic equivalent of <div align="center">. However, <center> is also numbered among the deprecated elements. So, if you are trying to write an XHTML page that will validate, you need to avoid this element.

Position Tables with Attributes (Deprecated)

By using the align attribute inside the <table> tag, you also can position a table in the center or on the right side of the page. An added advantage of using the align attribute is that, just like with images, it influences text wrapping. If you set your table to align="right", any text outside the table will wrap to the left. To right-align the sample table, modify the opening <table> tag to read <table align="right">. The next illustration shows what the page looks like with some text added.

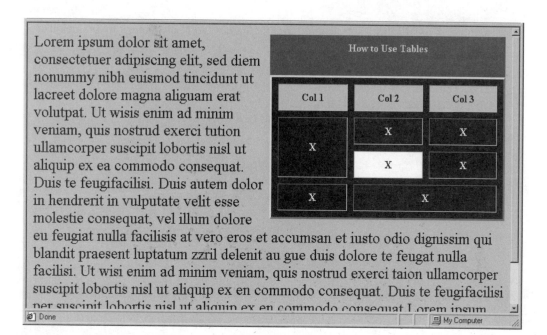

Modify Borders and Cell Divisions

Earlier in the chapter you learned how easy it is to create a border for your table. Simply use the border attribute with a value of one or more pixels. Sometimes, though, you might want only a partial border or just rule lines drawn between the cells. How do you do that? There are ways to accomplish this using both HTML and CSS.

Use the HTML frame Attribute to Adjust Table Borders

If you want to make changes to how the outer border of a table displays, the HTML frame=" " attribute gives you quite a few options. By inserting the following attributes, you can select portions of the table border to display, while others remain invisible:

- **To display only the top**   frame="above"
- **To display only the bottom**   frame="below"
- **To display only the left side**   frame="lhs"
- **To display only the right side**   frame="rhs"
- **To display both the left and right sides**   frame="vsides"
- **To display both the top and bottom sides**   frame="hsides"
- **To display no outside border at all**   frame="void"

For example, if you display a simple table with the frame="void" attribute, it might look like the following illustration:

```
<table frame="void">
<tr> <td>X</td> <td>X</td> <td>X</td> </tr>
<tr> <td>X</td> <td>X</td> <td>X</td> </tr>
<tr> <td>X</td> <td>X</td> <td>X</td> </tr>
</table>
```

NOTE *The values "box" and "border" both display a border all the way around the table.*

Use the rules Attribute to Adjust Interior Borders

Just as frame enables you to control the outer borders of a table, rules gives you control over the interior borders, or rules, between the cells. With the rules attribute you can remove all the interior borders, just the horizontal ones, or just the vertical ones:

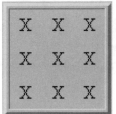

■ **To display vertical rules**   rules="cols"

■ **To display horizontal rules**   rules="rows"

■ **To display no rules**   rules="none"

■ **To display rules between table groups**   rules="groups"

Use CSS Border Properties for Tables

Borders are another area where HTML cannot hold a candle to CSS. In fact, the possibilities for creating attractive borders for your tables are so many and varied, it would be impractical to try to deal with them all in this chapter. Chapter 10 goes into detail about how to create borders with CSS; for a sample, use the following code to create a simple four-celled table using CSS' border properties. This code also is a good test for how well your browser supports CSS. If your display does not resemble the following example, your browser's CSS support is weak:

```
<html>
    <head>
```

```
      <title>CSS Table Border</title>
      <style type="text/css">
table   { border-width: medium;
          border-color: navy;
          border-style: groove; }
td      { text-align: center;
          background-color: yellow; }
      </style>
   </head>
   <body>
     <table>
        <tr><td>CSS</td><td>IS</td></tr>
        <tr><td>VERY</td><td>COOL</td></tr>
     </table>
   <body>
</html>
```

Add Images and Links

If you've read the chapters on graphics and links, you know almost all you need to know about adding them to tables. Of course, if you are using tables to create your layout, you will need to choose the cells where you place your images or links carefully. It may help you to sketch out what your table will look like before you write the markup. That way you can visualize the results you hope to achieve.

Add Images with <img />

You add images to a table the same way you place them anywhere else in your page: with the <img /> element. The only difference is that <img /> must go between a set of <td> or <th> tags. To put an image into a table cell:

```
<td><image src="picture.gif" height="#" width="#" alt=" "></td>
```

Although it is not required, be sure to specify the height and width of the picture, just as you would any other time you place an image on a page. If an image seems too large for your layout, remember that you can reduce the image's display size by reducing the values in *height* and *width*. Another (and better) option is to use your image-editing software to create a smaller version of the graphic. That way, it will take less time to load, and it will generally be a clearer picture.

Add Links with \<a\> \</a\>

To add links to your table, use the anchor, the \<a\> element with a URL, the same way you create any other link. The anchor tag and its URL are cell contents; thus, they go between the \<td\> or \<th\> tags on your table. You also can use the \<img /\> element if you want to create a graphical link.

To put a text link inside a table cell:

```
<td><a href="cj.htm">Visit CJ's Page</a></td>
```

To put a graphical link inside a table cell:

```
<td><a href="cj.htm"><img src="cjhat.jpg"></a></td>
```

In the preceding example, the different elements are nested inside each other. Nesting is very important when working with tables because if tags overlap, your entire table structure could become confused. If you're not sure what nesting is, see Chapter 1.

This code creates a four-celled "Family Album" table with both text and graphical links, as shown in the following illustration. Try typing the code yourself and substituting your own pictures and filenames. As you type the code, try to think about what each element is doing and why it is there. Comment lines have been added so you can easily identify the different parts of the code. If you don't want to type the code, you can download it from the author's Web site at www.jamespence.com.

```
<table border="3" cellpadding="10" bgcolor="gold">
<!-- This is the table caption -->
    <caption>FAMILY ALBUM</caption>
<!-- This is the top row and first cell -->
      <tr>
        <td align="center"><a href="cj.htm">
          <img src="cjhat.jpg" height="110"
            width="90" alt="CJ" />
          </a><br /> CJ
        </td>
<!-- This is the top row and second cell -->
        <td><a href="cj.htm">Visit CJ's Page</a>
          </td>
      </tr>
<!-- This is the second row and first cell -->
      <tr>
        <td align="center"> <a href="cm.htm">
          <img src="cm1.jpg" height="100"
            width="100" alt="CM" />
          </a><br />CM
        </td>
```

```
<!-- This is the second text link cell -->
        <td> <a href="cm.htm">Visit CM's Page</a>
        </td>
    </tr>
</table>
```

FAMILY ALBUM

Use Tables for Faster Image Loading

Suppose you have a very large image that you don't want to reduce. How can you avoid having your visitors view a blank screen while the picture loads? You use a table. Just use a graphics editor to slice the image up into some smaller pieces. Then place one part of the image in each cell and put it back together, just as you would a jigsaw puzzle. To make the image appear seamless, you must specify the following attributes in the opening table tag:

```
<table border="0" cellpadding="0" cellspacing="0">.
```

In the illustration that follows, the cellpadding and cellspacing attributes are left at their default sizes of one pixel, so you can see how each cell holds part of the picture.

Miscellaneous Table Features

Several features of tables are worth noting, but at this writing do not enjoy very broad browser support. Attributes such as summary and bordercolor and the <thead>, <tfoot>, and <tbody> elements can be useful. As you would with CSS, however, be cautious in using them.

Summarize Tables with the summary Attribute

The summary attribute goes in the opening table tag and is supposed to contain a description of the table for nonvisual browsers. This will help people who visit your site with Braille or aural browsers to get an idea of what your table contains. For example, for the preceding family album table, you could write a summary that reads as follows:

```
<table summary="This is my online family album with pictures
and links to my children's pages.  CJ's picture and link is
first and CM's picture and link is second">
```

Summary promises to be an important aspect of tables in the future, but it is not yet well supported. Still, it won't hurt to take advantage of it now. It will save you the trouble of going back and modifying your pages later.

Set Border Colors with the bordercolor Attribute

The *bordercolor* attribute is an Internet Explorer extension to HTML. In other words, it is not part of the XHTML recommendation and should be considered a deprecated attribute. Bordercolor enables you to use HTML to set a color for your table borders. The *bordercolorlight* and *bordercolordark* attributes are also IE Extensions. They enable you to create a 3-D effect by choosing two different colors to apply to the border. These attributes are safe to use as long as you remember that your XHTML pages will not validate when you use them, and some of your visitors will not see the colored border. To see bordercolor in action, modify the code for the family album table by changing the opening table tag to read as follows:

```
<table border="3" cellpadding="10" bgcolor="yellow"
       bordercolor="red">
```

If your browser supports this attribute, you should see a red border around the table. if you're using IE, you can give the border a 3-D look by trying the bordercolorlight and bordercolordark attributes. See how it works by changing the preceding attributes to read as follows:

```
bordercolorlight="red" bordercolordark="maroon"
```

*As of this writing, the bordercolorlight and bordercolordark attributes are supported
only by Internet Explorer. However, Netscape 7 has added support for the bordercolor
attribute.*

Group rows with <thead>, <tfoot>, and <tbody>

Some useful (although not well supported) elements are the <thead>, <tfoot>, and <tbody>
elements. These elements enable you to display a large table with a permanent or static header
and footer. If you have a lot of data on a page, the header and footer will remain stationary while
the table data scrolls. You have to set up this type of table a little differently, with the <thead>
and <tfoot> elements at the top, followed by the <tbody> element. A simple construction is given
in the following. Notice how the browser puts the footer cell at the bottom, even though in the code
it comes second:

```
<table>
   <thead><tr><td>Header</td><tr></thead>
   <tfoot><tr><td>Footer</td></tr></tfoot>
   <tbody><tr><td>Body</td></tr></tbody>
</table>
```

Group Columns with <colgroup> and <col />

The <colgroup> and <col /> elements make it possible for you to form groups of table columns
and set their attributes collectively. For example, say you used a table to create a five-column
spreadsheet. You have decided that you would like to have the first two columns display with a
red background, but the next three columns to remain white. By adding the following two lines
of markup, you can control the background colors of these columns as if they were two groups
rather than five individual columns:

```
<table>
<colgroup span="2" bgcolor="red" />
<colgroup span="3" />
<tr>(Beginning of first row)
```

CAUTION   *Notice that <colgroup /> is written as an empty element.*

8

If you look at the following illustration you will see that the first two columns have been colored red while the next three are white. This is because the span attribute in the first <colgroup> is set to a value of 2, which means that this element controls two columns. The second <colgroup /> has span set to 3, giving it control over three columns.

Column A	Column B	Column C	Column D	Column E

As you can see, the <colgroup /> element is useful in applying attributes to groups of columns, but what if you want to modify the contents of just one column? Perhaps you would like to have the contents of columns C, D, and E centered, and give D background color of yellow, but you want the other two columns (C and E) to retain a white background. To accomplish this, you use the <col /> element with <colgroup>.

The <col /> element performs the same function as does span. It specifies the number of columns in a group. However, the difference is that you have individual control over each column. You would write your markup this way:

```
<table>
   <colgroup span="2" bgcolor="red" />
   <colgroup>
     <col  align="center" />
     <col bgcolor="yellow" align="center" />
     <col  align="center" />
   </colgroup>
   <tr>(Beginning of first row)
```

In place of the span attribute, you use the <col /> element one time for each column to be represented. Then, in each of the <col /> tags, you can add the attributes you need. If you try this with a simple table, your results should look something like the following illustration:

Column A	Column B	Column C	Column D	Column E
X	X	X	X	X
X	X	X	X	X
X	X	X	X	X
X	X	X	X	X
X	X	X	X	X

When used with the span attribute, the <colgroup> element is written as an empty element: <colgroup span="#" />. However, when you are using the <col /> element instead of span, then you must use opening and closing tags for colgroup, as in the following:

```
<colgroup>
   <col />
   <col />
</colgroup>
```

Project 12: Create a Table-Based Web Page Layout

In this chapter, you have learned how to create tables and use them for data structure or page layout. In this project, you will apply what you have learned about XHTML and about tables as you create a simple table-based page layout. To complete this project you will need a banner graphic for your page's logo. If you'd rather not create your own, or don't have the necessary software, you can download the banner directly from the author's Web site at www.jamespence.com. When you have worked through the steps that follow, your page should resemble Figure 8-1.

> **TIP**   *The complete code for this exercise is included in the "Quick Reference" section that follows. If you get stuck, check the code.*

1. Open index.htm or create a new XHTML document named *index.htm*. If you create a new file, remember to save it in a different directory or you will overwrite your existing index.htm

2. Add a !DOCTYPE line identifying the document as XHTML 1.0 Transitional DTD. If you need to refresh your memory on how to do this, go back to Chapter 7 or check the code in the next section.

3. Set the <title> for the page to **Using Tables for Page Layout.**

4. Add a <style> element between the <head> tags and use the CSS background-color property to set the page background to white.

5. After the opening <body> tag insert an opening <div> tag and include a style attribute with the CSS text-align property set to center.

6. Next, add an opening <table> tag. Set the width to 100 percent, the border to 1 pixel, the cellpadding and cellspacing to 0 pixels, and add a summary that says **Page Layout.**

7. Now, set the dimensions of your vertical columns by using the <colgroup> element. Below the opening <colgroup> tag, add two <col /> elements. Set the width of the first to 15 percent and the second to 85 percent.

8. In the next few steps, you will define the header of your table and page with the <thead> element. First insert an opening <thead> tag.

9. Now, begin a row by adding an opening <tr> tag.

10. Because this row will have only one cell, add an opening <td> tag. Use the align attribute to center its contents, and set the colspan attribute to 2.

11. Add an <img /> element pointing to your banner. If you are using the banner file that is found in Figure 8-1, the file name is banner.gif. Don't forget to set the height and width attributes and to add a description with the alt attribute.

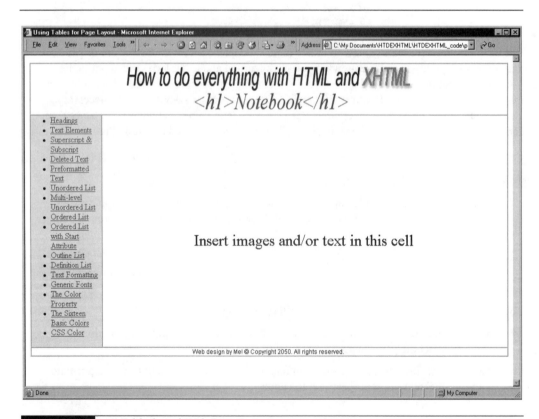

FIGURE 8-1   A Table-based Web Page Layout

12. Now supply closing </td>, </tr>, and </thead> tags.

13. Your table footer will come next. You will use the <tfoot> element for this. For the footer you are going to write a brief copyright notice. This would also be a great place to put a list of text-based links on a graphics heavy page. Begin by adding an opening <tfoot> element and follow it with a new opening <tr>.

14. Insert an opening <td> element and set the colspan attribute to 2. You might also try giving the footer a slightly different appearance from the rest of the text on the page. In this example, the style element has been used to set the font-family to Arial (or sansserif) and to reduce the size to .75em. The align attribute has been used to center the content. You might want to make some other changes, perhaps some different colors.

15. After the opening <td> element, add your copyright line. Don't forget to use the entity for the copyright symbol: ©.

16. Now, add closing </td>, </tr>, and </tfoot> tags to finish off this section of your page.

17. The body of your table is next, and you begin by adding an opening <tbody> tag, followed by opening <tr> and <td> tags. In the opening <td> tag, use the bgcolor attribute to set the cell color to aqua and the align attribute to set the alignment to left.

18. Now copy and paste the entire list of links from your original index.htm into your page, just past the opening <td> tag. Be sure to get the entire list, including the <ul> </ul> tags. After the closing </ul> tag, add a closing </td> tag to finish off that cell.

19. Begin a new cell by adding a new opening <td> tag. Use the valign attribute and a value of "middle" to vertically align the cell contents in the center of the cell.

20. Next, add an opening paragraph <p> tag. Apply the style attribute to set the font-size property to a value of 2em.

21. Add some text after the paragraph tag and then close the paragraph out with a closing </p> tag.

22. Finally, close out the rest of your tags by adding in this order: </td>, </tr>, </tbody>, </table>, </div>, and, if you need to, </body> and </html>.

23. Now save your page and view it in your browser. It should look something like Figure 8-1. If it doesn't, compare your code with the code in the next section to see if you can spot any mistakes.

Quick Reference: Tables

In this chapter you have learned how to use tables to display and format data. However, you have also learned how to use tables to create a stable layout for your Web pages. It is up to you whether or not you use tables as a design tool, but you will doubtless find many uses for them. If you find yourself losing track of all the different elements and attributes you can use with tables, or if you need help with the code for Project 12, the following sections provide a ready resource.

Create and Use Tables

Tables are simple to use and easy to learn. However, large tables can quickly become complex and difficult to manage or decipher. Use the following ready reference table to keep yourself familiar with the various elements and attributes used in creating XHTML tables:

To Do This	Use This
Create a table	`<table> </table>`
Create a row	`<tr> </tr>`
Create a data cell	`<td> </td>`
Create a heading	`<th> </th>`
Add a caption	`<caption> </caption>`

Align a table using the <div> element and the align attribute (deprecated)	`<div align="left">`
	`    <table>`
	`    </table>`
	`</div>`
	also: right or center

Align a table using the <div> element and the CSS text-align property	`<div style="text-align: left">`
	`    <table>`
	`    </table>`
	`</div>`
	also: right or center

Align cell contents horizontally	`<td align="left">` also: right or center Can also be used with <tr>, <thead>, <tfoot>, <tbody>, and <colgroup>
Align cell contents vertically	`<td valign="top">` or: middle, bottom, baseline Can also be used with <tr>, <thead>, <tfoot>, <tbody>, and <colgroup>
Set cell background colors	`<td bgcolor="colorValue">` Can also be used with <tr>, <thead>, <tfoot>, <tbody>, and <colgroup>
Turn borders off	`<table border="0">` or simply omit the border attribute
Adjust border thickness	`<table border="#">` (#=thickness in pixels)
Control display of outer table border	`<table frame="above">` or: below, lhs, rhs, hsides, vsides, void
Control display of inside cell borders (rules)	`<table rules="cols">` or: rows, groups, none
Add space between cells	`<table cellspacing="#">` (#=pixels)
Add space inside cells	`<table cellpadding="#">` (#=pixels)
Make a data cell span multiple columns	`<td colspan="#">` (#=number of columns)
Make a data cell span multiple rows	`<td rowspan="#">` (#=number of rows)

To Do This	Use This

Group rows together	`<thead> </thead>`
	`<tfoot> </tfoot>`
	`<tbody> </tbody>`

Group columns together	`<colgroup span="#" />` (#=number of columns) *or*
	`<colgroup>`
	    `<col />`
	    `<col />`
	`</colgroup>`

Add an image to a table cell	`<td><img src="picture.gif " /></td>`
And an image and text to a table cell	`<td><img src="picture.gif " />Text here</td>`
Add a link inside a table cell	`<td><a href="pageName.htm">Go Here</a></td>`
Add a graphical link inside a table cell	`<td><a href="pageName.htm"><img picture.gif /></a></td>`

Use a table to join together a sliced image	`<table cellpadding="0" cellspacing="0">`
	`<tr><td><img src="part1.gif " />`
	`</td></tr>`
	`<tr><td><img src="part2.gif" />`
	`</td></tr>`
	`</table>`

Code for Project 12

Project 12 provided a good test of your mastery of XHTML tables. If you found yourself stuck at any point, the code that created Figure 1 is reproduced here. Compare your code and see if there are any glitches that crept in.

```
<!DOCTYPE html PUBLIC "-//W3C//DTD XHTML 1.0 Transitional//EN"
    "http://www.w3.org/TR/xhtml1/DTD/xhtml1-transitional.dtd">
<html xmlns="http://www.w3.org/1999/xhtml">
  <head>
    <title>Using Tables for Page Layout</title>
      <style type="text/css">
        body {background-color: white;}
      </style>
  </head>
  <body>
   <div style="text-align: center;">
     <table summary="Page layout" width="100%"
          border="1" cellpadding="0" cellspacing="0">
```

```
<colgroup>
  <col width="15%" />
  <col width="85%" />
</colgroup>
<thead>
  <tr>
    <td align="center" colspan="2">
      <img src="banner.gif" height="100" width="600"
       alt="How to Do Everything with HTML Notebook" />
    </td>
  </tr>
</thead>
<tfoot>
  <tr>
    <td style="font-family: arial; font-size: .75em;"
      align="center" colspan="2">Web design by Me! &copy;
      Copyright 2050. All rights reserved.
    </td>
  </tr>
</tfoot>
<tbody>
  <tr>
    <td bgcolor="aqua" align="left">
    <ul>
      <li><a href="headings.htm">Headings</a></li>
      <li><a href="text.htm">Text Elements</a></li>
      <li><a href="sup.htm">Superscript &amp;
            Subscript</a></li>
      <li><a href="del.htm">Deleted Text</a></li>
      <li><a href="pre.htm">Preformatted Text</a></li>
      <li><a href="ulist.htm">Unordered List</a></li>
      <li><a href="ulist2.htm">Multi-level
            Unordered List</a></li>
      <li><a href="olist.htm">Ordered List</a></li>
      <li><a href="olist2.htm">Ordered List with Start
            Attribute</a></li>
      <li><a href="olist3.htm">Outline List</a></li>
      <li><a href="dlist.htm">Definition List</a></li>
      <li><a href="text-format.htm">Text
            Formatting</a></li>
      <li><a href="generic-fonts.htm">Generic
            Fonts</a></li>
      <li><a href="font-colors.htm">The Color
            Property</a></li>
```

```
            <li><a href="16colors.htm">The Sixteen
                    Basic Colors</a></li>
            <li><a href="css-color.htm">CSS Color</a></li>
          </ul>
        </td>
        <td valign="middle">
          <p style="font-size: 2em">Insert images and/or
            text in this cell</p>
        </td>
      </tr>
    </tbody>
  </table>
  </div>
  </body>
</html>
```

8

Chapter 9

Create Framesets and Frames Pages

How to...

- Understand frames and the XHTML frameset DTD
- Create a basic frameset
- Modify your frames
- Provide content for noncompatible browsers
- Use floating frames
- Create a frames-based navigation layout

If you've surfed the Web at all, you have encountered frames. Chances are you have also formed a strong opinion about them; you probably either love them or hate them. Why do frames provoke such strong emotional reactions from people? Possibly because they are misused so often. When frames are used incorrectly, they can be very frustrating to those trying to sort through them. The frustration is like opening a large gift-wrapped box only to find a slightly smaller box inside it. When you open the second box, you find another, even smaller one inside, and so on. By the time you actually get to the box with the gift in it, you might not even care anymore.

Nevertheless, frames provide an excellent tool for site navigation. They enable you to create, among other things, a navigation bar that is always present, pages that load faster, and a permanently reserved space for your site's logo or banner. Just be careful to not get carried away—if the adage "you can't see the forest for the trees" were ever applicable to Web design, it is when a visitor can't see your site because of the frames.

Understand Frames

Although frames look intimidating on the surface, they really are simple to construct. In fact, one of the reasons for their overuse might be that when people find out how easy they are to create, they go "frame crazy" and use them all the time. However, frames are not an all-purpose site creation tool, but rather a means for creating dynamic layouts and efficient navigation systems.

Frames Allow for Multiple Page Display

What, exactly, are frames? Simply put, frames enable you to display more than one page at a time in the same window. Until now, when you have displayed your XHTML pages, you've done it one at a time. To display more than one document at a time, you would have to open multiple browser windows. Frames change all that. With a fairly simple set of elements, you can display two, four, eight, or even more pages in the same browser window. But why would you want to do this?

Say you are an author, and you want to put together a Web site to publicize your book. As you design the site, you decide that you want your book's cover to appear on every page, but you'd like to include a lot of different content. Perhaps you want to put some reviews on one page, an excerpt on another, and reader comments on another, but you always want to keep your book's cover in front of your potential customer.

You could design a site with tables, creating five or ten separate pages, each with the same layout but different content. Or you could construct a three-frame page that features the cover of your book and a banner with your name at the top, content on the right side, and a navigation bar on the left side. Then, when a visitor clicks a link in the navigation bar, only the content frame will change; everything else stays where it is. In this case, you have made your life easier by not creating the same layout ten times. You also have made things easier for your visitor because your pages will download more quickly. Remember, only the text content has to reload—not the images in the other frames. Less content equals faster load time.

Disadvantages of Frames

Although frames provide for more efficient site design and navigation, they come with some noteworthy disadvantages attached. In fact, if you are not careful, you actually can make getting around your site more difficult. Consider some of the following ways in which frames can make site navigation confusing:

- Too many frames on a page present a dizzying array of visual options and choices, often causing the focus of your site to be obscured.

- Overuse of frames slows down loading time. Keep in mind that each frame is loaded with a separate HTML document. Each of these documents takes time to download. Thus, the more frames you use, the longer it is going to take for your site to be fully loaded on the user's machine.

- Frames pages don't mix well with search engines. Some search engines won't even look at a frames-based site. Others will, but as you will learn later in this chapter, your frameset document provides no content in and of itself. If this is also the main page for your site, search engines don't have much to work with.

- Frames pages can pose navigation problems for someone who enters your site through a "back door." If a search engine's spider has indexed the content pages on your Web site, visitors might come to your site indirectly through one of these pages, rather than through your home page. In this case the page will display apart from the frame structure you created. If you are relying solely on frames for navigation purposes, your visitors will find no navigation bar. In other words, their visit to your site will be a dead end.

- Frames pages are difficult to bookmark. Visitors to your site might want to mark a page on your site as one of their favorites. Because the basic building block of a frames-based site is a frameset document, they will actually be marking the location of the frameset, not the content they are viewing. If your site is a simple one, that might not be a problem; however, if your navigation system is complex, your visitors might have to wade through a lot of pages to get back to the one they *thought* they had bookmarked.

■ Although the numbers are small, there are still browsers out there that don't support frames. Someone coming to your site with one of these browsers will find it inaccessible. Nonvisual browsers for the handicapped also have trouble with frames.

You might be wondering why you should even bother with frames. After all, there are plenty of other ways to present a Web site without using them. In fact, many excellent sites use no frames at all. So why use them?

Advantages of Frames

There are any number of reasons you would want to use frames on your site. Frames can help you do things that would be difficult or impossible to do without them. For example, frames enable you to create some of the following effects:

■ Frames allow you to display multiple pages in a single browser window.

■ Frames allow you to keep some content static as other content changes.

■ Frames allow your visitors to access content from a different Web site without leaving yours or opening a second browser window. Thus, if you have a second site and want to include content from it, frames make it easy.

■ When you use seamless frames you can create the impression of a single page with dynamically changing content.

■ Frames enable you to update the navigation system for your entire site by editing only *one* document.

> **TIP**   *If you prefer to have a link open in a separate window rather than in one of your frames, just use the target="_blank" attribute in your link tag. For example, the link <a href"www.osborne.com" target="_blank">Open Osborne's Web Site</a> will cause a new window to open. Be sure to include the underscore character (_) before the word "blank."*

To keep frames in perspective, remember that, although frames are useful tools, no tool is right for every task. If frames help you create a better site, by all means use them. But don't load your site with frames just because you think they're cool.

Understand Frame Elements and Attributes

Like tables, HTML frames are very easy to build. As a matter of fact, they are so easy that you will wonder why you haven't used them before now. In many ways, creating a site based on frames is easier than building it with tables. Although a frames-based site can become complicated, the basic concept is simple. First, you create the frames with a master document, called a *frameset*. This establishes the layout. Next you create standard a XHTML documents to fill the frames you've just designed.

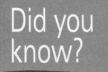

Who Developed the Idea of Frames?

Frames originally were developed by Netscape and first supported in Netscape 2. Later, they were made part of the HTML 4 standard. Virtually all new browsers support frames, but there are still some older browsers in use that do not.

Understand the Frameset DTD

You learned in Chapter 7 that XHTML has three Document Type Descriptions or DTDs: Transitional, Strict, and Frameset. In Chapter 8, you applied the Transitional DTD to your table-based layout. For your frames pages, you need to use the Frameset DTD. This means that the very first line of your HTML document (even before the opening <html> tag) needs to be a *document type declaration*, identifying the document as a frameset. This declaration should be typed in *exactly* as you see it in the following code listing:

```
<!DOCTYPE HTML PUBLIC "-//W3C//DTD XHTML 1.0 Frameset//EN"
  "DTD/xhtml1-frameset.dtd">
```

CAUTION *You need only* one *frameset document for a frames-based page. The documents that actually fill the frames should be normal XHTML documents, using either the Transitional or Strict DTD. If you find this confusing, think of the frameset document as if it were a picture frame capable of holding more than one photo. You've seen these in stores: one big frame, several places for pictures. That's how a frameset works. The frameset is like a big picture frame, divided into multiple sections. Your XHTML documents are the "photos" that go into the various parts of the frame.*

Understand the Frameset Document

Another unique part of the frameset is how the document is constructed. By now, you are accustomed to using the standard sequence of XHTML document elements:

```
<html>
    <head>
        <title>Standard XHTML Document</title>
    </head>
    <body>
    </body>
</html>
```

There is one significant difference in how a frameset document is built. The frameset document does not have a <body> element. Instead, you use the <frameset> and <frame /> elements. A basic frameset document (with no frames defined) would look like the following code:

```
<html>
    <head>
        <title>Basic Frameset Document</title>
    </head>
    <frameset>
    </frameset>
</html>
```

TIP *As you'll see in the next section, to add frames to your frameset, you insert one <frame /> element for each frame. The <frame /> elements are nested between the <frameset> tags.*

Understand Basic Frame Elements

The first step in learning how to work with frames is in understanding the elements used to create them. You need only two elements to create a page with frames: <frameset> and <frame />. The basic frame elements (and what they do) are listed here:

■ **<frameset>** The *frameset* element is what actually creates the multiple frames. When creating a frames-based page, you use this element *instead* of the <body> </body> element.

■ **<frame />** The *frame* element is used to specify each of the frames that will be visible on your page. Like the <img /> element, <frame /> is an empty element and requires no closing tag.

Understand Basic Frame Attributes

Two attributes are essential to creating frames, while others enable you to fine-tune your frames. The essential attributes are the *columns* and *rows* attributes. These attributes enable you to control the layout, size, and number of frames that will appear on your page.

NOTE *Actually, you only need one of these two attributes. Unlike HTML tables, you do not need to have both rows and columns; you can create a frame page with either rows or columns.*

■ **cols= "column width"** This attribute defines a frameset in columns. The default setting is one column, which takes up 100 percent of the page. If you want more than one column, specify the width of each column, separated by commas. You can specify width in pixels or percentages. By using the asterisk (*) as a wildcard, you can create a column that dynamically adjusts to whatever space is left over. In the following example, the columns attribute will create three vertical frames, one taking up 20 percent of the screen, the next using 30 percent, and the last using the remaining 50 percent:

```
<frameset cols="20%, 30%, *">
```

■ **rows="row height"**   The rows attribute defines a frameset in rows. The default setting is one row, taking up 100 percent of the page. As with columns, you can define row height with pixels (fixed design) or percentages (dynamic design) and use an asterisk as a wildcard.

TIP	*Whenever possible, specify row and column dimensions with percentages and the asterisk. The advantage of using dynamic design is that your frames will adjust to fit browser windows, no matter how they are sized. If you give absolute dimensions in pixels and a visitor has resized his or her browser, your frames might be cropped. Also, how a page will be displayed is determined by the screen resolution your visitor is using. Visitors making a quick scan of your site might miss parts of the page that scroll off screen if they are using a low resolution (640×480).*

Although there are some other elements, and quite a few other attributes, that can be applied to frames, these are more for fine-tuning the frames and how they display and are covered later in this chapter. All you need for creating your first frames page are the elements and attributes we've covered so far.

Project 13: Create a Simple Frameset

The best way to learn HTML frames is by experimentation. By constructing a simple page with four frames, you will learn what you can do with them and how to modify them. For this example, you will start by creating some display documents.

Build Your Display Documents

Frames need something to display to work correctly. Before you begin constructing a frameset, you will want to create some simple HTML pages. For this example, these pages needn't be complicated or filled with content. A plain page with the text "This is page 1" (or something equally simple) will suffice. Just for fun, you might want to specify a different background color for each of the pages.

To create a set of display documents, follow these steps:

1. Create a directory on your hard drive named *Framesample*.

2. Open template.htm and save it as *frame1.htm*.

3. In the <body> </body> portion of the page, add this line: **<h1>This is page 1.</h1>**.

4. To add visual interest, choose a background color for the page by adding a the <style> element in the <head> portion of your page. In between the two <style> tags, add a rule that uses the CSS *background-color* property to define a background color, as in the following example.

```
<style>
     body {background-color: white;}
</style>
```

5. If you set a page to a dark color (such as black, navy, green, maroon, or purple), you also might want to specify white or another light color as a text color, as in the following listing:

```
<style>
     body {background-color: black;
             color: white}
</style>
```

> **TIP** *For other color possibilities, read Chapter 4.*

6. Save the page as *frame1.htm*, in the Framesample directory.

7. Create seven more pages, saving them as *frame2.htm*, *frame3.htm*, and so on.

The following code creates a black page with white text. Change the bgcolor and text values to create different combinations:

```
<html>
     <head>
          <title>Frames</title>
          <style>
body {background-color: black;
     color: white}
          </style
     </head>
<body>
<h1>This is page 1</h1>
</body>
</html>
```

After you have some documents to display, it's time to move on to the next step in making frames pages: constructing the frameset.

Construct a Frameset

The heart of a frames page is the *frameset*. Think of it as a master document that controls the display of your frames. Although a frameset document is an HTML page in its own right, it displays no content of its own. The frameset's contents are the frames. Keep in mind that when you are doing frames you must *always* have one extra document: the frameset.

Build a Frameset

You construct a frameset document the same way you do any other HTML page—with one important exception: A frameset page uses the <frameset> element in place of the <body> element. The reason for this is that your frames make up the body of the frameset document.

 A frameset page can use the <body> </body> element, but only if it is contained within the <noframes> </noframes> element. This is to provide content for browsers that do not support frames.

At its simplest, with no frames defined, a frameset will look like the following code listing. Using template.htm, create a frameset by replacing the <body> element with the <frameset> </frameset> element. Save it as *framesample.htm*.

```
<html>
    <head>
        <title>Frame Sample</title>
    </head>
    <frameset>
    </frameset>
</html>
```

However, if you try to display this, you won't see much of anything because the frames have not yet been defined.

Define Frame Structure

As mentioned earlier, you define frames using the cols=" " and rows=" " attributes. If you read Chapter 8, the idea of table columns and rows will be familiar. However, frames work a bit differently. You can have either columns or rows or a combination of both. For example, to construct a frameset with four equal columns, you would modify the opening <frameset> tag to read:

```
<frameset cols="25%, 25%, 25%, 25%">
```

If you want instead to have a frameset with four equal rows, change to the rows attribute:

```
<frameset rows="25%, 25%, 25%, 25%">
```

To divide your frameset into four equal parts with both columns and rows, you would modify the <frameset> tag to look like this:

```
<frameset rows="50%, 50%" cols="50, 50%">
```

If you add this code to your page and try to display it, you will still get a blank page. Why? Because defining a frameset is not enough. You also must specify what pages your different frames will load. For that, you use the <frame> </frame> element.

Specify Frame Content

Your frames provide the content for your page. If you define frame structure in the <frameset> element but don't tell the browser what to put into the frames, it will ignore the frameset altogether. Because the last example uses both rows and columns to construct four frames, you will use the <frame /> element four times.

For each <frame /> you create, you must also use the src attribute to tell the browser which file to load in that frame. For example, to use frame1.htm in one of your frames, you would include the following tag: <frame src="frame1.htm" /> .

Try including the preceding line plus three others in your frameset. Your complete frameset should look like the following code and illustration:

```html
<html>
    <head>
        <title>Frame Sample</title>
    </head>
    <frameset rows="50%, 50%" cols="50%, 50%">
        <frame src="frame1.htm" />
        <frame src="frame2.htm" />
        <frame src="frame3.htm" />
        <frame src="frame4.htm" />
    </frameset>
</html>
```

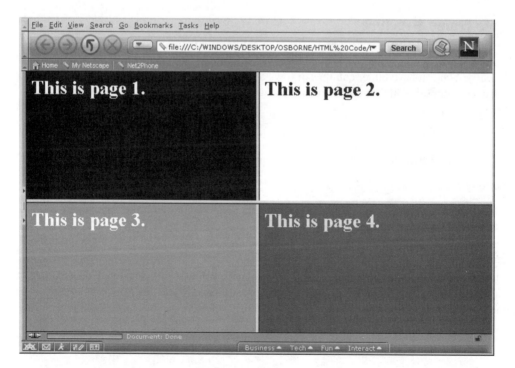

Create Nested Frames

You can create even more complicated framesets by nesting them. Chapter 1 covers the concept of nesting, which means putting complete sets of tags inside one another. To nest frames, you will place another set of frameset tags *inside* your existing frameset. For example, consider the preceding frameset, which created four equal-sized frames. What if you decide to divide the bottom-right frame into two smaller frames? One way to do it would be to add another <frameset> in place of the <frame /> tag for that frame. Your code will be changed to look like this:

```
<html>
    <head>
        <title>Frame Sample</title>
    </head>
    <frameset rows="50%, 50%" cols"50%, 50%">
        <frame src="frame1.htm" />
        <frame src="frame2.htm" />
        <frame src="frame3.htm" />
            <frameset cols="50%, 50%">
                <frame src="frame4.htm" />
                <frame src="frame5.htm" />
            </frameset>
    </frameset>
</html>
```

9

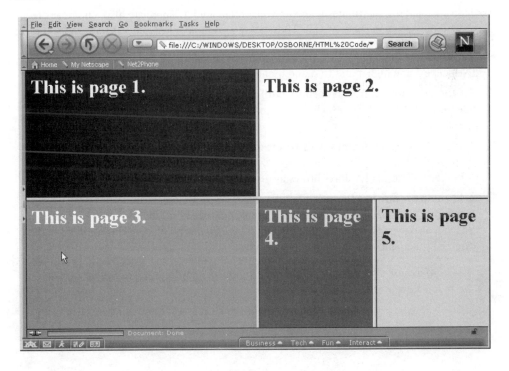

NOTE   *By changing the columns and rows attributes, you can come up with many different possible frame constructions. The preceding illustration is only one possibility.*

Although it is possible to come up with many different combinations of nested framesets, you might want to think twice about doing it. Nesting frames is one way to make your pages so complicated that you destroy their effectiveness. If you have a good reason to nest frames, by all means do it. Otherwise, let nested frames remain a curiosity, but not part of your regular Web arsenal.

CAUTION   *Don't forget to include closing tags (or closing slashes on empty elements). Also, don't forget to properly nest your elements. If you make any mistakes, your frames will not display properly.*

Modify Your Frames

Both the <frameset> and the <frame /> elements can be modified with attributes that allow you to control how your frames are displayed and how much your visitors can modify them. For example, you can add or remove borders, select border colors, determine whether your visitors can resize the frames on their browsers, and much more. These attributes give you the ability to fine-tune your layout.

Use Attributes with the <frameset> Element

You used the cols and rows attributes to create your frame layout. There are also a number of additional attributes you can choose from. These allows you to control general frame appearance:

- **Turn borders on and off with frameborder.**   The values are "1" for on and "0" for off. (Netscape 3 and higher and IE 4 and higher also support "yes" for on and "no" for off.)

- **Set the thickness of frame borders with border.**   With this attribute, you set the thickness of the border in pixels. For example, border="5" sets a border that is five pixels thick.

- **Add space between frames with framespacing.**   This also is specified in pixels. Thus, framespacing="20" adds a 20-pixel–wide space between frames. (This attribute is limited to Internet Explorer browsers.)

- **Add color to your borders with bordercolor.**   Specify colors for your frame borders with either color names or hexadecimal code. This affects all the frames on the page. You can also specify border colors for individual frames by placing this attribute in the <frame /> element.

NOTE   *The bordercolor=" " attribute works only in Internet Explorer 4 and higher and in Netscape 3 and higher.*

The following example shows how the previous illustration would look with added color, framespacing, and border thickness added. The modified <frameset> tag would look like this: <frameset bordercolor="navy" framespacing="10" border="5">.

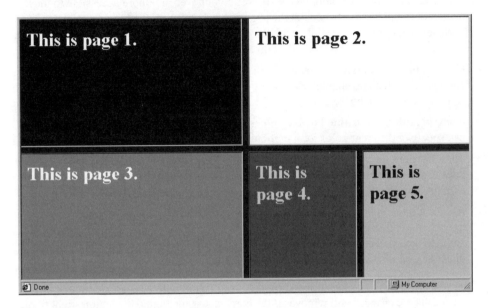

Use Attributes with the <frame /> Element

In addition to the src=" " attribute, the frame element takes a number of other attributes. Most of these relate to how the frame functions when displayed, although a few deal with general appearance. The attributes you can use with the <frame /> element are as follows:

- **Add white space with marginheight and marginwidth.** As their names imply, these attributes control the margins in your frames. You can use them in individual <frame /> elements to specify different margins for each. The values for these attributes can be given in pixels or percentages.

- **Prevent resizing with the noresize attribute.** To prevent viewers from resizing your frames according to their own tastes, use the noresize attribute. When you insert this into a <frame /> element, it acts like a toggle switch, fixing your frames at the proportions you set. This attribute should be written as noresize="noresize".

- **Add a scrolling bar with the scrolling attribute.** You actually have three options where scrolling bars are concerned. If you supply a "no" value here, your frame will never display a scrolling bar, no matter how much content the page has. If you put "yes" as a value, your frame will always display a scrolling bar. By choosing "auto" for the value, the browser will determine when a scroll bar is needed and insert one automatically.

SHORTCUT   *The default setting for scrolling is auto. There's no need to use the scrolling attribute unless you want to turn scrolling off or ensure that it's always on.*

■ **Add a description with longdesc.**   To make your Web site more accessible to those using nonvisual browsers, consider using this attribute. With the long description attribute, you can provide a link to a URL containing a description of the frame's contents. For example, <frame longdesc="description.htm" />.

■ **Control individual frame borders with frameborder.**   Used in the <frame /> element, this attribute enables you to turn individual frame borders on and off. If you want to turn off the borders for some, but not all of your frames, this is a useful attribute.

■ **Control individual frame border colors with bordercolor.**   With this attribute, you can specify a different color for a particular frame border.

■ **Turn borders on and off with frameborder.**   This attribute works the same way as it does in the <frameset> element, by toggling borders on and off. Here you can control an individual frame.

■ **Assign names to your frames with the name attribute.**   This is probably the most important of all the attributes you can use with the <frame /> element. By assigning a name to a particular frame and using the *target* attribute in your hyperlinks, you can direct any number of different pages to display in that frame.

To see some of these attributes at work, modify your framesample.htm code to look like the following code. These changes will remove all the borders, except around the bottom-right frame. A scroll bar will be added to the bottom-left frame.

```
<html>
   <head>
      <title>Frame Sample</title>
   </head>
   <frameset rows="50%, 50%" cols="50, 50%" frameborder="0"
         framespacing="0" border="0">
     <frame src="frame1.htm" marginheight="100"
           marginwidth="100" />
     <frame src="frame2.htm" noresize="noresize"/>
     <frame src="frame3.htm" scrolling="yes"/>
         <frameset cols="50%, 50%" frameborder="0">
             <frame src="frame4.htm" />
             <frame src="frame5.htm" frameborder="1"/>
         </frameset>
   </frameset>
</html>
```

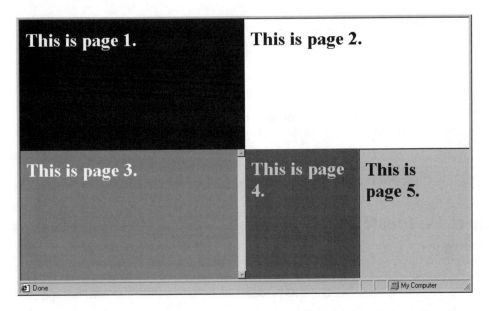

By using the different frame attributes, you can control many aspects of your frames' display. Try experimenting with the framesample.htm page by adding some of the attributes yourself and seeing what changes they make as the page is displayed.

Address Noncompatible Browsers with <noframes>

Although the numbers are small, there still are browsers in use that do not support frames. If someone tries to access your site with one of these, they will not be able to view your pages. As a courtesy to people using these older browsers, it is wise to include special directions inside the <noframes> element. You can either provide alternative content between these or offer directions or even a link to a nonframes version of your site. A sample <noframes> instruction is given here:

```
<html>
   <head>
      <title>No Frames</title>
   </head>
   <frameset>
      <frame src=" " />
      <frame src=" " />
   </frameset>
   <noframes>
     <body>
       <h1 style="text-align: center">
       Your browser does not support frames.<br /> Click this
```

```
        link for an alternate <a href="noframes.htm">non frames
        version</a> of this site.</h1>
     </body>
   </noframes>
</html>
```

The content in the <noframes> element will be displayed only on browsers that do not support frames. Frame-supporting browsers will ignore it.

Your browser does not support frames.
Click this link for an alternate <u>non-frames version</u> of this site.

Project 14: Create an Inline Frame

Frames were first incorporated by Netscape. Not to be left out, the developers of Internet Explorer threw their own version of frames into the mix. However, IE's concept is quite different from Netscape's. Instead of dividing a single window into multiple frames, IE developed the concept of the *inline* or *floating* frame. And, like its predecessor, the inline frame has been incorporated into the XHTML recommendation.

An inline frame is more like a mini-window that you can place inside a block of text or the layout of a page. Like regular frames, floating frames draw their content from a separate XHTML document; unlike them, the page they are placed on can have its own content. The easiest way to picture how a floating frame works is to think of it as a sidebar in a magazine article. It provides its own content, but in the context of other content.

To create an inline frame, you use the <iframe> element. This element is a bit of an anomaly because even though it functions as an empty element (you don't put anything between the two tags), you still must have the closing tag. All the frame attributes given earlier can be applied to inline frames. You also can use the *align* attribute to position it on the page and cause text to wrap around it (although align has been deprecated in favor of style sheets). To create a sample page that uses a floating frame, follow these steps:

1. Open template.htm and save it as *iframe.htm*.

2. Set the body backgroundcolor to white with the <style> element and the CSS background-color property

3. Add the following line just below the first <body> tag:

   ```
   <iframe src="frame1.htm" width="200" height="300"> </iframe>
   ```

4. Add some text below this line to simulate content for the iframe.htm page.

5. Save the file in your Framesample directory and display iframe.htm on your browser.

The following illustration was created from this code.

```html
<html>
      <head>
<title>Inline Frames</title>
      </head>
      <body>
         <!-- Comment: notice that the iframe references
               lorem.htm as its source. Any HTML file can
               go there. -->
         <iframe src="lorem.htm"
         width="200" height="300">
         </iframe>
         <pstyle="font-size: 1.5em"/>
<!-- Comment: lorem.txt was pasted in here.
      Supply your own text or go to the author's Web
site:www.jamespence.com, and download the lorem.txt file. -->>
         </p>
      </body>
</html>
```

9

Lorem ipsum dolor sit amet, consectetuer adipiscing elit, sed diem nonummy nibh euismod tincidunt ut lacreet dolore magna aliguam erat volutpat. Ut wisis enim ad minim veniam, quis nostrud exerci tution ullamcorper suscipit lobortis nisl ut aliquip ex ea commodo consequat. Duis te feugifacilisi. Duis autem dolor in hendrerit in vulputate velit esse molestie consequat, vel illum dolore eu feugiat nulla facilisis at vero eros et accumsan et iusto odio dignissim qui blandit praesent luptatum zzril delenit au gue duis dolore te feugat nulla facilisi.Ut wisi enim ad minim veniam, quis nostrud exerci taion ullamcorper suscipit lobortis nisl ut aliquip ex en commodo consequat. Duis te feugifacilisi per suscipit lobortis nisl ut aliquip ex en commodo consequat.Lorem ipsum dolor sit amet, consectetuer adipiscing elit, sed diem nonummy nibh euismod tincidunt ut lacreet dolore magna aliguam

Inline frames can be very useful, but they do have one big disadvantage. Until recently, Internet Explorer was about the only browser that supported them, even though they have been made part of the HTML 4.01 standard. Things are changing, though, as both Netscape and Opera now display inline frames. If you decide to use them, keep in mind the people who visit your site; be sure to provide alternatives for those who won't see your floating frames.

Project 15: Create a Frame-Based Web Site

Perhaps the best use of frames is in providing an efficient and easily updated means of site navigation. Many sites that use frames will have a column of links on one side of the page and offer content on the other. Although this can be done with tables, as you learned in Chapter 8, you must insert the links on every page where you want the navigation bar to appear. The key to making this work is in using the name attribute with each of your frames and the target attribute with your links.

In Chapter 8 you learned how to design a table-based page with a banner at the top, a navigation bar on the left, content on the right, and a copyright notice at the bottom. For this project, you will duplicate that layout with a frameset, which helps you to compare and contrast frames layout with table layouts. To begin, you need to create four XHTML documents that will make up the "substance" of your layout. You'll need a banner page, a navigation page, a content page, and a copyright page. The following steps give you the specifics:

1. Create an XHTML page named *banner.htm*. The only other thing you need to do on this page is to insert the banner.gif image that you used in Chapter 8. Your code for the banner.htm page should look something like the following code listing:

```
<html>
   <head>
      <title>Banner Page</title>
   </head>
   <body>
      <div style="text-align: center">
         <img src="banner.gif" />
      </div>
   </body>
</html>
```

2. Create a second page named *nav.htm*. All of your links will go on this page. The easiest way to get them there is to open index.htm and then just copy and paste them into the new page. However, you will need to make one small addition to each link. You'll need to add the target attribute to point the link to the proper frame. Because your primary frame will be named "content," modify your links to look like the ones in the code that follows:

```
<html>
   <head>
      <title>Navigation Document</title>
```

```
        <style>
          body {background-color: aqua}
        </style>
    </head>
    <body>
      <ul>
<li><a href="headings.htm" target="content">Headings</a></li>
<li><a href="text.htm" target="content">Text Elements</a></li>
<li><a href="sup.htm" target="content">
        Superscript &amp; Subscript</a></li>
<li><a href="del.htm" target="content">Deleted Text</a></li>
<li><a href="pre.htm" target="content">
        Preformatted Text</a></li>
<li><a href="ulist.htm" target="content">Unordered List</a></li>
<li><a href="ulist2.htm" target="content">Multi-level
        Unordered List</a></li>
<li><a href="olist.htm" target="content">Ordered List</a></li>
<li><a href="olist2.htm" target="content">Ordered List
        with Start Attribute</a></li>
<li><a href="olist3.htm" target="content">Outline List</a></li>
<li><a href="dlist.htm" target="content">Definition
        List</a></li>
<li><a href="text-format.htm" target="content">Text
        Formatting</a></li>
<li><a href="generic-fonts.htm" target="content">Generic
        Fonts</a></li>
<li><a href="font-colors.htm" target="content">The Color
        Property</a></li>
<li><a href="16colors.htm" target="content">The Sixteen
        Basic Colors</a></li>
<li><a href="css-color.htm" target="content">CSS Color</a></li>
      </ul>
    </body>
</html>
```

3. Next you need to create a page that will be loaded when the frameset loads. Name this page *welcome.htm*. This can be a welcome page, a simple orientation to your site, or whatever you wish. For this project, all you need to do is add a paragraph that says, "This is a frames-based layout." The code for this page is as follows:

```
<html>
    <head>
        <title>Welcome Page</title>
```

```
        </head>
        <body>
            <h1 style="text-align: center">This is a
                frames-based layout.</h1>
        </body>
    </html>
```

4. Finally, you need to create your copyright line. Name this page *copyright.htm*. Again, this requires very little in the way of coding. Just a line that has your name, perhaps some contact information, and a copyright notice. Your page should look like the following code:

```
<html>
    <head>
        <title>Copyright Page</title>
        <style>
            body {text-align: center}
        </style>
    </head>
    <body>
    <p>Web Design by Me! &copy; Copyright 2050.
        All Rights Reserved.</p>
    </body>
</html>
```

After you have your content pages written, it's time to put together your frameset. You can create your frame page by following the steps below. If you get confused, check the completed code below the numbered instructions:

1. Open template.htm and save it as *framesite.htm*.

2. Add a title such as <title>Mini Frames Site</title>.

3. Delete the <body> tags; in their place add a set of <frameset> tags.

4. Modify the opening <frameset> tag to read

   ```
   <frameset rows="20%, 70%, *">
   ```

5. Create a frame and link it to banner.htm as follows:

   ```
   <frame src="banner.htm" /> (This will be your banner space.)
   ```

6. Now, to construct the navigation bar and content frames, you need to nest another frameset in the existing one. Just below the frame element you just typed, add another set of <frameset> tags.

7. Modify the opening <frameset> tag to read

```
<frameset cols="20%, *">
```

8. Define a frame for your navigation bar:

```
<frame src="nav.htm" />
```

9. Now comes the part that makes the whole system work. You want to define another frame, this time for your content. However, this frame needs to have a name so you can "target" links at it. For the sake of simplicity, name this frame *content*. The <frame /> element will look like this:

```
<frame src="welcome.htm" name="content" />
```

10. Finally, add a closing frameset tag to complete this nested frame.

11. Now, add one more <frame /> element to the main frameset. This one will hold your copyright notice. The element should look like the following line:

```
<frame src="copyright.htm" />
```

12. Make sure you have properly nested all of your tags and that you have closing tags for both framesets. Save and close this document.

13. Now you're ready to try out your miniframes site. Load framesite.htm in your browser. The window should resemble the following illustration. (For the illustration, frame1.htm was modified to read "This is your banner frame.")

```
<html>
<head>
<title>Mini Frames Site</title>
</head>
<frameset rows="20%, 70%, *">
        <frame src="banner.htm" />
            <frameset cols="20%, *">
                <frame src="nav.htm" />
                <frame src="welcome.htm" name="content" />
            </frameset>
        <frame src="copyright.htm" />
    </frameset>
</html>
```

9

Quick Reference: Creating Frame-Based Pages

Frames are another example of simple HTML that can become very complex. Complicated framesets with nested frames can be quite confusing to set up. However, a basic frameset is easy to do. The following table lists the necessary elements and attributes:

To Do This	Use This
Add an XHTML frameset <!DOCTYPE> declaration	`<!DOCTYPE html PUBLIC "-//W3C// DTD XHTML 1.0 Frameset//EN" "DTD/xhtml1-frameset.dtd">`
Create a frameset	`<frameset> </frameset>`
Create a frame	`<frame />`
Specify a frame's source file	`<frame src="page1.htm" />`
Assign a name to your frame	`<frame name="frame1" />`
Provide content for noncompatible browsers	`<noframes> </noframes>`
Specify rows	`<frameset rows="#">` (Pixels or percentages)
Specify columns	`<frameset cols="#">` (Pixels or percentages)
Turn borders off	`<frame frameborder="no" />` (Default is "yes")
Prevent resizing	`<frame noresize />`
Add or remove scroll bar	`<frame scrolling="auto	yes	no" />` (Default is "auto")
Control margins	`<frame marginheight="#" marginwidth="#" />` (# = pixels)

Create a two column frameset	`<frameset cols="#, #">`
	`    <frame src="webpage1.htm" />`
	`     <frame src="webpage2.htm" />`
	`</frameset>`

Create a two row frameset	`<frameset rows="#, #">`
	`    <frame src="webpage1.htm" />`
	`     <frame src="webpage2.htm" />`
	`</frameset>`

Create a nested frameset	`<frameset cols="#, #">`
	`    <frame src="webpage1.htm" />`
	`     <frame src="webpage2.htm" />`
	`        <frameset rows="#, #">`
	`            <frame src="webpage3.htm />`
	`            <frame src="webpage4.htm />`
	`        </frameset>`
	`</frameset>`

Chapter 10

Control Presentation with Style Sheets

How to…

- Understand CSS
- Add inline styles
- Embed a style sheet
- Link to a style sheet
- Apply CSS properties

HTML was developed to define the structure of a document when Web and Internet documents were entirely text-based. The advent of graphical browsers and Web design stretched HTML far beyond its capacity. To accommodate the needs of Web designers, extensions were added to HTML to increase its ability to address a document's appearance and structure. Unfortunately, this was roughly similar to doing interior decorating with two-by-fours and six-penny nails. You might be able to do it, but it won't look good—two-by-fours and big nails are useful in building the structure of a house, but for finished carpentry you want quality woods, molding, paint, wallpaper, and stain.

Likewise, HTML was not developed for controlling the appearance of a document. HTML is the equivalent of the two-by-fours and large nails. For finished Web "decorating," you need better materials and tools. Enter Cascading Style Sheets. CSS offer a set of tools that enable you to refine, finish, and polish the appearance of an element, a page, even an entire Web site.

Understand CSS

If you've been working through this book from the beginning, you've already used CSS and experienced the freedom it gives you in Web design. However, if you just jumped in here at Chapter 10, a brief orientation is in order. Newcomers to XHTML often find CSS intimidating when they come across it in a book such as this. It seems so much more complicated than XHTML that many readers just give CSS a curious glance before skipping forward to the next chapter. However, because you have been working with CSS almost from the first chapter of this book, you have already discovered that style sheets are not difficult. They're just *different*. Now that CSS have been "demystified," it's time for you to learn more of its "nuts and bolts."

HTML and the Problem of Style

HTML simply was never intended to address a document's style or presentation. Granted, the extensions added to HTML over the past decade have enabled it to handle some style issues, but HTML provides clumsy presentation control at best. It only makes sense to use the proper tool for the job you need to do. In the case of presentation, that tool is CSS. However, there are a few other strong reasons to learn how to use CSS. They can be summarized in three words: *deprecation, accessibility,* and *necessity.*

■ **Deprecation**   By now you have become quite familiar with the term *deprecated*. If you go to the W3C's site (www.w3.org) and read the current recommendation for XHTML, you'll discover that most presentational elements and attributes have been deprecated in favor of style sheets. When XHTML 2.0 becomes the official recommendation of the W3C, *all* presentational elements and attributes will be removed.

■ **Accessibility**   CSS2 (the second official CSS recommendation) addresses much more than style. It deals with accessibility issues such as how to develop pages for aural (sound) browsers. Although CSS2 is poorly supported at present, that will change. One day you will be able to create style sheets targeted toward different types of browsers and link your pages to them, opening your Web site to a much broader audience.

■ **Necessity**   While XHTML 1.0 and 1.1 are very similar to HTML in that the idea of a style sheet is optional, this will change with XHTML 2.0. XHTML 2.0 will be much closer to its parent language, XML. One distinction of XML is that all XML documents *require* style sheets. You can use either CSS or a language called XSL (the Extensible Stylesheet Language), but you will not have the option of ignoring style sheets then. Thus, you will find it helpful to learn CSS sooner rather than later. Of course, there is one more excellent reason to learn to use style sheets: They're fun.

Understand the Idea of Style Sheets

Style sheets take their name from the idea of style sheets in publishing. A publisher—Osborne, for example—has a particular style for its publications. In addition, the publisher is not limited to a single style. It might use a general style that is reflected in all its publications, but more specific styles for certain series. For example, if you were to examine all the books in the *How to Do Everything* series, you would notice that even though subject matter differs among books, they all reflect the same basic style in fonts, layouts, headings, and so on. If you check out some of Osborne's other books, you will notice a similarity in style at certain points, but each series has its own distinctive look and feel.

Cascading Style Sheets are intended to help you accomplish the same effect with your Web site. With CSS, you can plan a color scheme, set margins, create a layout, choose and modify fonts, and much more. All you have to do is save that style sheet as a separate document, link all your pages to it, and, voilà, your entire Web site takes on the characteristics you specified in the style sheet.

Understand CSS Terminology

One reason CSS confuse people who have been learning HTML is that many of the terms are different. When they read about style sheets, it's almost as if they are starting again from the ground floor. After getting used to elements, attributes, and values, it can be frustrating when the terminology shifts to selectors, properties, declarations, and rules. Actually, CSS terms need not be confusing as long as you learn to understand them in the context of HTML. Try understanding the basic CSS in the way described here.

10

■ **Selector**   Think element here. At its simplest, a *selector* is an element's name. For example, say you want to choose a style for the <h4> element. Then you use the h4 selector. The only difference is that you don't place the "less than" and "greater than" signs around it, like you would if it were a tag. Instead, <h4> is simply written as h4. As you'll discover later in this chapter, there can be more to it than this, but this is a good starting point.

■ **Property**   Properties are essentially the same as attributes. Remember that with HTML, an attribute identifies a characteristic assigned to an element, such as width. In CSS, you have *properties* instead of attributes. These are also written differently. In HTML the width attribute is written with an equals sign (=) and quotation marks (" "), like this: width=" ". In CSS, the width property is written inside curly braces with a colon following it, like this: {width: }.

■ **Value**   This one's easy. A *value* is the same in HTML and CSS. It is the specific characteristic assigned to an element or a selector. For example, 100 pixels can be a value assigned to an HTML attribute: width="100" or a CSS property: {width: 100px}.

■ **Declaration**   A *declaration* is a combination of at least one property and value. In other words, {width: 100px} is a declaration. You can include as many property/value combinations as you wish in a single style rule; however, keep in mind that if you have more than one property/value combination, you must separate them with semicolons (;). The semicolon tells the Web browser where one declaration ends and another begins. For example, if you want to specify purple text with a bold font for the same selector (element), you would separate the property/value combinations this way: {color:purple; font-weight: bold}.

■ **Rule**   A *rule* is the complete "sentence" combining a selector and declaration (properties and values). A complete declaration is enclosed in curly braces. For example, the following statement would be called a rule: h1 {color: purple; font-size: 24pt; margin-left: .5in;}. If you break down the preceding rule, h1 is the selector (for the level-one heading element); the properties are color, font-size, and margin-left; and the values are purple, 24pt, and .5in, respectively.

There are some other terms, such as *classes, pseudo-classes, pseudo-elements, descendent, ancestor,* and *inheritance*. These will be covered later in this chapter.

 You can put as many declarations in a rule as you want, as long as they are separated from one another by semicolons (;) and enclosed in curly braces ({ }). The single exception to this is with inline style sheets, in which you use quotation marks (" ") instead of curly braces to enclose the declarations.

Learn Style Sheet Types

There are three ways to implement style sheets in your HTML document: *inline, embedded,* and *linked.* The primary difference between these style sheets lies in where they are placed, how much of a document they affect, and the priority given to them by the browser.

Figure 1

Graphics displaying at a resolution of "millions of colors"

Figure 2

Graphics displaying at a resolution of 256 colors

Figure 3

Graphics displaying at a resolution of 16 colors

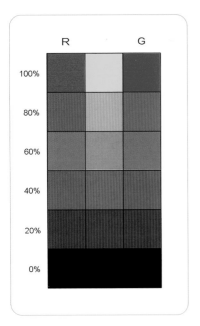

Figure 4

Mix red and green to make yellow.

Various shades of yellow can be made by mixing equal amounts of red and green.

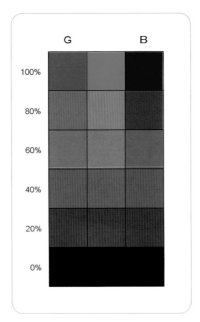

Figure 5

Mix green and blue to produce shades of aqua.

Green and blue combine to produce cyan (aqua).

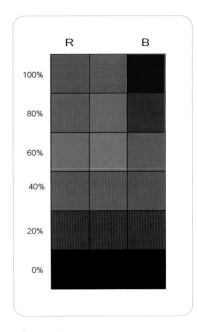

Figure 6

Mix red and blue to produce magenta (fuschia).

Equal amounts of red and blue produce magenta.

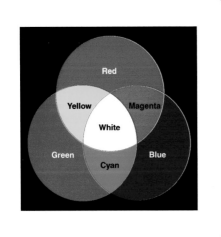

Figure 7

Mix red and green to make yellow, red and blue to create magenta, and blue and green to produce cyan.

Hue is a measure of pure color (orange, green, yellow, chartreuse—like in a tube of paint).

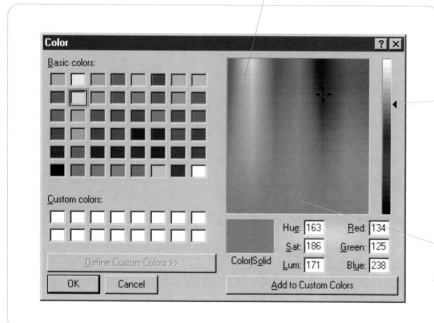

Figure 8

Understanding hue, saturation, and lightness

Brightness is a measure of how much "light" is reflected.

Saturation is a measure of how much color (hue) is present. Think of an intense color vs. a pastel.

Figure 9

The 16 basic (but not Web-safe) colors

The 16 basic or "Windows" colors are made up of either 100% or 50% combinations of red, green, and blue.

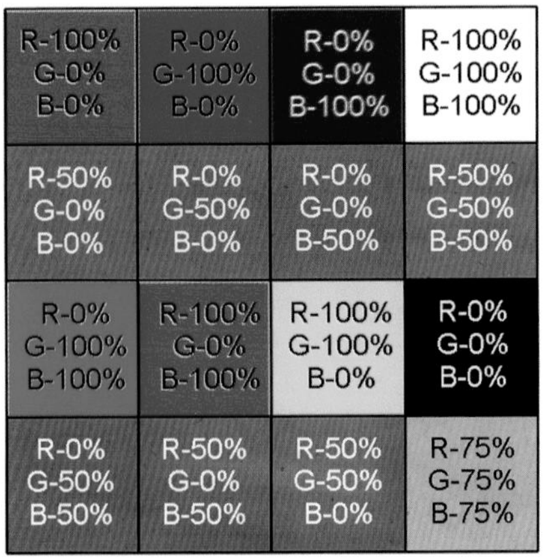

The 50% colors are not considered Web-safe.

R-100% G-0% B-0%	R-0% G-100% B-0%	R-0% G-0% B-100%	R-100% G-100% B-100%
R-50% G-0% B-0%	R-0% G-50% B-0%	R-0% G-0% B-50%	R-50% G-50% B-50%
R-0% G-100% B-100%	R-100% G-0% B-100%	R-100% G-100% B-0%	R-0% G-0% B-0%
R-0% G-50% B-50%	R-50% G-0% B-50%	R-50% G-50% B-0%	R-75% G-75% B-75%

One exception is "silver," which is made up of a 75% mixture of red, green, and blue.

Figure 10

Figuring rgb color in hex, percentages, and decimal

To use hexadecimal codes for Web-safe colors, list the appropriate amounts of red, green, and blue like this: #00ff00 (this is the code for green).

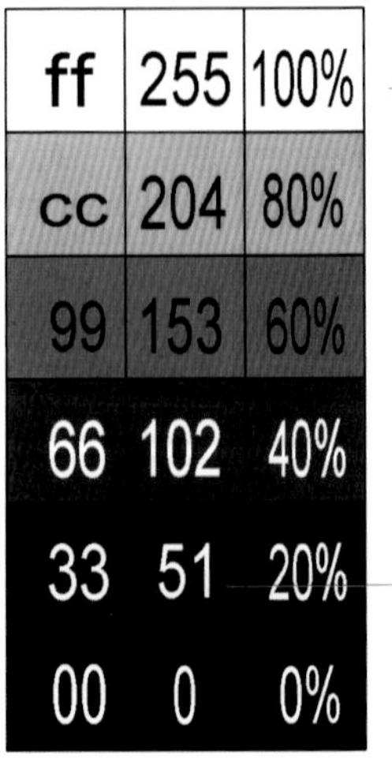

ff	255	100%
cc	204	80%
99	153	60%
66	102	40%
33	51	20%
00	0	0%

Figuring RGB amounts by percentage is easy. In CSS, the color red looks like this: rgb(100%,0%,0%).

If you want to express Web-safe color in decimal notation, just think "51." Adding 51 to the previous number creates each step of 20%. Then write it like this: rgb(0,0,255) (this is the code for blue).

255,255,204 100%,100%, 80% #ffffcc	255,204,153 100%,80%, 60% #ffcc99	255,204,204 100%,80%, 80% #ffcccc	255,153,204 100%,60%, 80% #ff99cc	255,51,204 100%,20%, 80% #ff33cc	204,0,51 80%,0%, 20% #cc0033
255,255,153 100%,100% 60% #ffff99	204,153,102 80%,60%, 40% #cc9966	204,153,153 80%,60%, 60% #cc9999	255,153,153 100%,60%, 60% #ff9999	255,51,153 100%,20%, 60% #ff3399	204,0,102 80%,0%, 40% #cc0066
255,255,102 100%,100%, 40% #ffff66	204,204,153 80%,80%, 60% #cccc99	255,102,204 100%,40%, 80% #ff66cc	204,102,153 80%,40%, 60% #cc6699	204,51,153 80%,20%, 60% #cc3399	204,0,153 80%,0%, 60% #cc0099
255,255,51 100%,100% 20% #ffff33	255,153,102 100%,60%, 40% #ff9966	255,102,102 100%,40%, 40% #ff6666	255,102,153 100%,40%, 60% #ff6699	255,51,102 100%,20%, 40% #ff3366	153,0,51 60%,0%, 20% #990033
255,204,51 100%,80%, 20% #ffcc33	255,204,102 100%,80%, 40% #ffcc66	204,102,102 80%,40%, 40% #cc6666	153,51,102 60%,20%, 40% #993366	204,51,102 80%,20%, 40% #cc3366	153,0,102 60%,0%, 40% #990066
255,204,0 100%,80%, 0% #ffcc00	204,204,102 80%,80%, 40% #cccc66	153,102,102 60%,40%, 40% #996666	204,51,51 80%,20%, 20% #cc3333	255,51,51 100%,20%, 20% #ff3333	153,51,51 60%,20%, 20% #993333
255,153,0 100%,60%, 0% #ff9900	204,153,0 80%,60%, 0% #cc9900	102,51,51 40%,20%, 20% #663333	102,51,0 40%,20%, 0% #663300	153,51,0 60%,20%, 0% #993300	204,51,204 80%,20%, 80% #cc33cc
255,102,0 100%,40%, 0% #ff6600	255,102,51 100%,40%, 20% #ff6633	204,204,51 80%,80%, 20% #cccc33	153,153,51 60%,60% 20% #999933	102,102,51 40%,40%, 20% #666633	204,153,51 80%,60%, 20% #cc9933
255,51,0 100%,20%, 0% #ff3300	204,102,0 80%,40%, 0% #cc6600	204,102,51 80%,40%, 20% #cc6633	255,153,51 100%,60%, 20% #ff9933	153,102,51 60%,40%, 20% #996633	153,102,0 60%,40%, 0% #996600

Figure 12

Web-safe color mixtures
in decimal, percentage,
and hexadecimal

255,255,255 100%,100%, 100% #ffffff	204,204,204 80%,80%, 80% #cccccc	153,153,153 60%,60%, 60% #999999	102,102,102 40%,40%, 40% #666666	51,51,51, 20%,20%, 20% #333333	0,0,0 0%,0%,0% #000000
204,255,204 80%,100%, 80% #ccffcc	153,255,153 60%,100%, 60% #99ff99	102,255,153 40%,100%, 60% #66ff99	51,255,102 20%,100%, 40% #33ff66	51,153,51 20%,60%, 20% #339933	0,102,51 0%,40%, 20% #006633
204,255,153 80%,100%, 60% #ccff99	0,255,102 0%,100%, 40% #00ff66	102,204,102 40%,80%, 40% #66cc66	102,255,102 40%,100%, 40% #66ff66	51,102,51 20%,40%, 20% #336633	0,204,51 0%,80%, 20% #00cc33
153,255,51 60%,100%, 20% #99ff33	153,204,51 60%,80%, 20% #99cc33	102,204,51 40%,80%, 20% #66cc33	51,204,51 20%80%, 20% #33cc33	51,255,51 20%,100%, 20% #33ff33	0,255,51 0%,100%, 20% #00ff33
153,255,102 60%,100%, 40% #99ff66	153,204,102 60%,80%, 40% #99cc66	102,153,51 40%,60%, 20% #669933	102,255,51 40%,100%, 20% #66ff33	51,255,0 20%,100%, 0% #33ff00	0,255,0 0%,100%, 0% #00ff00
0,153,51 0%,60%, 20% #009933	102,153,102 40%,60%, 40% #669966	0,204,102 0%,80%, 40% #00cc66	102,255,0 40%,100%, 0% #66ff00	51,204,0 20%,80%, 0% #33cc00	0,204,0 0%,80%, 0% #00cc00
204,255,102 80%,100%, 40% #ccff66	51,204,102 20%,80%, 40% #33cc66	153,255,0 60%,100%, 0% #99ff00	102,204,0 40%,80%, 0% #66cc00	51,153,0 20%,60%, 0% #339900	0,153,0 0%,60%, 0% #009900
204,255,51 80%,100%, 20% #ccff33	204,255,0 80%100%, 0% #ccff00	153,204,0 60%,80%, 0% #99cc00	102,153,0 40%,60%, 0% #669900	51,102,0 20%,40%, 0% #336600	0,102,0 0%,40%, 0% #006600
255,255,0 100%,100%, 0%, #ffff00	204,204,0 80%,80%, 0% #cccc00	153,153,0 60%,60%, 0% #999900	102,102,0 40%,40%, 0% #666600	51,51,0 20%20%, 0% #333300	0,51,0 0%,20%, 0% #003300

Figure 13

Web-safe color mixtures in decimal, percentage, and hexadecimal

102,51,102 40%,20%,40% #663366	153,51,153 60%,20%,60% #993399	153,204,255 60%,80%,100% #99ccff	204,153,204 80%,60%,80% #cc99cc	204,102,255 80%,40%,100% #cc66ff	255,204,255 100%,80%,100% #ffccff
51,102,153 20%,40%,60% #336699	153,102,153 60%,40%,60% #996699	153,102,204 60%,40%,80% #9966cc	204,153,255 80%,60%,100% #cc99ff	255,153,255 100%,60%,100% #ff99ff	255,102,255 100%,40%,100% #ff66ff
102,153,204 40%,60%,80% #6699cc	153,0,153 60%,0%,60% #990099	153,0,255 60%,0%,100% #9900ff	153,51,255 60%,20%,100% #9933ff	204,102,204 80%,40%,80% #cc66cc	255,51,255 100%,20%,100% #ff33ff
102,102,153 40%,40%,60% #666699	153,153,204 60%,60%,80% #9999cc	153,102,255 60%,40%,100% #9966ff	153,51,204 60%,20%,80% #9933cc	204,51,255 80%,20%,100% #cc33ff	255,0,255 100%,0%,100% #ff00ff
51,0,255 20%,0%,100% #3300ff	102,102,204 40%,40%,80% #6666cc	102,0,255 40%,0%,100% #6600ff	102,51,255 40%,20%,100% #6633ff	204,0,255 80%,0%,100% #cc00ff	255,0,204 100%,0%,80% #ff00cc
51,0,204 20%,0%,80% #3300cc	51,51,204 20%,20%,80% #3333cc	102,0,204 40%,0%,80% #6600cc	102,51,204 40%,20%,80% #6633cc	153,0,204 60%,0%,80% #9900cc	255,0,153 100%,0%,60% #ff0099
51,0,153 20%,0%,60% #330099	51,51,153 20%,20%,60% #333399	102,0,102 40%,0%,40% #660066	102,51,153 40%,20%,60% #663399	204,0,204 80%,0%,80% #cc00cc	255,0,102 100%,0%,40% #ff0066
51,0,102 20%,0%,40% #330066	51,51,102 20%,20%,40% #333366	102,0,51 40%,0%,20% #660033	102,0,153 40%,0%,60% #660099	204,51,0 80%,20%,0% #cc3300	255,0,51 100%,0%,20% #ff0033
51,0,51 20%,0%,20% #330033	51,0,0 20%,0%,0% #330000	102,0,0 40%,0%,0% #660000	153,0,0 60%,0%,0% #990000	204,0,0 80%,0%,0% #cc0000	255,0,0 100%,0%,0% #ff0000

Figure 14

Web-safe color mixtures
in decimal, percentage,
and hexadecimal

204,255,255 80%,100%, 100% #ccffff	153,255,204 60%,100%, 80% #99ffcc	51,153,204 20%,60%, 80% #3399cc	51,102,204 20%,40%, 80% #3366cc	153,204,153 60%,80%, 60% #99cc99	204,204,255 80%,80% 100% #ccccff
153,255,255 60%100%, 100% #99ffff	102,255,204 40%,100%, 80% #66ffcc	0,255,204 0%,100%, 80% #00ffcc	0,153,102 0%,60%, 40% #009966	102,204,153 40%,80%, 60% #66cc99	153,153,255 60%,60% 100% #9999ff
102,255,255 40%,100% 100% #66ffff	51,255,153 20%,100%, 60% #33ff99	0,255,153 0%,100%, 60% #00ff99	0,204,153 0%,80%, 60% #00cc99	51,153,102 20%,60%, 40% #339966	102,102,255 40%,40%, 100% #6666ff
51,255,255 20%,100% 100% #33ffff	51,255,204 20%,100%, 80% #33ffcc	51,204,153 20%,80%, 60% #33cc99	102,204,255 40%,80%, 100% #66ccff	51,153,255 20%,60% 100% #3399ff	51,51,255 20%,20%, 100% #3333ff
0,255,255 0%,100%, 100% #00ffff	0,204,255 0%,80%, 100% #00ccff	0,153,255 0%,60%, 100% #0099ff	51,204,255 20%,80%, 100% #33ccff	51,102,255 20%,40%, 100% #3366ff	0,0,255 0%,0%, 100% #0000ff
0,204,204 0%,80%, 80% #00cccc	0,153,204 0%60% 80% #0099cc	51,204,204 20%,80% 80% #33cccc	102,153,255 40%,60%, 100% #6699ff	0,51,255 0%,20%, 100% #0033ff	0,0,204 0%,0%, 80% #0000cc
0,153,153 0%,60%, 60% #009999	102,204,204 40%,80%, 80% #66cccc	51,163,153 20%,60%, 60% #339999	0,102,255 0%,40%, 100% #0066ff	0,51,204 0%,20% 80% #0033cc	0,0,153 0%,0%, 60% #000099
0,102,102 0%,40%, 40% #006666	153,204,204 60%,80%, 80% #99cccc	51,102,102 20%,40%, 40% #336666	0,102,204 0%,40%, 80% #0066cc	0,51,153 0%,20%, 60% #003399	0,0,102 0%,0%, 40% #000066
0,51,51 0%,20%,20% #003333	102,153,153 40%,60%, 60% #669999	153,153,102 60%,60% 40% #999966	0,102,153 0%,40%, 60% #006699	0,51,102 0%,20%, 40% #003366	0,0,51 0%,0%, 20% #000033

Control a Single Element with an Inline Style Sheet

To control a single element only one time, use an *inline* style sheet. Inline style sheets, as their name implies, are placed "in line" in the individual elements of an HTML page and control only the specific element to which they are applied. To create an inline style sheet, you use the style=" " attribute. For example, to change the text for a single paragraph to a red, italicized font you would modify the opening <p> tag to read as follows:

```
<p style="color: red; font-style: italic;">
```

Generally, browsers give inline styles priority over embedded or linked style sheets. This makes them good for doing "spot" styling, where you only need to modify a small portion of a page.

Control an Entire Page with an Embedded Style Sheet

To control styles on an entire page, use an *embedded* style sheet. Embedded style sheets are placed between the <head> tags of an HTML page and make use of the <style>element. An embedded style sheet controls the elements to which it is applied throughout the entire page, although any inline styles generally take precedence over it. To set the paragraph style for an entire page to 12-point bold, navy text with a yellow background, you would create a style rule like the following one:

```
<style type="text/css">
p     {   color: navy;
          font-weight: bold;
          font-size: 12pt;
          background-color: yellow; } </style>
```

10

TIP *When using embedded and external style sheets, you also should include the type=" " attribute with the value set to "text/css", as in the preceding example. This tells the browser what type of style sheet to expect.*

Control Elements on Multiple Pages with a Linked Style Sheet

By creating a style sheet and saving it as a separate document, you can link multiple pages to it and the pages will take on the style specified in that sheet. For example, you could have saved the style in the preceding paragraph as a separate file—say, my_style.css—and then linked your pages to it using <link> element. The <link> element should be placed in between the <head> tags of each page you want linked to a style sheet and would be written as follows:

```
<link rel="stylesheet" type="text/css" href="my_style.css">
```

NOTE

The rel=" " attribute tells the browser the relationship between the <link> element and whatever is being linked. Because it is possible to use this element to link more than just style sheets to a Web page, it is necessary to add the value "stylesheet" to the rel attribute. The href attribute is added to tell the browser where to find the style sheet. The value for this attribute would be the URL where the style sheet is located. In most cases, that will simply be the name of the file, as in the preceding example.

As you read this, perhaps you are beginning to see a potential problem with style sheets. With so many possibilities for specifying style, which one takes priority? That's where the *cascade* comes in.

Understand the Cascade

Why are style sheets called cascading? *Cascading* refers to the order of priority in which styles are applied. Consider all the possible conflicting style rules that can be applied to one Web page: The browser might have its own style, the author can specify a style, and the readers who visit your site might have specified their own styles for browser display. On top of that, it is possible to have different styles specified in linked, embedded, and inline style sheets. In other words, on any given page you could have six or seven different styles all competing for the right to determine what an <h1> element should look like. So, which style gets the last word? The following questions give some guidelines for how a style's precedence is determined:

- ■ **Who wrote the rule?** In most cases, the page author's styles take priority over the reader's styles; both have priority over the browser's default styles.

- ■ **What kind of style is it?** An inline style generally (but not always) takes precedence over an embedded style; both take precedence over a linked style.

- ■ **How specific is the selector?** The selector with more detail takes priority over the selector with less detail.

- ■ **Which style occurs last?** Generally, the last declaration takes precedence over earlier ones in a document.

Project 16: Create and Use Style Sheets

The easiest way to see CSS in action and learn how to use it is to create a sample Web page and progressively add different style rules. By doing this, you will see how the different styles affect the overall look of your page. You will also gain a feel for how certain styles take precedence over others. To create a CSS sample page, follow these steps:

1. Open template.htm and save it as *css_sample.htm*.

2. Cut and paste several paragraphs of plain text in between the <body> tags of your HTML document. These paragraphs can be from any text document you want. The next illustration uses lorem.txt.

3. Format your text into at least three paragraphs by using the <p> </p> element.

4. Write three headlines and insert one before each paragraph. Enclose all your headlines in the <h1> element.

Your HTML code should resemble this:

```
<html>
   <head>
      <title>CSS Sample Page</title>
   </head>
   <body>
        <h1>This is going to be a headline.</h1>
        <p>Paste a paragraph of text here.</p>
        <h1>This will be another headline.</h1>
        <p>Paste another paragraph of text here.</p>
        <h1>This is a headline, too</h1>
        <p>Paste a third paragraph here.</p>
   </body>
</html>
```

When you view the page in your Web browser, you should see something similar to the following illustration. When you have saved your basic page, you're ready to begin styling.

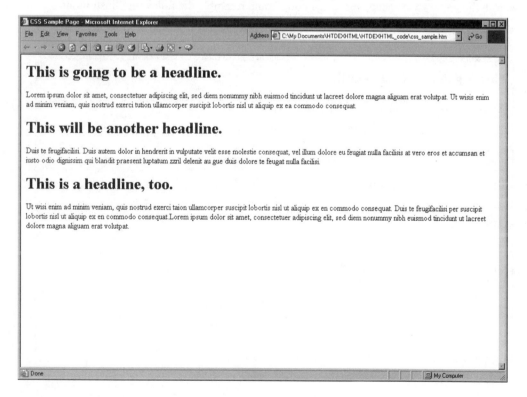

Your ability to reproduce the results you see in this chapter depends directly on your browser's capability to support style sheets. Although most browsers have some degree of support for CSS, for best results use the most recent version of Internet Explorer. If you want to test your browser for its style sheet support, the W3C has a great testing site. Just go to www.w3.org/Style/CSS/Test and click the various links. It will load test pages linked to external style sheets. You'll be able to measure your own browser's support for CSS easily with this free tool.

Apply an Inline Style Sheet

Begin styling your sample page by adding an inline style to the second headline, changing its font to Arial, size to 18pt, color to blue, and position to center. To do this, use the *style* attribute with the font size, color, and text align properties. The <h1> headline with an inline style sheet added should look like the following line of code:

Be sure to enclose all the declarations in a single set of quotation marks and separate them by semicolons; otherwise, your style will not display properly.

```
<h1 style="font-family: arial; font-size: 18pt; color: blue; text-align:
center;">This will be another
      headline.</h1>
```

With the inline style added, your page now should resemble the following illustration:

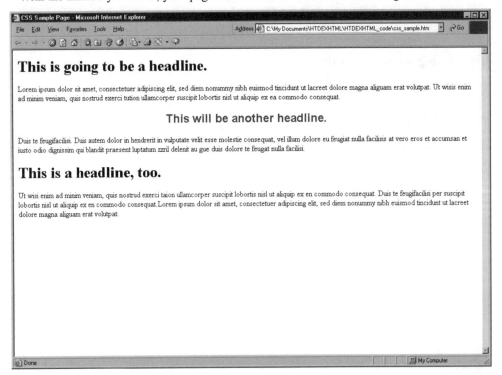

Add an Embedded Style Sheet

To add an embedded style sheet to this document, you use the same syntax except that instead of enclosing declarations in quotation marks you use curly braces and place your style rules in between the <style>tags in the <head>portion of your page. For your sample page, try setting a page background color of yellow, a default font for the <p> element, and a default font size and color for the <h1> element. You can do this by following these steps:

1. Insert a set of <style></style> tags in between the <head></head> tags on your page.

2. Modify the opening <style> tag to read <style type="text/css">. Because there can be different kinds of style sheets, the *type* attribute tells the browser to expect text-based commands and the CSS language.

3. To set the background color to yellow, you will need to write the following style rule for the body selector:

```
body { background-color: yellow; }
```

4. To set a style for the h1 selector that gives it an aqua background, with navy blue text, set at a size of 1.5 ems, add the following line:

```
h1 { background-color: aqua; font-size: 1.5em; color: navy; }
```

TIP
> *You may have noticed that this style uses "em" instead of points to set the font size. An em is equivalent to the document's default font size and is calculated in relation to the width of the font's capital* M. *Thus, a setting of 1.5 ems is equal to one-and-one-half times the size of your body text. Because ems are* relative *units of measurement, Web designers generally prefer them to points, which are* absolute *units of measurement. A similar but less popular measurement is the "ex," which is calculated relative to the height of a font's lowercase letter* x.

10

5. Now, tell the browser to display the p element as bold, italicized text by adding the following rule:

```
p { font-weight: bold; font-style: italic; }
```

The completed header for your page should look like the following code listing:

```
<head>
    <title>CSS Sample</title>
    <style type="text/css">
body { background-color: yellow; }
h1 { background-color: aqua; font-size: 1.5em; color: navy; }
p { font-weight: bold; font-style: italic; }
    </style>
</head>
```

When you save and display your page, your style changes should look like this:

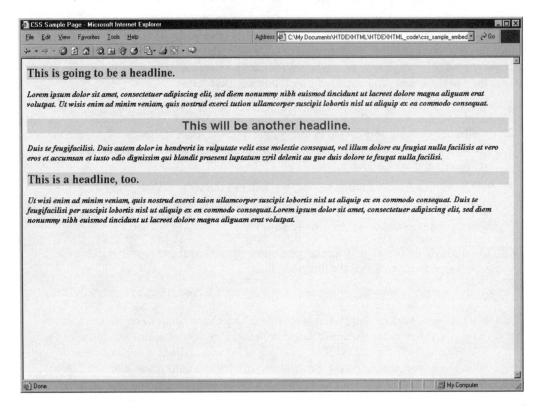

As you examine your results, you will see that your style specifications were all incorporated in the page, with one exception: The middle headline will still be blue with an 18-point Arial font. Remember that an inline style sheet overrides an embedded style sheet, so your first specification remains unchanged. You will see this even more clearly when you create and link to an external style sheet, which is covered next.

Create and Link to an External Style Sheet

There's nothing difficult or mystical about creating an external style sheet; it's merely a text document that contains a set of style rules. As with HTML, you can produce an external style sheet with a simple text editor. You need only to make certain that you save the document with a .css extension so the browser can identify it.

To construct a simple external style sheet, follow this procedure:

1. Create a new file in Notepad or another text editor. Save it as a plain text file named *my_styles.css*.

2. Copy in the following lines exactly as written:

```
body     { margin-left: 15%;
            background-color: rgb(80%,80%,80%) }


h1       { background-color: black;
            color: white;
            font-size: 2.2em; }


p.green {
            color: green;
            font-family: arial;
            font-weight: bold;
            border-style: double;
            border-width: thick;
            border-color: red; }


p.large {
            color: navy;
            font-size: 1.25em;
            background: yellow; }
```

3. Save your style sheet and open css_sample.htm.

How to ... **Use Classes**

In the preceding code, the selectors p.green and p.large are called *class* selectors. This is a way of modifying a standard selector, in this case "p," and setting it apart as a separate class with its own properties. To call a class selector's characteristics forth in a Web page, just add the class=" " attribute to the appropriate element. For example, to apply the characteristics of p.large to a paragraph, you would write **<p class="large"> Content </p>**. Using classes gives you a virtually unlimited ability to specify style details for your page.

10

4. Remove both the embedded and inline style sheets from css_sample.htm. (This is just so you can see the effects of the external style sheet without having to worry about the other styles overriding it.)

5. Add the following line in the <head></head> portion of the page:

   ```
   <link rel="stylesheet" type="text/css" href="my_styles.css" />
   ```

6. Now, to apply the class in your sample page, change the first <p> to read <p class="green"> and the second <p> to read <p class="large">.

> **TIP**
> *It's not necessary to put each declaration on a separate line, but it does make it easier to identify which styles you have assigned to the selectors and check your code for errors. As long as you have written the rules correctly and keep individual declarations together, the browser doesn't care whether they're on one line or several.*

Your revised code should resemble the following code listing:

```
<html>
   <head>
      <title>CSS Sample Page</title>
     <link rel="stylesheet" type="text/css"
           href="my_styles.css" />
   </head>
   <body>
      <h1>This is going to be a headline.</h1>
      <p class="green">Paste a paragraph of text here.</p>
      <h1>This will be another headline.</h1>
      <p class="large">Paste another paragraph of text here.</p>
      <h1>This will be a headline, too</h1>
      <p>Paste a third paragraph here.</p>
   </body>
</html>
```

Save css_sample.htm and display it in your browser. Your page should look somewhat like the following illustration:

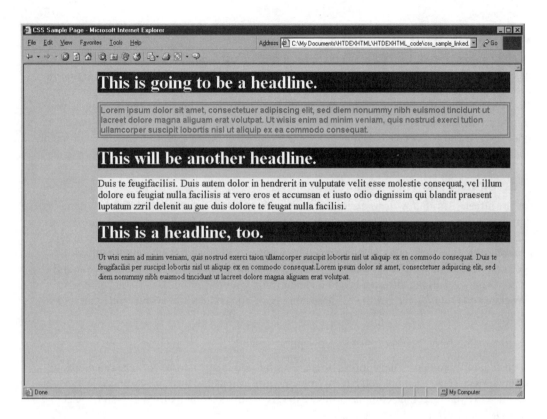

After you view your page, experiment by adding the embedded and inline styles back into the document to see how it affects your ultimate result.

When editing CSS and XHTML documents simultaneously, you can save time by using Wordpad for your XHTML document and Notepad for the style sheet. Keep both programs open at the same time, along with a browser to view the document in, and you'll have a much easier time editing your styles.

Understand CSS Basics

The challenge in writing a chapter on CSS is providing you with enough detail to enable you to use them without flooding you with every single possibility. After all, the current CSS specification weighs in at a whopping 331 pages. Trying to cover even a small portion of the details is challenging enough. Attempting to cover everything in one chapter is impossible. However, it is possible to give you enough information to get you started on the learning process.

10

Apply Style with Selectors

If you're going to work with CSS, the place to start is with *selectors*. At the most basic level, selectors are simply element names without the < and > around them. By beginning a style rule with an element name, you are "selecting" that element and assigning one or more styles to it. However, selectors can be much more specific than just a simple element name. In fact, as you learn to create and use specialized selectors, you can target specific portions of a Web page for style—even if you didn't create the page! The paragraphs that follow list just a few of the different kinds of selectors you can use to apply style in a Web page.

Understand *Type* (Element) Selectors

You are already familiar with *type* selectors, although you may not know them by that name. Type selectors are made up of one or more element names. If you have worked on some of the CSS projects in this chapter, you have primarily used type selectors, although you have used them one at a time. One great time saver with type selectors is that you can group multiple selectors together in a single style rule by merely separating them with commas. For example, suppose you want all the different heading elements on your page to be blue. You could write a separate style rule for each of the h1–h6 elements, or you could write a single rule that looks like this:

```
h1, h2, h3, h4, h5, h6 {color: blue}
```

Incidentally, you don't have to stop there. You can add in any number of other elements to that style rule. The only thing you have to remember is to separate them by commas. Why is this important? If you forget the commas, you are inadvertently creating a different kind of selector: a *descendent* selector.

Understand Descendent Selectors

Descendent selectors used to be called *contextual* selectors because they are based on an element's context. The name was changed to *descendent*, which more accurately describes the function of this kind of selector. A descendent selector focuses on an element that is a descendent of (in other words, nested inside) another element. For example, suppose you want to modify the <strong> element to display with bold red text, but you want it to display this way only when it is used inside an <h1> element. You would use a descendent selector and write your style rule this way:

```
h1 strong  {color: red; font-weight: bold;}
```

When applying style to this selector, a browser would modify only the <strong> element when it is a descendent of <h1>.

NOTE   *In the preceding example, it is not necessary for a <strong> to be an immediate descendent of <h1>. It could be nested inside any number of other elements and the style would still be applied. It is only required that <h1> be strong's ancestor, not parent.*

Create Custom Selectors with Class Selectors

Class selectors enable you to create your own selectors based on classes or unique identification names you assign. Suppose you're creating a Web site with a list of recipes, and you want all the recipe names to be formatted a certain way. Rather than taking the time to add an inline style for each recipe name, you can simply create a class selector for that particular style information. To create a class, you simply preface the class name you have chosen with a period, as in the following style rule:

```
.recipeName  {font-family: arial; color: blue; font-size: 1.5em}
```

Then, to apply that style in your Web page, you simply add the *class* attribute wherever you want that particular style to appear, as in the following:

```
<p class="recipeName">Style will be applied here</p>
```

If you want to, you can also attach a class to a specific element name by connecting the element name and class name with a period, like this:

```
p.recipeName {font-family: arial; color: blue; font-size: 1.5em}
```

This class name limits the use of the recipeName class to the <p> element. Whichever way you choose to apply them, class selectors can greatly simplify your work with CSS.

Use the ID Selector for Greater Specificity

10

Remember the section earlier in this chapter that covered the *cascade*—the order of preference given to competing style rules? One way in which browsers choose between competing selectors is by determining which selector has a greater *specificity*. In other words, which selector is more specific or detailed? The greater a selector's specificity, the higher the priority a browser gives it. The ID selector, a close cousin of the class selector, is a good choice if you want to ensure a higher degree of specificity in your selectors. The reason for this is that the ID must be unique in any one document. In other words, you can only use a particular ID once on a page.

You create an ID selector by placing a crosshatch (tic-tac-toe) symbol before the ID name. As with class selectors, your ID name can be anything you wish, provided you begin it with a crosshatch. Thus, a style rule for a copyright notice might look like this:

```
#copyrightInfo  {font-size: .80em; font-family: arial}
```

To apply the style in your Web page, you use the *ID* attribute, as in the following element:

```
<p id="copyrightInfo">Style will be applied here.</p>
```

Use Pseudo-Classes for Links

Pseudo-class selectors were developed to address conditions that can occur on a Web page without being reflected in the XHTML code itself. The most obvious examples of this are hyperlinks. If you've surfed the Web very long, you have probably noticed that a link's color usually changes after you click on it. Even though the link's color has changed, you won't find this reflected anywhere in the page's XHTML markup. The color change is a function performed by the browser to remind you of the links you have already "visited." If you want to modify the color of a visited link, you use a pseudo-class selector. Although there are quite a few pseudo-class selectors, most are not well supported by browsers as of this writing, and even the ones that are supported work only with hyperlinks. The pseudo-classes you will find most useful are :link, :visited, :active, and :hover. If you combine these with the anchor (a) selector, you can adjust the colors and appearance of the links on your page, as in the following style rules:

```
a:link    {color: blue; font-style: italic}
a:visited {color: purple; font-style: normal}
a:active  {color: green; font-style: italic}
a:hover   {color: red; font-style: italic}
```

If you incorporate these rules into an embedded or linked style sheet, your unvisited links will be blue text with an italic font style, visited links will be purple with a normal font style, active (links that you have just clicked) will be green with italic font, and hover (mouseover) links will be red with italic font. Try it.

Although the list of possible selectors is longer than what has been presented here, many of them are considerably more complex that these. The preceding selectors are the ones you are most likely to use as you begin to learn how to use Cascading Style Sheets. If you want a more complete list of selectors, download the CSS reference section in at www.jamespence.com.

Understand CSS Measurement Units

When you are writing style rules for a Web page, CSS offers a number of different possibilities for specifying length measurements. In fact, so many options are available that you might find it confusing to decide which you should choose. When you can choose between percentages, pixels, points, picas, millimeters, centimeters, inches, ems, and exes, how do you even begin to sort them out? Actually, it's not all that difficult. First, all of these different measurements can be sorted into two basic groups: absolute and relative measurements.

Absolute Measurements Are Fixed

Absolute measurements are fixed lengths or sizes. Thus, this group of measurements includes points (1/72 in), picas (12 pts), millimeters, centimeters, and inches. If you use any of these measurements, remember that they do not adjust with window size display resolution or display size. They are *absolute*. Unless you are designing for a network and know exactly what kind of equipment your visitors will use, you will find it advisable to avoid absolute measurement units.

Relative Measurements Are Flexible

Relative measurements are flexible in that they are generally made *relative* to something else. For example, an *ex* measurement is made relative to the height of the letter *x* in an element's default font. Thus, a measurement of 2ex is equal to two x's stacked on top of one another. Another measurement, the *em,* is based generally on the browser's default font size. A value of 1.5em, then, would be one-and-one-half times the size of a browser's "body text" font. However, if you are working with an element where the font size has already been specified, then 1.5em would be equivalent to one-and-one-half times the font size for that element.

The third length measurement, pixels, might seem on the surface to be in the wrong group. After all, 100 pixels appears to be an absolute measurement. However, remember that there are several different possible resolution settings for browsers. One hundred pixels on a 640×480 screen takes up more space than on an 800×600 screen. Therefore, pixels are measured relative to a display screen's resolution. Although any of the measurements listed in this section will work for you, generally you will find that the *em*'s simplicity and flexibility make it your best choice for your CSS measurement need.

Understand <div>, <span>, and Inheritance

Two tools to keep ready for use in working with CSS are the <div> and <span> elements. These two elements have no function in and of themselves but are "generic" in nature. Essentially, you can make them do almost anything you want them to. Why are there two generic elements? The <div> element is a *block-level* element, while <span> is an *inline* element. Block-level elements create a separate division on the page and insert an extra space after the element. Thus, if you want to create a grouping of elements on your page to which you will add style, you would use <div>. For example, say there was a portion of your page where you wanted to have a different background color. You could apply the background color to each of the elements in that section individually, or you could simply enclose all of those elements inside a set of <div> tags. Then all you need to do is apply the new background color to <div>, and the other elements will *inherit* the new style, as in the following code listing:

```
<div style="background-color: blue">
<h1>All of this content</h1>
<h2>will have a</h2>
<p>blue background</p>
</div>
<p>This content returns to the default background.</p>
```

On the other hand, if you want to apply a style inside a paragraph, you would use <span>. For example, say that you want to italicize one sentence in a paragraph. Simply enclose the sentence you want to modify inside a set of <span> tags and assign whatever style you want, as in the following listing:

```
<p>This is a generic paragraph using the page's default
font. <span style="font-style: italic">However, this text
will display in italics.</span> This text returns to the
default font style.</p>
```

10

Another important concept to understand here is that of *inheritance*. In most cases, an element that is a descendent of (nested inside) another element inherits that element's styles. Although this is not always the case, it is helpful to remember that the styles you assign will often influence more page elements than you expect them to.

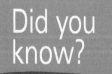 TIP   *Often, in CSS, you will see terms like* parent, child, ancestor, *and* descendent. *If you find these terms confusing, just think of a family. Anytime an element is nested inside another element, it is considered a "child" element. Thus, the terms* parent *and* child *refer to elements that are members of an "immediate family." The terms ancestor and descendent can refer to immediate family, but they can also refer to grandparents and grandchildren, great-grandparents and great-grandchildren, and so on.*

Understand and Use CSS Properties

As you have discovered, selectors enable you to apply styles to specific portions of an XHTML document. In the sections that follow, you will learn how to use properties. To keep it simple, think of properties as governing four general areas of page design: fonts, text, colors-backgrounds, and box properties (margins, padding, borders, and so on). There is much more to CSS than these four groups of properties, but this will give you plenty to start with.

In addition, this next section is designed to give you some more practical experience with CSS. As you read through the list of properties, type in the code following each one; gradually you will build a sample style sheet to incorporate into the plain Web page you created at the beginning of the chapter.

Use Font Properties for Controlling Font Display

Font properties enable you to apply styles to the fonts on your page. With these properties you can specify different fonts: their sizes, styles, weights, and so on. As each of the properties is listed, it will be added to the style rule for the <p> element. To see how it displays, import it

Did you know?

What's the difference between CSS 1, CSS 2, and CSS 3?

The different numbers refer to three successive CSS "versions" or "recommendations" by the W3C. The current version is CSS 2. CSS 3 is still under development. Because many of the new properties added in CSS 2 are not widely supported by the browsers, much of CSS 2 still cannot be used effectively in Web pages. For the most part, this book focuses on the selectors and properties of CSS 1. A complete listing of CSS 1 selectors and properties, along with some of the better-supported properties of CSS 2, can be downloaded from the author's Web site at www.jamespence.com, or Osborne's Web site at www.osborne.com.

into your original sample page. Try experimenting with CSS by substituting different values in the various declarations. Your choices for font properties are as follows:

NOTE

Throughout these property sections, you will be able to build some style rules for a sample document. It is not necessary to rewrite each line of code; the new additions are indicated in bold type. Also, you will notice that these style rules make use of most of the different length measurements. This is so that you can experiment with them and see the results that they give you.

- **Font-family**   Allows you to specify the font you want to display. Although you can choose any font you'd like, remember that if the font is not on your visitor's system, the browser will substitute a default font. Generic values for font-family are serif, sans-serif, monospaced, cursive, and fantasy.

  ```
  p { font-family: sans-serif; }
  ```

- **Font-style**   Toggles between normal and italic fonts. A third possible value is *oblique*, but this generally displays as italic.

  ```
  p {font-family: sans-serif; font-style: italic; }
  ```

- **Font-variant**   Enables you to display a font as small caps. The possible values to choose from are, as you would expect, normal and small caps.

  ```
  p {font-family: sans-serif; font-style: italic;
  font-variant: small-caps; }
  ```

- **Font-weight**   Offers a greater range of choices than HTML's bold <b> element. You can specify values by descriptive terms such as normal, bold, lighter, and bolder, or with a numerical value of 100 through 900 (in increments of 100).

  ```
  p {font-family: sans-serif; font-style: italic;
  font-variant: small-caps; font-weight: 700;}
  ```

10

What Is the Difference Between the Generic Fonts?

A serif font has decorative strokes at the ends of each character. These strokes are called *ascenders* and *descenders*, but are generally known as *serifs*. For example, *Times New Roman* is a serif font (and is used here). A sans-serif font has no ascenders or descenders. Arial is an example of a sans-serif font. A *monospace* font generally is a courier or "typewriter"-style font. Cursive fonts attempt to simulate handwritten script. Fantasy fonts tend to be anything a particular browser finds that doesn't fit into one of the preceding categories.

■ **Font-size** Sets you free from HTML's seven-step font sizes. This property enables you to specify font sizes with nine different measurements: inches (in), millimeters (mm), centimeters (cm), points (pt), picas (pc), pixels (px), ems (em), exs (ex), and percentages (#%).

```
p {font-family: sans-serif; font-style: italic;
font-variant: small-caps; font-weight: 700;
font-size: 14pt;}
```

■ **Color** Enables you to choose colors for your fonts by using color names or their hexadecimal or RGB values.

```
p {font-family: sans-serif; font-style: italic;
font-variant: small-caps; font-weight: 700;
font-size: 14pt; color: blue;}
```

Applying this style rule to the original plain text HTML page produces these results:

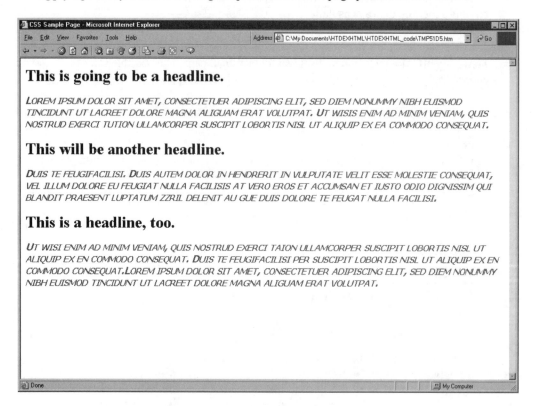

Apply Text Properties for Spacing and Alignment

Whereas font properties deal with size, color, weight, and style of fonts, text properties handle the more mundane tasks of dealing with character and line spacing, alignment, justification, and so on. The text properties enable you to arrange your page with far greater precision than you ever could with HTML. For example, you can specify details such as the following:

- **Word-spacing**   With this property you can specify additional space between words using the same types of measurements as with font-size. The default is normal.

  ```
  h1 {word-spacing: .1em;}
  ```

- **Letter-spacing**   As its name suggests, letter-spacing allows you to add to the default spacing between letters. Again, normal is the default.

  ```
  h1 {word-spacing: .1em; letter-spacing: .2cm; }
  ```

- **Text-decoration**   With text-decoration you can add the values of underline, overline, line-through, and blink. The default value is text-decoration: none.

  ```
  h1 {word-spacing: .1em; letter-spacing: .2cm;
  text-decoration: underline; }
  ```

- **Vertical-align**   This allows you to apply the same vertical alignment properties to text elements as you did with text alignment attributes in HTML. Values include baseline, sub, super, top, text-top, middle, bottom, text-bottom, and percentage.

  ```
  h1 em {vertical-align: super;}
  ```

<table><tr><td>NOTE</td><td>*Notice that in addition to the h1 selector, this line also has em added. This is called a descendent selector. By adding an element to the selector, you can create styles for specific contexts. To create a superscript in an h1 headline, simply enclose the words you want to superscript in a set of <em></em> tags.*</td></tr></table>

- **Text-transform**   With the text-transform property, you can automatically capitalize every word in any given element, change them all to uppercase, or make them all lowercase.

  ```
  h1 {word-spacing: .1em; letter-spacing: .2cm;
  text-decoration: underline;
  text-transform: capitalize;}
  ```

- **Text-align**   The text-align property works essentially the same way as the align attribute. You can choose from values of left, right, center, and justify.

  ```
  h1 {word-spacing: .1em; letter-spacing: .2cm;
  text-decoration: underline;
  text-transform: capitalize;
  text-align: center; }
  ```

10

■ **Text-indent**   Using text-indent frees you from the old convention of using the non-breaking space entity, , for indenting. Using this property, you can specify exactly what kind of indent you would like. The possible values are a number, a measurement, and a percentage.

```
p {font-family: sans-serif; font-style: italic;
    font-variant: small-caps; font-weight: 700;
    font-size: 14pt; color: blue;
    text-indent: .5in;}
```

■ **Line-height**   If you want to space lines farther apart than the default setting for a browser, use the line-height property. You can specify line-height by a number, a measurement, or a percentage.

```
p {font-family: sans-serif; font-style: italic;
    font-variant: small-caps; font-weight: 700;
    font-size: 14pt; color: blue;
    text-indent: .5 in; line-height: 1em;}
```

Try adding these modified rules to your css_sample.htm document and compare your results to the following illustration:

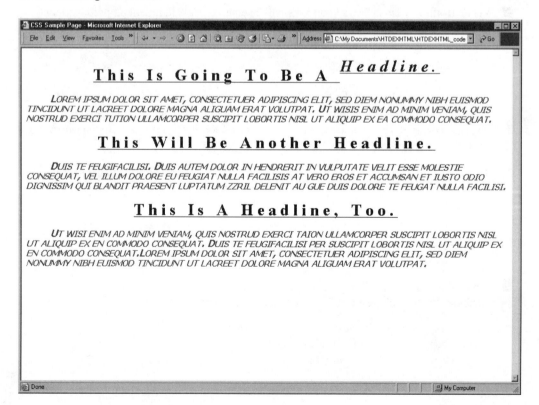

Use Color and Background Properties

As you might imagine from the name, color and background properties enable you to control the display of background images and colors. These properties work much the same way as the bgcolor and background attributes but give you many more options to work with. The color and background properties are as follows:

- **Background-color** With HTML you were able to set the background color for only an entire page or individual table cells. The CSS background-color property enables you to set a background color for any element.

    ```
    body {background-color: yellow; }
    ```

- **Background-image** With this property you can set a background image for any element, not just for a page.

TIP *If you are working through this example, you can supply any image you have in place of weavetile.gif. If you want to try to copy the page exactly, then you can download weavetile2.gif, along with the rest of the code and images, from this book at the author's Web site, www.jamespence.com.*

    ```
    body {background-color: yellow;
          background-image: url(weavetile2.gif); }
    ```

- **Background-repeat** This property allows you a much greater range of choices in how a background image repeats on your page. You can choose to have the image repeat (tile) through the entire page, repeat horizontally or vertically, or not at all. The values are repeat, repeat-x (horizontal), repeat-y (vertical), and no-repeat.

    ```
    body {background-color: yellow;
          background-image: url(weavetile2.gif);
          background-repeat: repeat-y; }
    ```

- **Background-attachment** To create a watermark effect with a fixed background image that allows content to scroll, you can use the background-attachment property. Your options are scroll or fixed.

    ```
    body {background-color: yellow;
          background-image: url(weavetile2.gif);
          background-repeat: repeat-y;
          background-attachment: scroll; }
    ```

- **Background-position** With the background-position property you can specify where an image occurs in an element. You can describe the position in terms of top/center/bottom and left/center/right. In other words, you can specify an image to show up in the top right, center, bottom left, and so on.

    ```
    body {background-color: yellow;
          background-image: url(weavetile2.gif);
    ```

10

```
background-repeat: repeat-y;
background-attachment: scroll;
background-position: left;}
```

Copy the preceding style rule into your Web page, and then save and display it. It should resemble the following illustration:

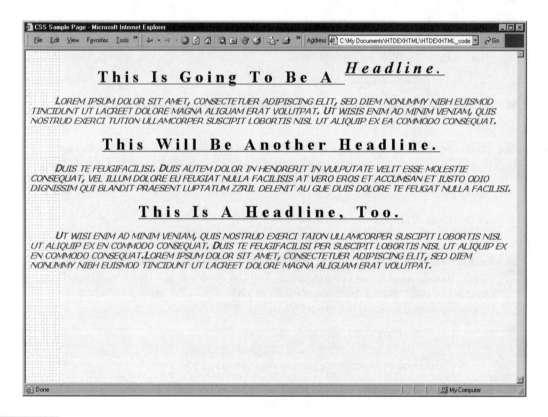

NOTE

With background-position and other position-related properties, the positioning is relative to an imaginary "box" that surrounds the element. If you would like to visualize what that box looks like with one element, open an HTML page and modify any <h1> element to read <h1 style "background-color: blue>". The h1 element will now appear with a blue rectangle behind it. That's the invisible box. When you specify background position with any element, the background image is placed relative to the invisible box around that element, not the entire page—unless, of course, you are modifying the <body> element.

Control Margins, Padding, and Borders with Box Properties

Perhaps the most complicated (and useful) properties are the box properties. These allow you much greater influence over positioning, layout, borders, text flow, and so on, than you ever could have with HTML. To better understand how the box properties work, envision each element on your page as being contained in a box. You can add *padding* around the element, a *border* around the edge of the box, and *margins* around the outside of the box (and between other elements). Figure 10-1 illustrates the CSS box model.

With the box properties, you can influence the layout of your entire page. These properties can take quite a while to master, but they are great tools to have at your disposal. They are as follows:

■ **Margin-top (right, bottom, left)**   With the margin properties, you can specify margins in measurements or percentages. If you don't specify margins, the browser will set them

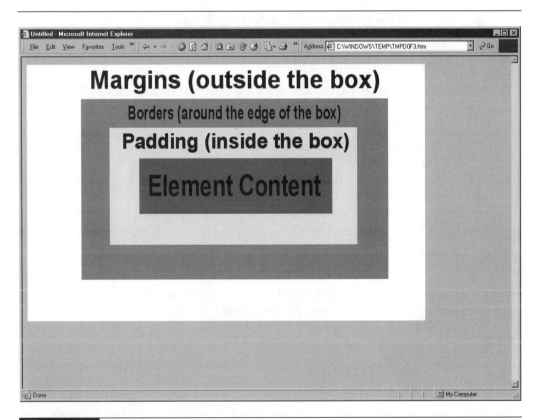

FIGURE 10-1   The Box Model

automatically (this can also be specified as "auto"). The following sets left and right margins to one inch:

```
body {background-color: yellow;
      background-image: url(weavetile2.gif);
      background-repeat: repeat-y;
      background-attachment: scroll;
      background-position: left;
      margin-left: 1in; margin-right: 1in;}
```

■ **Padding-top (right, bottom, left)**   If you think about tables and the cell-padding attribute, you will understand how padding works. Now, you don't need to be limited to individual cells—you can add padding to any element.

```
p {font-family: sans-serif; font-style: italic;
   font-variant: small-caps; font-weight: 700;
   font-size: 14pt; color: blue;
   text-indent: .5 in; line-height: 1em;
   padding: .25in .50in;}
```

■ **Border-style**   If you want to add a border to any element, you can do it with this property. You can choose from eight possible options: solid, dashed, dotted, inset, outset, ridge, groove, or double.

```
p {font-family: sans-serif; font-style: italic;
   font-variant: small-caps; font-weight: 700;
   font-size: 14pt; color: blue;
   text-indent: .5 in; line-height: 1em;
   padding: .25in .50in;
   border-style: inset;}
```

■ **Border-color**   This property enables you to set the color for a border. You can specify up to four values; they are assigned the same way as margin values.

```
p {font-family: sans-serif; font-style: italic;
   font-variant: small-caps; font-weight: 700;
   font-size: 14pt; color: blue;
   text-indent: .5 in; line-height: 1em;
   padding: .25in .50in;
   border-style: inset;
   border-color: red;}
```

■ **Border-top-width (right-width, bottom-width, left-width)**   You can set the width of a border as thin, medium, or thick, or you can specify a unit of measurement.

```
p {font-family: sans-serif; font-style: italic;
    font-variant: small-caps; font-weight: 700;
    font-size: 14pt; color: blue;
    text-indent: .5 in; line-height: 1em;
    padding: .25in .50in;
    border-style: inset;
    border-color: red;
    border-width: thick;}
```

When you've modified your style rules to match these, save your page and compare it in your browser. It should look something like the following illustration:

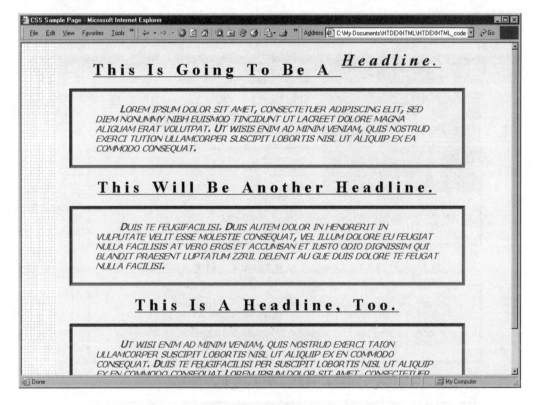

If you plan to add images, the height, width, float, and clear properties will prove quite useful. These properties correspond to the height, width, and align attributes in HTML—that is, they allow you to specify how an image will be displayed and whether text will wrap around it.

■ **Width**   This property functions much the same as the width attribute. Its best use is with graphics or to set the width of a block-level element.

```
img.pansy1 {height: 200px;}
```

■ **Height**   As with width, this property sets the height of an element.

```
img.pansy1 {height: 200px; width: 320px;}
```

■ **Float**   Similar to the align attribute, this property allows you to set an element to the left or right margin, with text flowing around the opposite side.

```
img.pansy1 {height: 200px; width: 320px;
        float: left;}
```

If you have added the preceding style rule to the page (and have supplied or downloaded a picture to go with it), you will notice that the image is overlapping part of the text box as in the following illustration:

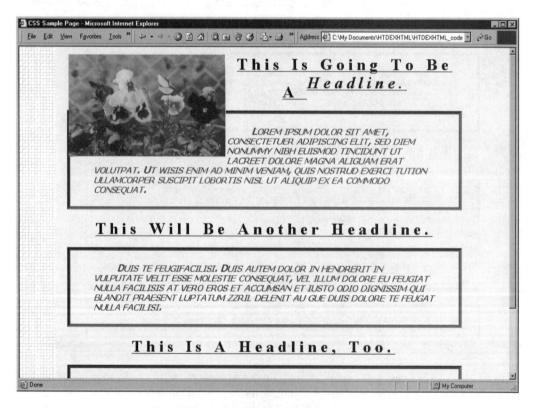

If you don't want the image to float with text wrapping, use the clear property.

■ **Clear**   The clear property will prevent an image from floating on top of another element, leaving one or both sides clear. The values for this property are *none*, *left*, *right*, and *both*.

```
p {font-family: sans-serif; font-style: italic;
font-variant: small-caps; font-weight: 700;
font-size: 14pt; color: blue;
text-indent: .5 in; line-height: 1em;
padding: .25in .50in;
border-style: inset;
border-color: red;
border-width: thick;
clear: left;}
```

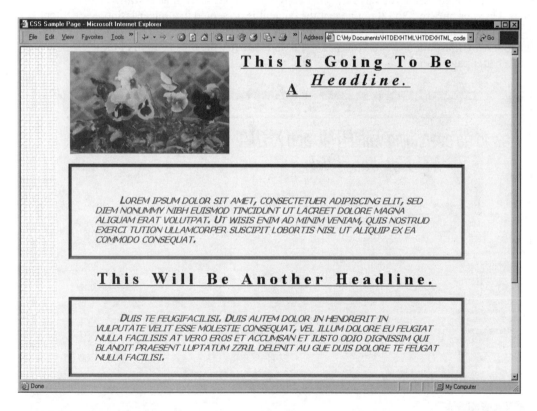

With the box properties, you now have the ability to create complex layouts for a Web page using nothing more than HTML and CSS. Now that you have had a chance to see the box properties in action, why don't you try creating a complete layout using CSS?

Project 17: Create a Layout with CSS

In Chapters 8 and 9 you learned how to create simple layouts with tables and frames. This project will show you how to create a similar layout using only CSS. You will create a Web page using the same basic elements you used in Chapters 8 and 9: a banner, a group of navigational links, some content, and a copyright section. Then you'll link to an external style sheet. However, to make things a bit more interesting, and to show you some of what CSS can do, we'll add in a picture and supply our own bullets for the navigation list.

Copy the XHTML Code

Because of the complexity of this project, the code for the Web page is reproduced in this section. As you copy the markup, be sure to observe how classes are implemented and how the <div> element is applied. After you have finished copying the code, save it as *css-layout.htm* and view it in your browser. You'll notice that the content is presented in a linear fashion—one item comes after another. In fact, the content can't even be presented in a single browser window, as the following illustration shows. You will use CSS to modify the presentation of these elements into a better page layout.

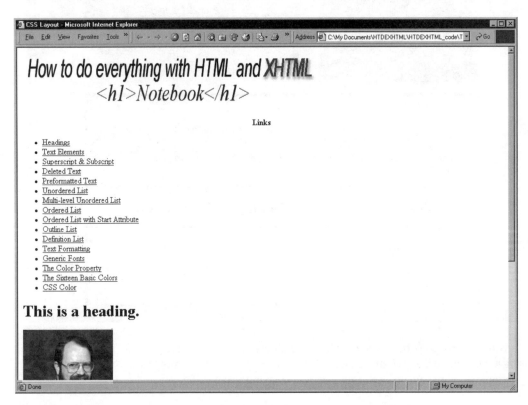

```
<!DOCTYPE html PUBLIC "-//W3C//DTD XHTML 1.0 Transitional//EN"
 "http://www.w3.org/TR/xhtml1/DTD/xhtml1-transitional.dtd">
<html xmlns="http://www.w3.org/1999/xhtml">
  <head>
    <title>CSS Layout</title>
      <link rel="stylesheet" type="text/css"
            href="CSS-layout1.css" />
  </head>
  <body>
    <div class="banner">
      <img alt="HTDEXHTML Banner" src="banner.gif"
                      height="100" width="600" />
    </div>
    <div class="nav">
      <p style="text-align: center"><strong>Links</strong></p>
      <ul>
<li><a href="headings.htm" target="_blank">Headings</a></li>
<li><a href="text.htm" target="_blank">Text Elements</a></li>
<li><a href="sup.htm" target="_blank">
                Superscript &amp;Subscript</a></li>
<li><a href="del.htm" target="_blank">Deleted Text</a></li>
<li><a href="pre.htm" target="_blank">Preformatted Text</a></li>
<li><a href="ulist.htm" target="_blank">Unordered List</a></li>
<li><a href="ulist2.htm" target="_blank">Multi-level Unordered
List</a></li>
<li><a href="olist.htm" target="_blank">Ordered List</a></li>
<li><a href="olist2.htm" target="_blank">Ordered List with Start
Attribute</a></li>
<li><a href="olist3.htm" target="_blank">Outline List</a></li>
<li><a href="dlist.htm" target="_blank">Definition List</a></li>
<li><a href="text-format.htm" target="_blank">Text
Formatting</a></li>
<li><a href="generic-fonts.htm" target="_blank">Generic
Fonts</a></li>
<li><a href="font-colors.htm" target="_blank">The Color
Property</a></li>
<li><a href="16colors.htm" target="_blank">The Sixteen Basic
Colors</a></li>
<li><a href="css-color.htm" target="_blank">CSS Color</a></li>
</ul>
    </div>
    <h1 class="heading">This is a heading.</h1>
```

10

```
<div class="content"><img class="jim" alt="jim (9K)"
          src="jim.jpg" height="200" width="183" />
    <p> This is just more meaningless text that I wrote to
use as filler for this illustration. It might not be very
profound, but then it doesn't need to be, does it? By the way,
the handsome guy in the photo on this page is yours truly.</p>
</div>
<p id="copyright">Web Design by Me! &copy; Copyright 2050. All
Rights Reserved.</p>
</body>
</html>
```

Write the Style Sheet

After you have copied and saved the XHTML page, you need to create a style sheet to go with it. Because you are using an external style sheet, simply use Notepad to create a blank file (no XHTML elements), and save it as *CSS-layout1.css*. Then work through the following steps to create your style rules. The style rules are written out for you below each step.

Write a style rule that sets the background color of the page to white.

```
body    {   background-color: white;
              }
```

1. In this step, you design a style for your navigation links. Create a class called "nav" and set the background color to aqua. Then set the margin-top property to 110 pixels and the width to 200 pixels. Set the font family to arial and sans-serif. Specify a font-size of .80 ems and use the float property to position the navigation bar on the left side of the page.

```
.nav {      background-color: aqua;
            margin-top: 70px;
            width: 200px;
            font-family: arial, sans-serif;
            font-size: .80em;
            float: left;
            }
```

2. This style rule enables you to substitute your own bullet for the list items instead of using the bullet supplied by the browser. For this to work, you will either need to download star.gif from the author's Web site (www.jamespence.com) or supply a small (20×20) image of your own. For the list item selector, use the list-style-type property to set the bullet to disc. This is a backup style, in case your visitor's browser doesn't load star.gif. Use the list-style-image property to point to star.gif as your bullet of choice. The last two properties position the bullet on the inside and in the middle (vertically) of the line. You won't notice the "inside" effect unless a list item extends to more than one line. If it does, the bullet will be positioned flush with the first letter of the second line.

```
li      {
            list-style-type: disc;
            list-style-image: url(star.gif);
            list-style-position: inside;
            vertical-align: middle
        }
```

The next rule uses the :hover pseudo-class to add a hover effect and color change when a mouse cursor passes over a link. The text-decoration: none declaration will remove the underline on a mouseover, and the color property will turn the link red.

```
a:hover {
            text-decoration: none;
            color: red;
        }
```

Now you will create a rule that allows you to format your content box. Create a class named **content** and set its background color to transparent. Set the text-align property to justify and the font family to arial. Add a 30 pixel top margin and add 15 pixels of padding to the left and right sides. Finally, set the width of your content box to 75 percent.

```
.content {  background-color: transparent;
            text-align: justify;
            font-family: arial;
            margin-top: 30px;
            padding-left: 15px;
            padding-right:15px;
            width: 75%;
        }
```

3. To set the styles for your copyright box, create an ID named **copyright**. Set its background color to transparent, and the font size to .75em. Center-align the text and change its color to navy.

```
#copyright {  background-color: transparent;
              font-size: .75em;
              text-align: center;
              color: navy;
            }
```

4. The following style rule uses a descendent selector to modify the word Links on the Web page. This rule sets the font size to 2 ems.

```
p strong {   font-size: 2em;
            }
```

5. The next rule modifies your heading by moving down from the top of the page and center-aligning it. Create a class named *h1.heading* and use the margin-top and text-align properties to set your values.

```
h1.heading { margin-top: 90px;
             text-align: center;
           }
```

6. Create a class named *img.jim* for the next rule. These style declarations add a bit of space around the picture and separate it from the surrounding text. You will also use the border shortcut property to add a thick, yellow outset border to the picture.

```
img.jim    { margin-left: 5px;
             margin-right: 5px;
             float: left;
             border: thick yellow outset
           }
```

7. The final style rule centers your banner and uses the clear property to make sure no other elements conflict with or overlap it.

```
.banner    { text-align: center;
             clear: both
           }
```

When you have finished writing your style sheet, save it and display CSS-layout.htm in your Web browser. Hopefully, your results will resemble the following illustration. If they don't,

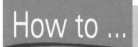 **Learn More About Style Sheets**

Because CSS are so extensive, you will find the Quick Reference chart for CSS at www .jamespence.com. This chart focuses primarily on CSS 1 selectors and properties. For a complete listing of CSS selectors and properties in downloadable form, go to www .blooberry.com and check out Index.DOT/CSS, a comprehensive online CSS reference. You can access this site for free online or download it (for a small fee).

remember that differences in browsers and display screens can create some variety in how a style sheet layout will look from system to system.

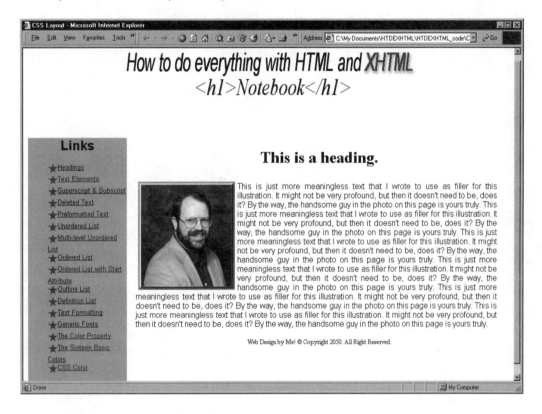

Part III

Bells and Whistles to Adorn Your Site

Chapter 11

Add Multimedia and other Objects

How to...

- Understand formats and delivery methods
- Find audio and video files
- Link to a sound or video file
- Add a background sound
- Embed sound and video
- Use streaming audio and video

Nowhere are the sweeping advances in the technology of the Web more evident than in the area of multimedia. When the Web started, it was little more than typewritten text on a screen. Next came graphics and the capability to add pictures and fonts of different sizes and colors. Now you can include animation, audio, and video to bring life to your designs. You might be tempted to avoid multimedia on the grounds that it's too difficult for you to learn and use; however, nothing could be further from the truth. In fact, if you know how to add a link to a Web page, you already know enough to link to an audio or a video file.

Understand Formats and Delivery Methods

As you explore multimedia, it's best to start with the different formats that are available. Just as with graphics, certain formats work best for certain purposes. For example, when deciding on sound files, you might be influenced by the desire for a quick download time as opposed to good sound quality. On the other hand, sound quality might be important to you and you really don't care how long it takes a file to download. Perhaps both are important to you. All of these factors will influence the choices you make.

Compare Audio Formats

You will encounter several different audio formats as you enter the world of multimedia. Some you will definitely use; others you just need to know about. The formats listed next do not represent all possible choices, only those most commonly used and best supported:

- **m-Law** Pronounced *moo-law*, this format is sort of the granddaddy of them all. If you're familiar at all with audio files, you might recognize its file extension, .au. This is the file type used on UNIX systems. Although this type of file is supported on most PCs, it doesn't offer great sound quality.

- **MIDI** Musical Instrument Digital Interface is a very different way of producing music and other sounds. Whereas most sound files actually record and reproduce sound and music, MIDI does not. Instead, a MIDI file is somewhat similar to storing the information from a printed page of music in digital format. Although that might be an oversimplification, that's the basic concept. MIDI doesn't store music; it stores instructions for creating music. The advantages of MIDI files are that they are very small and download quickly. The disadvantage is that you are limited in the sound you can reproduce because sound is not actually recorded. For example, because MIDI files are built around digitized virtual musical instruments, they cannot be used for voice recordings.

- **Waveform (Wave) Audio** If you use a Windows system, you already use Waveform (or Wave) Audio. Are you familiar with the little tune that Windows plays when it loads? That's a .wav file. These files allow for excellent sound quality but can be extremely large and slow to download.

- **Mp3** Mp3 has been in the news a lot lately. In fact, you might say that Mp3 files have put the music industry in a bit of a quandary. MPEG (Motion Picture Experts Group), better known as Mp3, files are compressed, enabling music to be downloaded easily. The amount of compression is striking. For example, a single song saved as a .wav file can use 40 megabytes of space or more. The same song saved as an .mp3 file might be 1 or 2 megabytes. In light of this, you can understand the Napster controversy. Who would want to take the time to download an album of 12 songs at 40 megabytes each? On the other hand, what if each song is only 1.5 megabytes?

- **AIFF** Originally developed for Macintosh systems, Audio Interchange File Format (.aif, .aiff) files provide high quality, although the file size tends to be large. Even though it was a Mac development, .aif files are supported in the Windows environment and can easily be converted to other formats.

- **RM** RealMedia files are a special file format designed by RealNetworks for streaming media. Helix Producer Basic, a limited versionprogram that creates these files, is available as freeware.

- **WMA** Windows Media Files are Microsoft's answer to RealNetworks' streaming media files. The technology is essentially the same, because Microsoft purchased from Real Networks the rights to use their technology.

So, which file type should you use when you are putting together sounds for your Web site? It all depends. If you want to have background music that begins when the page loads, you want a small file that downloads quickly. Your best bet is a MIDI file. If you don't like the computerized sound that tends to go along with MIDI files, try a very short WAV file. Also, if you want to emphasize sound quality, you'll lean toward WAV. If your sound clips are long, you will probably want to take advantage of Mp3's compression capabilities. MPEG files do lose some quality in the compression process, but it is not usually significant. If you want your visitors to be able to listen to the file as it downloads, then streaming media (Real or Windows Media) is your best option.

Compare Video Formats

A slightly less daunting array of choices awaits you when you consider the different video formats that are available. Again, although there are more formats than those discussed here, those listed next are the most common and enjoy the greatest support.

- **Audio/Video Interleaved** This format was developed for Microsoft's Video for Windows. Audio/Video Interleaved (.avi) is the standard for the Windows platform and is used for many applications requiring video. For example, if you have an encyclopedia on CD-ROM, you'll find that most (if not all) of the video clips contained on it are in the .avi format.

- **QuickTime** QuickTime (.mov) is used widely and works well on all platforms. Developed for the Macintosh, it is nevertheless supported in both Internet Explorer and Netscape. QuickTime's latest versions provide better quality at lower transfer rates because of some new compression routines. Add to that its ease of use and the availability of inexpensive encoding software make the .mov a good choice for newcomers to the world of multimedia.

- **RealMedia** Helix Producer 9 can encode video for streaming. Because video files tend to be very large, streaming is a good option if you plan to have video on your pages. Better yet, the basic version is free.

- **Windows Media** Likewise, you can use the Windows Media encoding software to create streaming video. As with audio, the software and support that Microsoft provides free of charge makes this an attractive option.

- **MPEG** Developed by the Moving Picture Experts Group, MPEG (.mpg) files, like their JPEG counterparts, can be compressed significantly yet lose little quality. In fact, MPEG-4 can provide DVD-quality images. If you are looking for high-quality video reproduction for your site, this is the format of choice. However, MPEG can be complicated, and you will need special software for encoding the videos. This makes MPEG an unlikely choice for a casual user.

NOTE *If you are interested in exploring MPEG in more detail, visit the MPEG4IP Web site at http://mpeg4ip.sourceforge.net and www.apple.com/mpeg4.*

Which format should you choose? The main consideration here probably is file size, as video files tend to be very large. For simply attaching a video link or embedding a file, you probably will want to use either QuickTime or AVI. The advantage of using QuickTime is that it is already supported on both Windows and Mac systems. However, if you use AVI clips on your site, Mac users will need to download a plug-in to enable them to view the files. For streaming video, you will probably want to use Windows Media or Real Media.

Understand Delivery Methods

There are two different ways to deliver audio or video to your visitors: *download* and *streaming*. Your choice of one or the other will be governed by the size of the file you are planning to use.

If you plan to use only very short clips of a few hundred kilobytes or less, use download as your delivery method. When you link to an audio or a video file, or when you embed multimedia into your pages, the normal method of delivery is by download. In other words, the entire file is downloaded into your visitor's computer before it is played. With short clips and small file sizes, most people won't mind waiting. However, if you're planning to include a long clip—perhaps a lecture, complete songs, or 15 minutes of your Hawaiian vacation video—your visitors likely will move on before the file has time to download. In cases such as this you might want to consider *streaming* audio and video.

The difference between streaming and downloadable media is very simple: Downloadable audio and video is like filling a glass of water before you take a drink. You wait until the glass is full; then you enjoy the water. On the other hand, using streaming media is like going to a water fountain. You drink the water as it streams up from the fountain's nozzle. No need to wait for a glass to fill up. With streaming media, the visitor gets to watch the video or listen to the music while the file is downloading.

 Even with downloadable files, it is to your advantage to use streaming media. Because streaming audio and video use the UDP protocol (no error checking, hence faster downloads) rather than TCP, the same size file will take less time to download to your visitor's browser. A longer clip could be used without hindering performance.

Find Multimedia Files

Obviously, if you're going to do the exercises in this chapter, you're going to need some audio and video files to work with. How do you go about finding them? It might not be as hard as you think. Consider some of these possible sources:

- **Your Own PC**   If your computer is of recent vintage, you might be astonished to learn how many multimedia files are already stored away on your hard drive. On Windows 98, just click Start | Find | Files or Folders. For Windows 2000 or XP, click Start | Search | For Files or Folders. On the line that reads Named:, type an asterisk followed by an audio or a video file extension (for example, ***.mov**). Click Find Now and watch as your computer searches for the files.

- **CD and DVD-ROMs**   These can be a great source of potential files. Just pop one in your drive and use the same process as outlined earlier (remembering to specify the CD/DVD-ROM drive as the one to search); you could find plenty of files to experiment with.

- **Online**   Web sites such as www.freeaudioclips.com and www.multimedialibrary.com are sources worth checking out. Also, although it won't always work, try right-clicking any links to videos on Web sites. Your browser usually will give you an option to download and save the video file.

- **Osborne's Web Site**   Some of the audio files used in the examples for this chapter are available on Osborne's site, www.osborne.com.

- **Create Your Own**   There are quite a few shareware and even freeware programs available that will enable you to create your own audio and video files. Try visiting some sites such as www.download.com, www.tucows.com, or www.zdnet.com/downloads, and search for audio and video editors or multimedia authoring tools. You'll find a large range of selections to choose from. Table 11-1 lists a few you might start with. Most of these programs offer at least a free trial version.

11

Program Name	What It Does	Publisher URL	Approximate Price
Cooledit 2000	Audio editor	www.syntrillium.com	$69
GoldWave	Audio editor	www.goldwave.com	$40
Total Recorder	Audio editor	www.highcriteria.com	$12
Ulead Video Studio 7	Video editor	www.ulead.com	$100
QuickTime Pro	Makes QuickTime movies	www.apple.com/quicktime/upgrade	$30
Windows Media Encoder 9 Series	Produces audio and video for Windows Media	www.microsoft.com	Freeware
Helix Producer 9	Creates streaming audio and video	www.real.com	Freeware

TABLE 11-1   Audio and Video Editors

TIP

If you want to create your own audio or video files, you will need both the hardware and software to get the job done. For audio, your computer must be equipped with a sound card (standard equipment nowadays), and you'll need audio editing software. For video, you must install a video capture card on your computer. This will enable you to plug a VCR, video camera, digital camera, and so on, into your system.

When you have some multimedia files to work with, you're ready to see how they function on a Web page.

CAUTION

When dealing with audio and video, copyright issues quickly become relevant. It might seem harmless for you to include your favorite song as background music for your site, but if you do not have permission to use it, you are violating the law. The same holds true for video, still photos, art, software, or just about anything that has been created by someone else. ASCAP (American Society of Composers, Authors, and Publishers) is a good place to start if you want to use copyrighted music on your site. Check out their Web site: www.ascap.com/weblicense.

Link to Audio or Video Files

Just as you can link to an external image, you can add audio and video to your page simply by linking to a file. This is without a doubt the easiest way to add multimedia to your site. For example, in Chapter 8 a family album page was created to demonstrate the use of tables for layout. What if you decided you would like to have a recorded message available as a link? The message wouldn't play automatically, nor would it be embedded as part of the page. Rather, it would be kept as a separate file; if anyone wanted to listen to it, they would just have to click the link.

Assuming you have already created the audio and video files you want to link to, all you need to do is use the anchor element <a> </a> with the href=" " attribute. The value for href=" " will be the filename of the audio/video clip. For an audio clip, your link might look like this one:

```
<a href="greeting.wav">Listen to a greeting.</a>
```

For a video clip, everything's the same except for the filename:

```
<a href="homemovie.mov">Watch my home movies.</a>
```

As you can see in the illustration that follows, your link will look like any other link. However, instead of taking your visitors to another page, a browser will load a plug-in (a special "helper" program) that plays the sound.

Listen to a greeting.
Watch my home movies.
Listen to music

Adding audio and video to a page can be that simple. Of course, although using an external link might be the easiest way to add multimedia to your site, it might not be the best way. In fact, one of the more important aspects of adding multimedia is learning to sort out the different ways of including it on your site and choosing the right one for your purposes.

Embed Sound in Your Page

Have you ever visited a Web site and found yourself listening to background music that started playing automatically? Or perhaps you heard a recorded greeting, welcoming you to the site? This is an easy way to begin using audio. As long as you keep the clips short, the resulting file size will be small and manageable. You won't need to worry about long download times delaying your sounds.

Embed Files with <object>

As you'll see later in this chapter, you can embed sound and video files with both the <bgsound> and <embed> elements. However, if you want to write "standards-compliant" XHTML, your method of choice should be the <object> element. The <object> element is in a class by itself. If you've worked through Chapter 10 on CSS, you learned about the <div> and <span> elements. They are *generic* elements that enable Web authors to apply styles apart from the limitations of more specific elements. <object> is also a generic element, but you use it for inserting *objects* in Web pages. You can define an "object" as being just about anything you want to put in a Web page. Its use is not restricted to audio or video files. You can use it instead of <img /> to insert pictures. The <object> element is also useful for including Active-X controls, Java applets, text, and even other Web pages in your page. This is truly an "all-purpose" element. Eventually, the <object> element will be the only way of embedding anything in a Web page.

Because <object> can embed many different types of objects, you must inform the browser just what kind of object you are putting in. To embed a sound file in a Web page with the object element, follow these steps:

1. Open template.htm and save it as *object.htm*.

2. Add the opening object tag:

```
<object>
```

3. Use the data=" " attribute to tell the browser where to find the file you want to embed. The value for this will be the URL of the file you want to embed:

```
<object data="greeting.wav">
```

4. Now that you've told the browser where to find the file, you must tell it what kind of file it will be embedding. For this, you use the type=" " attribute with the MIME type of the file. In this case, it will be audio/wav:

```
<object data="greeting.wav" type="audio/wav">
```

5. You should add the height and width attributes to specify the amount of space allotted to the plug-in:

```
<object data="greeting.wav" type="audio/wav"
        height="125" width="125">
```

6. Add the autostart="true" attribute to allow the sound to play as soon as it loads:

```
<object data="greeting.wav" type="audio/wav"
        height="125" width="125" autostart="true">
```

7. Add the closing tag. Even though the <object> element functions as an empty element, it still requires a closing tag:

```
<object data="greeting.wav" type="audio/wav"
        height="125" width="125" autostart="true">
</object>
```

Just to give the page some substance, try adding a line that reads <h1>This page shows the <object> element in action</h1>. Your finished code should resemble the illustration that follows the XHTML:

```
<object data="greeting.wav" type="audio/wav"
        height="125" width="150" autostart="true">
</object>
<h1>This page shows the &lt;object&gt;<br />
element in action.</h1>
```

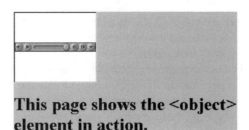

This page shows the <object> element in action.

TIP *Any time you want to display an HTML tag as part of a Web page, you must enclose the text with the character entities for the "less than," < , and "greater than," > , signs. If you typed in only the tag, the browser would interpret it as an element and not as part of the text of your document.*

Understand MIME Types

In the preceding example, you had to identify what kind of file the browser should expect by using the *type* attribute. The value you supplied was called the *MIME type*. MIME stands for *Multipurpose Internet Mail Extensions*. It was developed as a means for enabling non-text files to be transferred by e-mail. When you use the <object> element to embed a sound or video file, you must identify the file by its MIME type. This includes a basic file type such as audio, image, video, and so on, followed by a slash and a more specific type (often the file's normal extension). For example, the preceding entry was for a .wav file. In that case you entered type="audio/wav".

TIP *You can find a comprehensive list of MIME types at ftp://ftp.isi.edu/in-notes/iana/ assignments/media-types/media-types.*

11

The MIME types you generally encounter with audio and video files are listed in Table 11-2.

Add Background Sound with <bgsound /> (Internet Explorer Only)

If you want to add a "background track" to your Web page, and you're confident that your visitors will all be using Internet Explorer, you might want to experiment with the

Media Type	File Extension	MIME Type
m-Law	.au	audio/basic
Wave	.wav	audio/wav
MPEG	.mp3	audio/mpeg
QuickTime	.mov	video/quicktime
MPEG	.mpg	video/mpeg
Microsoft Video	.avi	video/msvideo

TABLE 11-2   MIME Types

element. This element is an IE extension to HTML. The good news about <bgsound /> is that it is very simple to use; the bad news is that it works only on Internet Explorer. However, it's a nice, easy way to practice working with audio files.

To insert a background sound with the <bgsound /> element, just use the *src* attribute to identify the sound file you want to attach. In the case of the following example, the name of the file is *bgsound.wav*, but you could put the name of any audio file in there as a value. One additional attribute is *loop*. The loop attribute allows you to specify how long the sound should play. If you want an endlessly repeating loop, add the value **infinite**. If you want the greeting to play only once when the page is loaded, insert a numerical value of **1**. By increasing the numerical value, you increase the number of times the sound plays. Thus, a value of 10 will cause the sound to play ten times.

Try typing in the following code to create a simple page with a background sound. Save it as *bgsound.htm*. Experiment with different sound files and different values for the loop attribute.

```
<html>
   <head>
      <title>Bgsound Sample</title>
   </head>
   <body>
      <h1>This is a sample of a page with a background sound</h1>
      <bgsound src="bgsound.wav" loop="3" />
</body>
</html>
```

Although the <bgsound /> element was never incorporated into the HTML recommendation, it remains the easiest way to embed a sound on a page. However, Netscape provides a different model for creating a page with inline sound.

Use <embed> for Inline Sounds (Netscape Extension)

What is an *inline* sound? It's simply a sound that has been placed in a page "inline," like any other element. Sometimes inline sounds are referred to as *embedded* sounds. The idea is the same as with external and inline images. If you merely write a hypertext link to an image file as you would with any other page, you are using an external image. When someone clicks on the link, the browser displays the image as a separate entity, rather than as part of the page that linked to it. On the other hand, if you use the <img /> element to actually place the image on your page, you are using an inline or embedded image. Sound files work the same way; however, instead of the <img /> element, you can embed sound files with the <embed>.

Add Inline Sound with <embed> </embed>

Netscape's <embed> </embed> extension is more versatile than IE's <bgsound />. With <bgsound /> you are limited (as its name implies) to embedding a background sound. The <embed> element, on the other hand, enables you to place different objects in your page, including audio and video files. Although <embed> is supported by both Netscape and IE, it has been deprecated in favor of the <object> element. Unfortunately, some older browsers will not recognize <object>. So, for the present it's not a bad idea to be familiar with <embed>. To experiment with the <embed> element, try the following steps:

1. Open bgsound.htm and save it as *embed.htm*.

2. Delete the line that reads

    ```
    <bgsound src="bgsound.wav" loop="3" />
    ```

3. In its place type

    `<embed src="embed.wav">`

> **TIP** *You can substitute any sound file you choose in place of embed.wav.*

4. Add the autostart="false" attribute to tell the browser not to start the audio clip automatically:

    ```
    <embed src="embed.wav" autostart="false">
    ```

5. Specify the size of the "player" the browser will display by using the height=" " and width=" " attributes:

    ```
    <embed src="embed.wav" autostart="false"   height="20"
    width="125">
    ```

6. Add a closing tag:

    ```
    <embed src="embed.wav" autostart="false"   height="20"
    width="125"> </embed>
    ```

> **CAUTION** *Even though embed works like an empty element (nothing in between the two tags), a closing tag is required.*

Your HTML for a page with an embedded sound file should resemble this code:

```
<html>
   <head>
      <title>Using the Embed Element</title>
   </head>
   <body>
      <embed src="embed.wav" autostart="false"
height="20" width="125"> </embed>
      <h1>This is a sample of a page<br />
         with an embedded sound</h1>
   </body>
</html>
```

11

When you save your page and display it in a browser, you should see a set of controls in the upper-left corner of the browser window. These controls function like the controls on a tape recorder and allow the visitor to play and replay a sound.

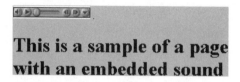

Use <embed> for Background Sound

What if you want to create a background sound using the <embed> element? You merely have to add one attribute and modify another. You must add the loop attribute as you did with <bgsound/>. With <embed>, however, loop uses a different set of values. Instead of numerical values or infinite, here loops can be given a value of only *true* or *false*. False turns the loop off; true makes the sound loop endlessly. In addition to adding the loop attribute, you must change the value in the autostart attribute to true. This will cause the sound to begin automatically. You can also delete the height and width attributes, as they are not needed for a background sound. Your modified code would look like this:

```
<embed src="embed.wav" autostart="true
     loop="true"> </embed>.
```

Use <embed> and <bgsound /> Together for Maximum Compatibility

Because both <embed> and <bgsound /> are extensions that are not part of the official HTML specification, you might encounter compatibility problems with some browsers if you use only one of them. If you plan to use these elements to add background sound to your pages, it would be wise to use both of them. For example, if you were to modify the original page created in this chapter, bgsound.htm, to include both <bgsound /> and <embed>, your code might look like the following:

```
<html>
   <head>
     <title>Bgsound Sample</title>
   </head>
   <body>
     <h1>This is a sample of a page
         with a background sound</h1>
     <bgsound src="bgsound.wav" loop="3" />
     <embed src="embed.wav" autostart="true"
               loop="true"> </embed>.
   </body>
</html>
```

Did you know?

Background Sounds Can Be Quite Annoying

As a rule, background sounds tend to be very irritating to your visitors. More often than not, an endlessly looping background sound will drive people away from your site rather than draw them to it. Unless you have a good reason to include background sound, you're probably better off avoiding it. Remember, you don't want to include effects on your Web page just because they're "cool." The whole idea is to get people to visit, hopefully more than once. If your sounds are an irritant, get rid of them.

Use <noembed> </noembed> for Non-Compatible Browsers

If you're concerned about visitors to your site who might be using browsers that do not support the <embed> element, you can provide substitute content for them with the <noembed> element. Similar to the <noframes> element, <noembed> displays alternative content in browsers that do not recognize the <embed> element. You could include a textual description or a title for your video, thus providing your visitors with some idea of what they are missing.

Project 18: Embed Video in Web Pages

After you have embedded some audio files in an HTML document, adding video is easy. For this project, you will create three basic Web pages and insert video in each one by using a different means. Your primary tools will be the <object> and <embed> elements. However, an easier option to start off with is one that, unfortunately, works only with Internet Explorer.

11

TIP *To complete this project, you will need a video file. The easiest source for video files is your own computer. If you're working with Windows, simply click Start | Find or Search. Choose Files or Folders in the pop-up menu. In the Named window, type *.avi or *.mov. Make sure that the Look In option is set to C:\ (or whatever drive letter you wish to search) and that the Include Sub-folders option is checked. Then click Find Now and you should quickly have a reasonable number of video files to choose from. If you don't find any .avi files on your C:\ drive, be sure and perform the same type of search for any CD-ROMs (particularly games) that you may have.*

Add Video with the dynsrc Attribute (Internet Exporer Only)

Internet Explorer has provided an uncomplicated way to include video on a page without using either <object> or <embed>. You can add video files using the <img /> element with the *dynamic source*, dynsrc, attribute. Unfortunately, dynsrc is not supported beyond Internet Explorer, so you might not want to use it extensively. However, it's an easy way to begin experimenting with video files. Besides, if you happen to be designing pages for a corporate intranet and you know everyone will be viewing your pages with IE, this is an easy way to add video to your pages.

Using the dynsrc=" " attribute to add video to a page is as easy as adding an image. If you have read Chapter 6 on adding graphics, you will remember that a graphical image can be embedded in a page with the <img /> (image) element. For a JPEG or GIF image, the element is written <img src="filename.jpg" />. To add a video instead of a still picture, use the *dynamic source* attribute instead of the *source* attribute. For example, to use dynsrc to add a video to a page, you would write the image element like this: <img dynsrc="myvideo.avi">. The following HTML code creates a page with the sample.mov file displaying as soon as the page is loaded:

```
<html>
    <head>
        <title>Use <em>dynsrc</em> for Video</title>
    </head>
    <body>
        <img dynsrc="myvideo.avi" />
        <h1>This video is added with the<br />
            dynsrc attribute.</h1>
    </body>
</html>
```

When you display this page, you should see something like this:

Some other attributes you can add to work along with dynsrc=" " are these:

- **loop=" "**   As with <bgsound />, you can specify infinite to create an endless loop or a numerical value for the number of times you want the video to play.

- **start=" "**   This allows you to specify when the video should start playing. Your choices are fileopen or mouseover. With fileopen (the default), the video begins playing as soon as the file loads. With mouseover, the image will not play until the mouse moves over it. Try modifying the preceding file to read <img dynsrc="sample.mov" start="mouseover" />. Save the file and load it. When the page has loaded, move your cursor over the image and see what happens.

Add Video with <object>

To add video with the <object> element, you proceed in much the same way as you would if you were embedding an audio file. The primary difference is that you use the data attribute to identify the file, you specify in the type attribute that you are using a video file, and you include the proper MIME type. For example, to insert the video from the preceding illustration with <object>, you would write the markup this way:

```
<html>
   <head>
      <title>Use &lt;object&gt; for Video</title>
   </head>
   <body>
      <object data="myvideo.avi" type="video/avi"
            height="200"  width="200" >
      </object>
      <h1>This video was added with the<br />
         &lt;object&gt; element.</h1>
   </body>
</html>
```

How to ... Avoid Problems with Browsers that Don't Support <object>

The <object> element is a versatile tool that will eventually become a key player in XHTML. Because <object> can be used to embed *any* object in a page, it will eventually replace elements such as the image <img /> element. Unfortunately, many older browsers do not support <object>, thus limiting its usefulness. If you want to use <object> but also want to accommodate older browsers, simply nest the <embed> element (along with the appropriate attributes) in between the <object> tags. Browsers that don't support <object> will ignore the tags altogether and display the contents of the <embed> element. The nested elements would look like this:

```
<object data="videoFile.avi" type="video/avi"
            height="##" width="##" >
     <embed src="videoFile.avi"
            height="##" width="##"
            autostart="true" loop="false" >
</embed>
</object>
```

11

As in the preceding code, you can use the height and width attributes to specify the display size for your video. Keep in mind that for your average visitor, the larger the display, the poorer the quality. Thus, you need to keep your height and width attributes to a reasonably small size. In the preceding illustration, the values for those attributes were set to 200×200 pixels.

Add Video with <embed>

The third alternative for embedding video on a page is Netscape's <embed> element. This element is similar to <object>, but you need to use some different attributes. Instead of the data attribute, you use the src attribute to point to the video file. Also, with <embed>, you don't need to use the type attribute. If you want the video to start automatically, use autostart="true". If not, make the value false. Also, a value of loop="true" causes the video to loop endlessly. False permits the video to loop only a single time. Use the following code to insert a video clip on a page with the <embed> element:

```
<html>
    <head>
        <title>Use &lt;embed&gt; for Video</title>
    </head>
    <body>
        <embed src="myvideo2.avi"
                height="200" width="200"
                autostart="true" loop="false"  >
        </embed>
        <h1>This video was added with the<br />
            &lt;embed&gt; element.</h1>
    </body>
</html>
```

The preceding options work well, provided you are using only very short video clips. If your clips will run even 15–30 seconds, however, your visitors may become very impatient waiting for them to download. For long clips—audio or video—you need to look into streaming media.

Add Streaming Audio and Video

Putting audio and video on your site presents a number of problems, the most serious is download time. Even short clips can result in fairly large file sizes. For example, the four-second clip used early in this chapter still came out to almost 100K. That's twice the recommended size for your entire page.

You can see how audio and video can slow your site down significantly. What is the solution? Streaming media. With streaming media your visitors can watch or listen to your files as they download. Are streaming files difficult to create? Not at all. Expensive? Definitely not. (Some of the best software for creating streaming media is freeware.)

What is the downside, then? Primarily that your Web host must be able to support streaming media, and not all currently do. If you spend a little money and invest in Apple's QuickTime Pro, you don't even have to worry about that. In any case, you shouldn't have to search long to find a server that supports streaming audio and video. With its increase in popularity, more and more Web hosts are upgrading their services to support streaming media.

If you want to provide streaming content on your site, a program such as Helix Producer 9 enables you to create the files you need. You can record your own sound with a microphone, plugged directly into your sound card. You can also input an audio through the sound card's line input jack with a CD, cassette, or even record player. If you have a video capture card, you can do the same with video input. After you have recorded your file, Helix Producer 9 converts it into a special format that is suitable for streaming. It even creates a special Web page to serve as the link to your streaming file. The wizards built in to the program enable you to easily and quickly create streaming audio or video files. When you save the file, the program uses the .rm extension, marking them out as RealMedia files.

When you have created your files and uploaded them to your Web server, you need to put a special link into your page to help it find the file. This is similar to linking to an external audio or video file, with one exception: You must create a special document and link to it. The document (also known as a *metafile*) serves as a pointer, directing the browser to your streaming file. Just create a blank file in Notepad or another text editor and type in the full URL for the file you are going to link to.

For example, say you converted video of your Hawaii vacation to RealVideo and saved it as hawaii_trip.rm. When it's uploaded to your server, the URL might be something such as http://www.cheapinternethost.com/hawaii_trip.rm. You simply type that line—and nothing else—into your text file and save it with a .ram extension—the filename could be *hawaii.ram*. Then simply link to the .ram file. When visitors click it, their browsers will launch a special "plug-in" that plays a streaming video of you enjoying Hawaii's sun and surf. The following code demonstrates how such a link might look:

```
<html>
   <head>
      <title>Streaming Video</title>
   </head>
   <body>
      <a href="hawaii.ram">Check out
         my Hawaiian vacation</a>
   </body>
</html>
```

Streaming media is the way to go if you plan to use a lot of audio and video files on your site. However, be sure that you have plenty of storage space on your Web server. Those files are large, and if you have very many, you might find yourself running out of storage space.

11

Quick Reference: Audio and Video

We live in a world dominated by audio-visual media. Movies, television, radio, CDs, videos, DVDs, video games, and, yes, the Internet are all a part of our media culture. As a result, the temptation to at least experiment with audio and video to your Web pages may be too great to resist. However, keep in mind that audio and video can drastically slow down your pages. If you are merely creating a personal Web site for your own use and enjoyment, then don't worry about it. Be creative and have a blast! On the other hand, if you are creating your site for business purposes, or if you are working as a Web developer for other people's sites, consider carefully whether audio-visual media will genuinely contribute to the site. If its only reason for being there is that it looks "cool," you may be better off leaving it out. In any case, here's a summary of how to add audio and video files to your Web pages:

To Do This	Use This
Link to an external audio file	`<a href="audioFile.wav">Link</a>`
Link to an external video file	`<a href="videoFile.avi">Link</a>`
Embed an audio file with `<object>`	`<object data="audioFile.wav" type="audio/wav" height="##" width="##" autostart="true"> </object>` (autostart="false" if you don't want the audio to start automatically)
Embed an audio file with `<bgsound />`	`<bgsound src="audioFile.wav" loop="#" />`
Embed an audio file with `<embed>`	`<embed src="audioFile.wav" autostart="false"` (or true) `height="##" width="##"> </embed>`
Embed a video file with *dynsrc*	`<img dynsrc="videoFile.avi" />`
Embed a video file with `<object>`	`<object data="videoFile.avi" type="video/avi" height="##" width="##" > </object>`
Embed a video file with `<embed>`	`<embed src="videoFile.avi" height="##" width="##" autostart="true"` (or false) `loop="false"` (or true) `> </embed>`

Chapter 12

Make Your Pages Come Alive with Animation

How to...

■ Understand GIF animation

■ Create and use GIF animations

■ Embed a Java applet

■ Add scrolling and blinking text

■ Understand vector graphics and Flash

■ Understand how to use animation

In the last decade, the World Wide Web has been swept by a whirlwind of change. Beginning with simple, linked text documents, it has seen the addition of graphics, sound, video, and more. The Web experience of the new millennium promises to be one of dynamic interactivity. Some of the most dramatic additions have been in the area of animation. Beginning with simple GIF animations and moving on to more exotic creations made with Macromedia's Flash technology, it is now possible to create a very "lively" Web site. However, be cautious in your use of animation. It is very easy to cross the line from interesting to annoying.

Create and Use GIF Animation

For many years, the animation workhorse of the Web has been GIF animation. If you've ever made a "flip-book" animation by drawing several sequential pictures (say, of a horse galloping), and then flipped through them quickly, you have a pretty good idea of how GIF animations work. GIF animations are simply a collection of GIF images organized in successive frames and combined into a single, animated image file.

Understand GIF Animation Tools

If you read Chapter 6, you already know that GIF stands for *Graphics Interchange Format,* a graphics format developed by CompuServe. GIF animations are easy to create and, if properly optimized, can be fairly small files. However, to create GIF animations, you do need graphics software capable of creating GIF images and animation software to assemble the animation. For suggestions on graphics software, see Chapter 6. Table 12-1 provides a list of a few of the possible software choices for creating animations. As you can see, most of these programs are in the $30–$40 range and can be downloaded as free demos.

Program	Publisher's Web Site	Approximate Cost
CoffeeCup GIF Animator	www.coffeecup.com	$30
Ulead GIF Animator	www.ulead.com	$40
Animagic GIF Animator	www.rtlsoft.com	$30
GIF Movie Gear	www.gamani.com	$40
Jasc Animation Shop (also comes bundled with PaintShop Pro)	www.jasc.com	$50

TABLE 12-1 GIF Animation Software Choices

There are three basic steps to making your own GIF animations. First, you must use a graphics editor to create the individual pictures' frames that will make up your animation. Second, use animation software to assemble the animation. Finally, you must optimize the animation. By *optimizing,* you reduce the file size as much as possible so it doesn't take too long for the animation to load onto your visitor's computer. After the animation has been created, you insert it in your Web page just as you would any other image.

Create Frames for an Animated Banner

The types of animations you could create are limited only by your imagination. However, on the Web GIF, animations are used most frequently for banners, buttons, icons, animated links, and so on. Although it is beyond the scope of this book to explore the details of how each of these might be created, it will be helpful for you to work through the steps of creating an animated GIF. For this exercise, you will create an animated banner. You will need to use a graphics editor capable of saving in the GIF format. If you want to create the banner as you work through the chapter, you should download a GIF program (see Table 12-1). The images that follow were created with Paint Shop Pro 6. CoffeeCup GIF Animator is used later in this chapter to animate the images.

To create an animated banner, follow these steps:

1. Start with a banner-sized blank frame. Open your graphics program and create a blank document that is 468 pixels long × 60 pixels high. Save the blank banner as *banneranim.gif.* It should look like this:

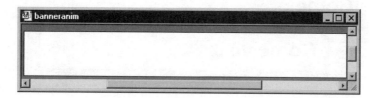

12

> **TIP** *The standard banner size for use on the Web is 468×60 pixels. If you plan to create banners for exchanges and advertising, always use these dimensions unless instructed otherwise.*

2. Select File | New and create another image with properties and dimensions identical to the first. (Or choose Edit | Copy, then paste a new picture.) A second blank frame identical to the first should appear on the screen.

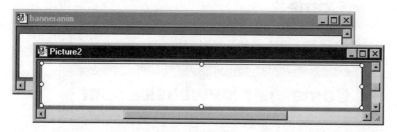

3. Use a text tool (generally represented as a capital letter on the image editor's toolbar) to add some text to your second frame. Click the Text tool for a Text Entry window to come up. Choose a font and color, set it at 26 points, and type **Come**. Your text should appear inside the banner (with some programs you might have to position the text). Save the image as *banneranim1.gif*. The following illustration shows what your second frame might look like:

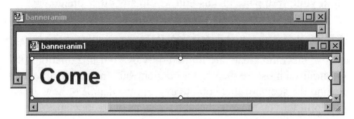

4. Repeat the preceding process, this time copying your second banner and pasting it as a new image. You now should have three banner frames in your window.

5. Using the text tool, add the word **visit** to your third banner frame. Position it and save this frame as *banneranim2.gif*. You've created three frames so far.

6. Create another frame by copying and pasting banneranim2.gif as a new image. Use the Text tool to add these words: **Mywebsite.com**. When you have positioned the text, save the image as *banneranim3.gif*. You now should have four frames, each adding to the previous one.

7. Now, to add a little color, copy and paste banneranim2.gif (the next to the last) as a new image. Select the text tool and click inside the banner. When the text entry box appears, change the color of Mywebsite.com. Depending on your graphics program, you might not have to retype the text. Be careful to position the text in exactly the same place as in banneranim3.gif. Remember to use the Zoom and Grid features of your image editor to help you position the letters accurately. If you don't, the letters will appear to move when the animation runs. While you may want that for some animations, for this one you simply want the text to appear to be changing color.

You have created the frames that will become your animation. Although this is a fairly simple animation, you can make it more complex by adding more frames. For example, you could have it spell the message out letter by letter, or you could use a series of pictures. Keep in mind, though, that the more frames you add, the larger your final file size will be, which in turn makes your animation take longer to load and slows the overall process of page loading. As you'll see later, there are steps you can take to optimize your file, but first you must create the animation.

Create a GIF Animation

You have created the raw materials for your animation, but now you need a way to combine and play them. A low-cost GIF animator does the job nicely and requires very little expertise on your part. The animation in the following illustrations was created with CoffeeCup Software's GIF Animator, but you can just as easily use a program listed in Table 12-1.

TIP *Most graphics software, such as PhotoShop Elements and Paint Shop Pro, include GIF animation programs as part of their total package.*

12

CoffeeCup's GIF Animator gets you up and running quickly with an Animation Wizard. Select File | New to bring up the wizard, then follow these steps:

1. Check the box that instructs the software to use the size of the first image for the entire animation. This automatically sets the frame size of all the images to match the first one.

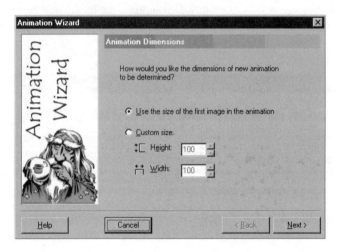

2. The second dialog box offers a choice of either a Transparent or Opaque background. Select Make The Animation Transparent.

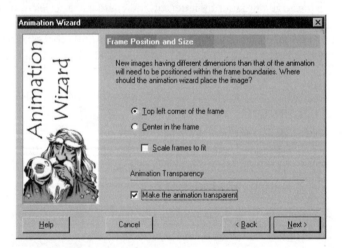

3. This box also deals with options that are necessary if you are using frames of different sizes and dimensions. Because all the frames in this animation have the same dimensions and are identical in size, you don't need to make any adjustments. Accept the default options by clicking Next.

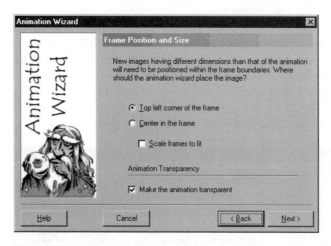

4. The next dialog box contains two very important options. First, you can either allow the animation to loop indefinitely or set it to run for a certain number of loops. As with the <blink> element, an endlessly looping animation can become very distracting, particularly if the person who is visiting your site plans to stay there a while. Set the animation to loop about five times and stop. Its purpose is to draw attention to the banner; several cycles should do it. Of course, there might be times when a continuous animation is warranted— but be sure it's necessary before you do it. The second option is for determining the amount of time between frames. The number you choose here should depend largely on the kind of animation you are trying to achieve. If you are doing a cartoon-type animation and you want to create the illusion of movement, you must use more frames and rotate them fairly quickly. For the kind of animation you are doing here, slower is better. Set the animation for 25 (¼ of a second). Click Next to move to the next dialog box.

12

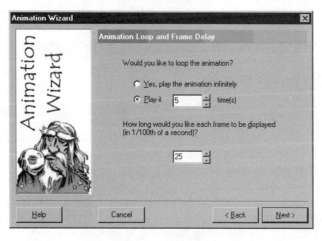

A motion picture runs at 24 frames per second (fps). Video moves at about 30 frames per second. For the Web, 15 fps is plenty fast.

5. Now you can add the files for your animation. Click Add Image in the dialog box and open the directory where you saved the frames you created earlier. Click the files you created in the order you want them to appear. You can insert the files as many times as you want. For example, banneranim3 and banneranim4 are repeated at the end, followed by the original blank frame. This will cause the color to change back and forth on the "Mywebsite" letters a few times; then the frame will blank out before the animation begins again. Click Next to move to the next dialog box.

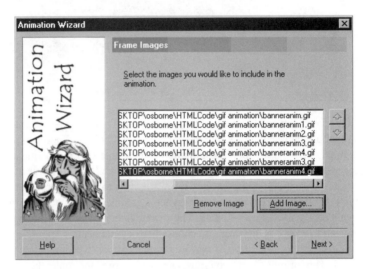

6. After the files are added, click Finish; the program will assemble the animation for you. It will display in a small window in which you can view your animation frame by frame. There also is a button on the toolbar that enables you to play the animation.

When you push the Play Animation button on the toolbar, the program plays back your animation. You can make adjustments, add new frames, and so on, working with the animation until it is exactly what you want.

Select the Preview in Browser option in the GIF Animation dialog box, and you will see a sample of your animation displayed. For the animation created with CoffeeCup's GIF Animator, you can preview it in the software itself. The following illustration shows the animated banner "running" in CoffeeCup's GIF Animator:

After you have viewed your animation and are satisfied with it, you are ready to optimize and save it.

Optimize Your GIF Animation

Animations can quickly become very large. Consider the sample animation you just built. Although you created only five frames, you added some of them more than once. What if you wanted to create a sophisticated animation that displayed 15 different frames per second? For a five-second animation, your final count would then be a whopping 75 frames. That might not sound like much until you remember that that means there are 75 GIF images making up that single animation. Can you imagine adding almost seventy separate pictures on one Web page? That's basically what you are doing. Those pictures take time to download before they ever display. If you plan to use detailed animations, and you want your visitors to hang around long enough to watch them, your animations better be pretty breathtaking. However, you *can* speed things up by taking the time to optimize your animation.

Understand Optimization

Many of the techniques used to optimize GIF animations are the same as what you would use to reduce the size of a single GIF image. Of course, there are some others that are unique to GIF animations. When optimizing your animation, you might consider some of the following adjustments:

- **Reduce the number of frames.** This perhaps is the simplest solution for reducing file size.
- **Reduce the size of the animation frames.** For something with a specified size, such as a banner, this isn't always an option. However, if you can make the actual frames smaller, they will load faster.
- **Reduce the number of different colors.** The greater the color depth in your images, the bigger the file. Use as few colors as possible without degrading the quality of your image. For more information on colors, read Chapter 4.
- **Turn off antialiasing when you create the images.** Antialiasing is the way graphics programs smooth out the choppy look that occurs when pixels are used to display letters and other curved lines. It results in a better look but takes up more space. If you can get away with it and still have a good-looking image, turn this option off.

Use an Optimization Wizard

In addition to the previous steps, you can further optimize your animations by taking advantage of your animation software's optimization wizard. The software can further reduce your file sizes by using some advanced compression options. For example, to optimize the animation created earlier with CoffeeCup's GIF Animator, follow these steps:

1. With the animation file still open, select Tools | Optimize Animation. In the opening dialog box, select the Replace Current Animation With Optimized Version check box. These check boxes allow you to choose whether to create an entirely new animation or merely optimize the one you just created. Unless you have a particular reason for saving your original animation, go ahead and replace it. Then click Next.

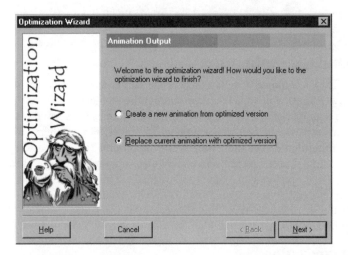

2. You see another dialog box that asks you what you want to do with the color palettes for the animation. Choose the first two options: Sort Palettes And Remove Unused Entries and Optimize All Palettes (Global And Local). This will optimize your colors. (See Chapter 6 for more about color depth in images.) Click Next to continue.

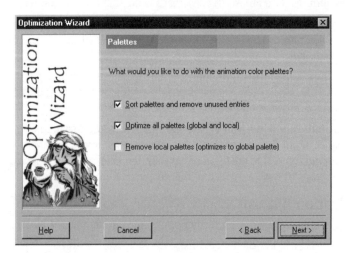

3. This box prompts you to optimize the frames by removing any unnecessary parts. Select at least the first two options, and then click Next.

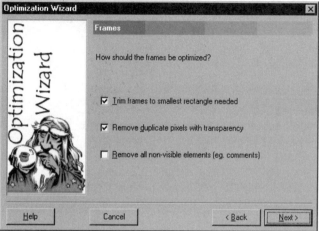

The final box shows you how much your file has "shrunk" since you began optimizing, plus an estimate of how long it will take to download. If you think the download time is too long, you can run the Optimization Wizard again and try to further reduce the size of the file. Otherwise, click Finish and save the file as *animation1.gif*.

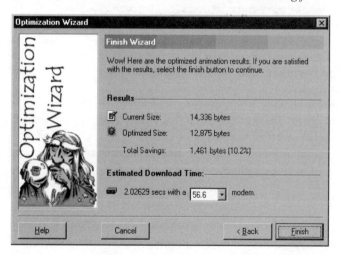

12

When your animated banner is complete, you are ready to try it out on a Web page to see how it works.

TIP

If you want to save time creating banners, Jasc's Animation Shop (bundled with Paint Shop Pro) has a banner wizard that enables you to create simple banners with nice effects very quickly.

Display Your Animation on a Web Page

Although creating an animation can be a time-consuming process, adding one to your Web page is simple. You treat it just as you would any other image. In fact, it is even saved with the same .GIF extension as a static image. To display your animation on a Web page, follow these steps:

1. Open template.htm and save it as *animation.htm*.

2. In between the <body> tags, add these lines:

```
<div align="center">
<img src="animation1.gif" width="468" height="60"
     alt="banner"/>
</div>
```

3. Use an embedded style sheet to change the background color to white:

```
<style type="text/css">
   body {background-color: rgb(100%,100%,100%)
<style>
```

Your finished code should resemble the following:

```
<!DOCTYPE html PUBLIC "-//W3C//DTD XHTML 1.0 Transitional//EN"
     "http://www.w3.org/TR/xhtml1/DTD/xhtml1-transitional.dtd">
<html xmlns="http://www.w3.org/1999/xhtml">
   <head>
     <title>Gif Animation</title>
     <style type="text/css">
      body {background-color: rgb(100%,100%,100%)}
     </style>
   </head>
   <body>
      <div align="center">
         <img src="animation1.gif" width="468" height="60"
              alt="banner" />
      </div>
   </body>
</html>
```

Save the page and open it in your browser. It should look like the following Web page illustration:

> TIP
>
> *Because you chose white as the background color for both the page and the banner, the banner disappears and the text appears to be part of the Web page. This is a nice trick for giving text a dynamic feel.*

Additional Animation Options

Although GIF animations certainly are the most frequently used on the Web, there are other ways to liven up your page that go far beyond GIF's capabilities. For example, say you want to create a slide show that uses JPEG images of your family photo album. Or perhaps you're a realtor and would like a page that displays pictures of some of the houses you're selling. Although creating GIF animations can be fun, there are other ways to liven up your page.

Project 19: Add a Java Applet

Java applets enable you to add animation and interactivity to your pages with little effort on your part. An *applet* is a "mini-program" that you place on your Web server and then embed in your Web page. When a browser loads your Web page, the applet is loaded and run on the client's (your visitor's) computer. The best thing about applets is that they are relatively easy to install, and that you don't need to know how to program in Java to be able to use them. Thousands of Java applets are available for download, and many of them are free.

After you download an applet, you can embed it on your page with either the deprecated <applet> element or the <object> element. In addition, the parameter <param /> element enables you to customize some of the applet's details. Although the HTML for adding a Java applet can become very complex, at its most basic it's not much more difficult than adding an image to your page.

Begin by opening template.htm and saving it as applet.htm. In addition, for this project you will need to download the free Java *Analog Clock* applet from Sun Microsystems' Web site. You can find it as a zip file at the following URL: http://java.sun.com/openstudio/applets/clock.html. After you have downloaded and unzipped the file, navigate to the Clock directory. There you will find another directory named Classes. Copy the four files in the Classes directory and paste them into the same directory where you saved applet.htm. Then follow these steps:

1. In between the <body> tags, add a set of <object> tags.

2. Inside the opening <object> tag, add the following attribute, which points the browser to the clock applet:

   ```
   classid="java:JavaClock.class
   ```

3. Set the size of the applet by using the width and height attributes with a value of 200 pixels each. This should also go inside the opening object tag.

4. In between the <object> tags, add the following alternate text: **Analog Clock Applet**. This text will show when the page is displayed on a browser that does not support Java.

5. Save your page and display it in your browser. You should see a clock face in the upper-left corner of the page. The time on the clock should be the same as that of your computer system.

6. After you've viewed the clock on your browser, return to the code and modify the clock's appearance with the parameter <param /> element. Most Java applets allow you to specify certain detail parameters for how the applet will display or operate. Among other things, this applet allows you to specify the applet's background color, font size, and type, as well as the color for the second hand, minute hand, hour hand, clock face, and border color. Try entering the following parameters and see how they change the appearance of the clock:

NOTE *Notice that hex code is used for the color values, and that the usual crosshatch # mark (#ff0033) is not present.*

```
<!-- Clock Font Size and type -->
<param  name="cfont"    value="TimesRoman|BOLD|18" />
<!-- Background Color -->
<param  name="bgcolor" value="000000" />
<!-- Seconds Hand Color -->
<param  name="shcolor" value="ffff00" />
<!-- Minutes Hand Color -->
```

```
<param  name="mhcolor" value="00ff00" />
<!-- Hours Hand Color -->
<param  name="hhcolor" value="0000ff" />
<!-- Clock Face Color -->
<param  name="ccolor"  value="dddddd" />
<!-- Clock Font and Border Color-->
<param  name="ncolor"  value="000000" />
```

Finally, when you've viewed the page with its default parameters, try adjusting some of them to your own tastes. Experiment with some of the color values by choosing colors from the Web Safe Color Chart in the color insert.

TIP   *The <param /> elements should be nested in between the <object> tags.*

```
<!DOCTYPE html PUBLIC "-//W3C//DTD XHTML 1.0 Transitional//EN"
    "http://www.w3.org/TR/xhtml1/DTD/xhtml1-transitional.dtd">
<html xmlns="http://www.w3.org/1999/xhtml">
   <head>
      <title>Applet Sample</title>
   </head>
   <body>
     <object classid="java:JavaClock.class"
         width="200" height="200">
       <!-- Clock Font Size and type -->
       <param  name="cfont"    value="TimesRoman|BOLD|18" />
       <!-- Background Color -->
       <param  name="bgcolor" value="000000" />
       <!-- Seconds Hand Color -->
       <param  name="shcolor" value="ffff00" />
       <!-- Minutes Hand Color -->
       <param  name="mhcolor" value="00ff00" />
       <!-- Hours Hand Color -->
       <param  name="hhcolor" value="0000ff" />
       <!-- Clock Face Color -->
       <param  name="ccolor"  value="dddddd" />
       <!-- Clock Font and Border Color-->
       <param  name="ncolor"  value="000000" />
       <p>Analog Clock Applet</p>
     </object>
   </body>
</html>
```

12

 **Use the <applet> Element**

The <applet> element has been deprecated in favor of the <object> element. However, because not all older browsers recognize <object>, it is good to be familiar with <applet>. To add the clock applet from the preceding example by using the <applet> element, your HTML would look like this:

```
<applet code="JavaClock.class" width="200" height=200>Alternate Text</applet>.
```

Parameters are added with the <param /> element the same way as with <object>.

Create a Scrolling Marquee (Discouraged)

A simple way to add animation to a Web page is with Internet Explorer's <marquee> element. Any text enclosed inside this element will scroll across the page, much the same way as a bar of text will move across your TV screen when the station wants to pass on some news without breaking into a program. Because <marquee> is proprietary, developed by Internet Explorer, only IE browsers support this element. Although Netscape 7+ now recognize <marquee>, older Netscape browsers do not. Opera ignores it entirely. Finally, because <marquee> is not part of the XHTML recommendation, its use is discouraged.

Use <marquee> to Make Text Scroll

Create a blank HTML page by opening template.htm and saving it as *marquee.htm*; then add the following line in the <body> </body> portion of the page:

```
<p><marquee>Welcome to my Web Site!</marquee></p>.
```

Save the page and view it with Internet Explorer. Your welcome line should be scrolling across the top of the page in an endless loop. Now, if you have Netscape or Opera on your computer, try viewing the page in either one or both. Those browsers will ignore the <marquee> element entirely and display the text as if it were a simple paragraph.

 While you are probably familiar with Netscape, you may not have heard of Opera. Opera is a nicely designed Web browser that is known for its speed in downloading pages. Although it costs around $40, it is also available as advertiser-supported freeware. If you're looking for an alternative to Internet Explorer and Netscape, you might want to download Opera and try it on your system. Their Web address is www.opera.com.

Modify the Marquee with Attributes

If you watch the marquee.htm page on IE very long, you will probably notice some eyestrain as you try to focus on the small moving letters. You'll also notice that your marquee's movements seem jerky. Most important, an endlessly looping string of text can become distracting to the point of being irritating. However, there are some attributes that will alter a marquee's appearance and behavior:

- **behavior=" "**   This attribute enables you to tell the browser how to scroll your text. *Scroll* (the default value) allows the text to scroll endlessly. Slide brings the text in from either the left or right side of the screen and slides it to the opposite margin. Alternate keeps the text moving between the left and right margins (as if it were bouncing off both sides).

- **loop=" "**   You can use this attribute to determine how many times you want the text to scroll, slide, or alternate. *Infinite* (the default value) keeps the text moving indefinitely. A numerical value causes the action to be performed for that number of times. For example, loop="10" will scroll the message ten times.

- **direction=" "**   With this attribute you can choose the direction in which your text will move. The values are left and right.

- **scrollamount=" "**   If the motion of the scrolling text seems too jerky, you can use scrollamount to smooth it out. Add a numerical value to represent the number of pixels you want the text to move each time. For example, scrollamount="2" will move the text a distance of two pixels each time it moves.

- **scrolldelay=" "**   The scrolldelay attribute also can be used to control the movement of the text, this time by delaying each separate movement for a specified period of time. The values for this attribute must be in milliseconds; thus, a delay of 100 milliseconds would be equivalent to one tenth of a second.

Some other attributes that can be used to modify the size and positioning of the marquee are height=" " (height of the marquee in pixels), width=" " (width of the marquee in pixels), hspace=" " (adds space on the sides of the marquee), vspace=" " (adds space above and below the marquee), and bgcolor=" " (enables you to specify a background color for the marquee).

To modify the appearance and behavior of the simple marquee created in the previous example, try the following steps:

1. Set the marquee's background color to red:

```
<marquee bgcolor="#ff0000">
```

TIP   *#ff0000 is the hexadecimal code for the color red. For more on color and hex codes, see Chapter 4.*

2. Change the direction so the text scrolls from left to right:

```
<marquee bgcolor="#ff0000" direction="right">
```

3. Let's slow down the motion of the text so it's not so hard on your visitors' eyes:

```
<marquee bgcolor="#ff0000" direction="right" scrolldelay="100"
scrollamount="2">
```

12

4. To reduce the annoyance factor, set the text to scroll across the window and stop at the opposite side:

```
<marquee bgcolor="#ff0000" direction="right" scrolldelay="100"
scrollamount="2" behavior="slide">
```

5. Just for fun, let's throw in a little style with CSS:

```
<marquee bgcolor="#ff0000" direction="right" scrolldelay="100"
scrollamount="2" behavior="slide" style="color: white;
font-family: arial; font-size: 24pt;">
```

6. Save the page as *marquee2.htm* and view it in Internet Explorer.

For a good example of why you must be careful with using <marquee>, try displaying the page in Netscape 6 or lower, or in Opera. Because neither browser supports the <marquee> element, all you will see is a line of plain text. In Opera 7, you will see nothing.

 *Netscape 7 now supports the <marquee> element.*

So why bother learning about <marquee> if the browser support is so weak? First, if it's tastefully used, you can use it to create a nice animation effect that a fair portion of visitors to your Web site will see. Second, it's a good way to learn about how irritating animation can be if it is carelessly thrown in. To see for yourself, go back into your code for marquee.htm and change the value in the behavior attribute to either scroll or alternate. You also might want to remove the scrollamount and scrolldelay attributes, allowing the text to scroll at its default speed; then load the page in IE and watch it for a while. It shouldn't take very long before you are ready to leave the page behind.

If you think that an endlessly scrolling line of text is irritating, you haven't seen anything until you've seen what results from Netscape's infamous <blink> element.

Create Blinking Text (Discouraged)

Internet Explorer has not cornered the market on obnoxious animation effects. In fact, Netscape's <blink> element has a worse reputation than <marquee> could ever have hoped for. Pick up any number of books on Web design and you'll find authors virtually pleading with you to never use the <blink> element. Do you wonder why?

Add Blinking Text with Netscape's <blink> </blink> Element

Try adding the following line to the marquee.htm page just below the line for your scrolling marquee:

```
<p style="font-size: 24pt;">This is a sample of
<blink style="color: red;">red, blinking text.</blink>
```

Save the page as *blink.htm* and view it in your browser. You will need to use Netscape to see the blinking text, as neither IE nor Opera support the <blink> element. As with the previous example, just watch the page for a little while if you want to get a feel for how annoying constantly blinking text can be.

Whereas the <marquee> element can at least be modified to make it less objectionable, <blink> takes no attributes. The only thing you can do with it is make the text blink on and off—endlessly. Are you beginning to understand why so many Web authoring and design books preach against using it?

Add Blinking Text with CSS

Despite the <blink> element's capability to irritate most Web surfers, for some reason the capability to create blinking text was included in the CSS recommendation. So, instead of using <blink> to create the effect, you can write a style rule that will do it. To see it work, add the following line to blink.htm:

```
<p style="text-decoration: blink; color:blue;
font-size: 24pt;">
This is a sample of blue blinking text,
done with CSS</p>
```

However, even using CSS, you will not find much more browser support. Internet Explorer does not support blinking text in either CSS or with the <blink> element, although Opera and Netscape 7 do.

Use Downloadable GIF Animations

Suppose you want to use some GIF animations on your site, but you have neither the time nor the inclination to do your own. What then? Are you left out in the cold with a static, immobile Web site? Not in the least. As with almost any other Web resource out there, you can find a host of animated GIFs (many of them free of charge) just waiting for you to download and insert on your page. Table 12-2 provides a list of some of the sites where you can find ready-to-use animations.

NOTE   *If you visit some of the sites mentioned in Table 12-2, you'll notice that GIF animations are sometimes referred to as GIF89a animations. This refers to the "version" of the GIF format that supports animation. An earlier version, GIF87a, did not support animation.*

Resource	URL
GIF Animations for Free Download	www.webdeveloper.com/animations
Espresso Graphics	www.espressographics.com/gif
Club Unlimited Animated GIFs	www.clubunlimited.com
GifsNow.com	www.gifsnow.com
GIFAnimations.com	www.gifanimations.com
Cool Archive	www.coolarchive.com
GIF Animation on the WWW	http://members.aol.com/royalef/gifanim.htm

TABLE 12-2   Sources for Animated GIFs

12

As good as GIF animations can be, at their best they still leave something to be desired. They are necessarily small and limited in scope. If you find that GIF animations seem too choppy or simplistic for your tastes, and you desire something "flashier," *scalable vector graphics (SVG)* is what you want to explore.

Understand Flash and Shockwave Animation

Although you might never have heard of vector graphics animation, if you've spent any time on the Internet recently, you've undoubtedly seen it. When you load a Web page and a smooth, professional-looking graphical animation greets you—and you feel as if you're watching a movie or TV program—you've probably just come face to face with vector graphics animation. The best known of these are Macromedia Shockwave and Flash animations.

Macromedia Shockwave and its somewhat less intricate sibling Flash are too complex to deal with in detail here. Also, the software is a bit pricey for the casual user (more than $300 for Flash). Macromedia Director, which produces Shockwave files, is considerably more expensive. However, lower-priced software such as CoffeeCup Firestarter is making Flash technology available to a broader audience. What makes Flash appealing is its ability to create very sophisticated animation yet maintain a reasonably small file size. However, even though Flash animations have relatively small file sizes, they still can take a long time to load. If you design a *splash page* for a Web site that takes two minutes to download to a user's machine, you need to ask yourself if your animation is so compelling that an average visitor would be willing to kill two minutes waiting for it to come up. If you are interested in experimenting with Flash animation, you can download a fully functional demonstration copy from Macromedia's site at www.macromedia.com, or if Macromedia's software is out of your price range, go to Coffee Cup Software and download a demo copy of the lower-priced CoffeeCup Firestarter at www.coffeecup.com.

Principles for Using Animation

In this chapter you have learned how to create several different types of animation and add them to your Web pages. Should you? When you decide to use animation in a Web page, you tread the very thin line between making your site attractive and making it gaudy.

What Is a "Splash" Page?

A *splash page* is an introductory page that functions somewhat like a book cover. It tends to be artistic in nature and then gives way to the site's main or index page. Many splash pages use sophisticated animation to act as a welcome mat to the Web site. However, because nearly 50 percent of Internet access is still done through slow, dialup modems, you might want to think twice before making your visitors wait for an artistic splash page to load.

There are certain givens about human beings. One of them is that people tend to be irritated by things that repeat endlessly. Think of that dripping faucet in the kitchen or the too-loud ticking of the clock on your wall. How about a neon light right outside your bedroom window, blinking on and off all night? What about your neighbor's dog, which has been barking incessantly since two in the morning? Do you get the idea?

There is nothing more irritating than visiting a Web site that is loaded down with images that are constantly blinking, flashing, changing colors, or scooting about the page. It's like trying to read a book with 20 people shouting in your face. Eventually you say, "Enough already. I'm outta here."

That's generally what visitors will say to a Web site whose designer is in love with animation. There's nothing wrong with animation—just keep the irritation factor in mind when you use it. You can do that by remembering some of these principles:

- Limit your use of animation. The purpose of animation is to attract the visitor's attention. If you have 10 or 15 different animated GIFs on each page, all you'll succeed in doing is driving your visitor crazy.

- Don't allow animations to loop endlessly. When you create them, set them to run about four, maybe five, times. That should be enough to draw a Web surfer's attention.

- If you create Flash animations, make sure that they are not so large that your visitors have to wait a long time for them to download.

- If you want to use <marquee>, use it with the slide value. That will allow your text to slide onto the page, making a nice entrance without making people feel as if they're staring at a theater marquee.

- Please, please don't use the <blink> element.

Quick Reference: Adding Animation

Animation is tricky to use but, if done tastefully, can enhance your site. Animated GIFs are the simplest and most common forms of animation on the Web. However, you can also add animation through Java applets and Flash animation. HTML animations such as <marquee> and <blink> are discouraged because they are presentational elements. In the transitional world of XHTML 1.0, they are discouraged; in the strict world of XHTML 1.1 and even stricter world of XHTML 2.0, they are not permitted. The following table lists some of the basic code you will need to add animations to your Web pages:

To Do This	Use This
Add an animated GIF	`<img src="animation.gif" />`
Add a Java applet with <object>	`<object classid="java:applet.class" width="##" height="##"> </object>`
Add a Java applet with <applet> (deprecated)	`<applet code="applet.class" width="##" height="##"> </applet>`
Add parameters to an applet	`<param name="name" value="value" />`
Add a scrolling marquee (discouraged)	`<marquee>Text</marquee>`

12

To Do This	Use This
Control a marquee's behavior	`<marquee behavior="value">` (values are `scroll`, `slide`, or `alternate`)
Control a marquee's direction	`<marquee direction="value">` (values are `left` and `right`)
Control a marquee's speed in pixels	`<marquee scrollamount="value">` (value in pixels)
Control a marquee's speed in milliseconds	`<marquee scrolldelay="value">` (value in milliseconds)
Create blinking text with <blink> (discouraged)	`<blink>Blinking Text</blink>`
Create blinking text with CSS	`selector {text-decoration: blink}`

Chapter 13

All About Image Maps

How to...

- Understand image maps
- Map different shapes
- Create a client-side image map
- Create an image map with mapping software

Have you ever visited a Web page and found a single picture that contained multiple links? Maybe it was a map of the United States, or perhaps it looked like a bookshelf. Whenever you clicked on a different part of the picture, it took you to a different page. You were navigating by means of an *image map*. Image mapping is another Web design technique that looks difficult but is really easy—once you know how to do it.

Understand Image Maps

What exactly is an image map? It is a single image or graphic that has had portions mapped out and identified in your XHTML code. The mapped portions, sometimes known as *hot spots,* are linked to other Web pages. When visitors to your site click on different parts of the graphic, they are taken to different places depending on where they clicked. With careful planning, an image map can add a professional look to your Web site.

Understand Image-Mapping Terms

Creating an image map is not difficult, although it can become complex depending on how you design it. A good starting point for learning to create image maps is to become familiar with some of the basic terminology. As you work with image maps, keep these key terms in mind:

- **Server-side image maps** The original method for creating image maps, server-side image maps reside and operate on your Web host. You create the map, but the Web server actually processes it. This kind of image map is somewhat complicated to create. Also, because the work is done on the server, it can be slower to respond. The W3C recommends that you use client-side image maps instead.

- **Client-side image maps** A client-side image map resides and operates on your visitor's computer. You write the code for the map and include it in the XHTML for your page. Client-side image maps are faster, reduce the load on the server, and are easier to create. This chapter focuses on creating client-side image maps.

- **Hot spots** A hot spot is a portion of an image that has been mapped and linked to another page. When visitors click on a hot spot, they are taken to the new page.

- **Coordinates** You use coordinates to map out the portions of your image that you want to turn into hot spots. The coordinates are simply numbers that are associated with the pixels used to create the image. Coordinates always begin at 0,0 at the upper-left corner of an image and increase in number toward the lower-right corner. (The horizontal coordinate comes first; vertical comes second.)

- **Shapes** You can map coordinates in three basic shapes: circles, rectangles, and polygons. Circles and rectangles are self-explanatory. Polygons include complex shapes that won't fit into the preceding definitions.

Understand Image Map Elements

As you might expect, there are special XHTML elements for both server-side and client-side image maps. By becoming familiar with each of these elements, you can demystify the process of creating your own image map. The image map elements are as follows:

- **<map> </map>** Defines a client-side image map on your Web page.
- **<area />** Used for specifying the coordinates of hot spots in client-side image maps. You use one <area /> element for each hot spot on the image. Note that <area /> is an empty element.
- **<img />** Used element to specify the image you want to use for your image map.

Understand Image Map Attributes

A number of different attributes come into play when you construct an image map. These do everything from assigning a special name for your map to laying out the coordinates for your hot spots. The image map attributes are as follows:

- **ismap** This attribute is used with server-side image maps. Even though this chapter does not discuss how to create server-side maps, as you will see later, the ismap attribute can prove useful in helping you identify the coordinates for your hotspots.

13

How to ... Understand Coordinates

If you're having trouble with the concept of coordinates, think of the game Battleship. There is a grid mapped out into squares with numbers along the vertical axis and letters along the horizontal axis. To fire at an opponent, you name a coordinate. For example, A-5 would be the first line, five squares from the left. Image coordinates work the same way, except that you use numbers for both horizontal and vertical. Coordinates of 47, 22 represent a position on an image that is 47 pixels across from the upper-left corner and 22 pixels down from the top.

- **shape**   The shape attribute is used with <area /> and can take values of circle, rect (rectangle), and poly (polygon, the default). You use it to define the shape of your hot spots.

- **coords**   The coordinates attribute is used within the <area /> element to plot the coordinates for your hot spots. The values are the pixel numbers of the coordinates, separated by commas. Circles, rectangles, and polygons all are plotted differently, as will be demonstrated later in the chapter in "Plot Coordinates."

- **name**   The name attribute works in the <map> element to assign a name by which browsers will recognize your map. You can choose whatever name you wish for your map. An easy-to-remember, descriptive term is usually the best choice. For example, for this chapter you will be working with a map named practicemap.

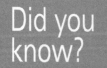

Because the name *attribute has been deprecated in XHTML 1.0 and totally removed in XHTML 1.1, the W3C recommends that you use the* id *attribute instead of* name.

- **usemap**   The usemap attribute is placed within the <img /> element and tells the browser which map to look for when applying the coordinates. The proper way to identify the map is with the name (or id) you created for it, preceded by a pound sign (#). For example, if you were telling a browser to use the practicemap mentioned earlier, you would write **usemap="#practicemap"**.

Project 20: Create a Client-Side Image Map

If you want to use a client-side image map on your page, you must either use image-mapping software or map the coordinates yourself. There are quite a few different programs available that create image maps for you and take care of writing all the necessary HTML code. These generally are inexpensive ($30–$50) and will speed up the process considerably. If you plan to do a lot of Web design and will be creating image maps frequently, undoubtedly these are the

Did you know?

What Is the Difference Between a Client and Server?

Any time you hear the term *client* in Web design, it means the computer of the person who is visiting your site. The term *server* refers to the Web server that hosts your site. When an application (such as an image map or a script) is referred to as *server-side*, it is operating on your Web host's computer. A *client-side* application is downloaded with your Web page and uses the resources of your visitor's computer. Client-side applications tend to operate faster because information does not have to pass between your visitor's computer to the server and back again. Thus, they are generally the better choice for Web authors.

way to go. However, if you are doing only a few image maps and time isn't a problem, you might enjoy the process of creating them on your own.

Choose an Image

Because image maps are used for navigation, it's important to choose or create your image with that in mind. For some reason, image maps seem to bring out the artistic side of Web authors. Although that is not a problem in itself, it can become one. If you are so artsy with your image map that visitors can't figure out your navigation scheme, you've defeated your purpose.

> **TIP**   *Choose your images carefully. Don't select a beautiful landscape for your image map just because you think it's attractive. If you are going to depend on images for navigation, they should be reasonably self-explanatory.*

Yet it's not uncommon to find many sites whose authors have decided to use image-based navigation alone, allowing the visitors to figure out the system on their own. You can avoid this by choosing or creating an image that provides a self-explanatory means of navigation. For example, say you took a wonderful summer trip through four southern states—Texas, Oklahoma, Arkansas, and Louisiana—and you want to put together a Web site that displays stories and pictures from each state you visited. You could create a simple map of the four states and make each state a separate hot spot on your image map, as in the following illustration:

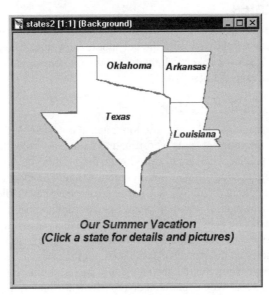

13

You can just as easily use a photograph for your image map. However, because a photo is not self-explanatory, you might want to use an image editor to add some directions for your visitors, as shown here:

 *You can use any image format that will work on a Web page. Your primary choices are GIF, JPEG, and PNG images.*

Find the Coordinates

The most time-consuming process of doing image maps is determining the coordinates for your hotspots. Depending on how refined you want the hot spot to be, you can find yourself sorting through a lot of numbers—the trick is keeping them straight. Of course, the other challenge is figuring out the coordinates in the first place.

Determine Coordinates with ISMAP

If you know the size of your image and don't care too much about accuracy, you can always determine the coordinates for your hot spots by estimating them. As a rule, though, you are going to want to be a little more precise when creating an image map. Thus you need to have some way to determine the exact coordinates of different spots on your image. The most common way of doing this is with an image-editing program (see Chapter 6 for a list of available software) or with image-mapping software. However, if you don't want to invest in either of these, there is a way to determine pixel coordinates by using your Web browser and the *ismap* attribute.

Ismap is used with server-side image maps, but it can also be used to tell your browser to display an image's coordinates on the status bar at the bottom of the screen. To do this you merely need to create an HTML page using the image you want to plot as a link. It's not necessary for the link to actually point to a real Web page. Include the ismap attribute to fool the browser into thinking the image is linked to a server-side image map. The browser will display the image's coordinates on the status bar.

Ismap should be included in the <img /> element, enclosed in a practice "link," as follows:

```
<a href="nolink.htm">
    <img alt="Coordinate shortcut"
```

```
      src="practicemap.gif" ismap="ismap" />
</a>
```

NOTE *The practice link does not really need to link to anything. It just needs to be there.*

To see this work, try typing in the following code and saving it as *coordinatemap.htm*. You can include any image file in the src=" " attribute. The image file used for the following illustration is practicemap.gif, which can be downloaded from the author's Web site at www.jamespence.com.

When you have saved your page and displayed it in your browser, move your mouse cursor over the image. You should see a set of numbers in the status bar at the bottom of the page. Those numbers should change whenever you move the mouse over the image; they should disappear entirely if you move the cursor off the image. Notice in the following illustration that the status bar lists the coordinates where the cursor is pointing as 304, 313. That means the cursor is placed at a point that is 304 pixels from the left and 313 pixels down from the top.

```
<html>
    <head>
        <title>Determining Coordinates with ISMAP</title>
    </head>
    <body>
        <p style="font-size: 14pt; text-align: left;">This is a
            trick for determining coordinates.</p><br />
        <p><a href="nolink.htm" ismap="ismap">
            <img alt="Coordinate Shortcut" src="practicemap.gif" />
        </a></p>
    </body>
</html>
```

13

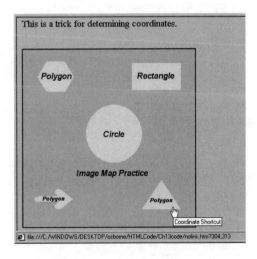

Determine Coordinates with Image Editing Software

Another way to determine pixel coordinates is with an image editor such as PaintShop Pro. All you have to do is open the image in the program, move the mouse over the image, and you will see the pixel coordinates displayed at the bottom of the screen. As with the preceding illustration, whenever you move the cursor, the coordinate numbers change. The following illustration shows what you should see when using an image editor:

Plot Coordinates

When you have a way of finding coordinates, the next step is to plot them. Plotting coordinates is simply a matter of deciding on the key portions of your image that you want to turn into hot spots. Then you determine their coordinates and write them down in a way that a Web browser can understand them. You plot coordinates differently, depending on the kind of shape you are trying to map. With a rectangle you always go from upper-left to lower-right. For a circle you begin at the center. If you are mapping a complex shape, such as a polygon, you proceed in a clockwise direction, beginning from the upper left.

Plot a Rectangle

The simplest shape to plot is a rectangle. You only need to find two sets of coordinates: the upper-left corner and the lower-right corner. Find these by putting the mouse cursor over the upper-left corner and noting the two numbers. For example, in Figure 13-1 (practicemap.gif) the coordinates for the upper-left corner of the rectangle are 221, 27. The coordinates for the lower-right corner are 320, 79.

> **TIP** *If you are using an image editor, you will find it much easier to be exact if you enlarge the image several times. The pixel count won't change and you'll greatly increase your accuracy with complex images.*

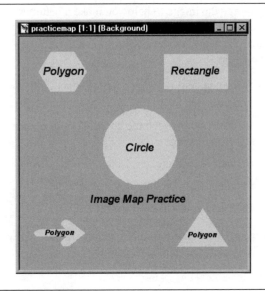

FIGURE 13-1   Practice Image Map

To plot this rectangle and turn it into a hot spot, you would write a line of code using the <area /> element along with the shape, coords, and href attributes, like this:

```
<area shape="rect"
      coords="221, 27,  320, 79"
      href="rectangle.htm" />
```

The *shape* attribute tells the browser what kind of shape to look for. The *coords* attribute gives the location of the shape. Finally, the *href* attribute provides the link that makes the shape a hot spot. Be sure to separate your coordinates by commas.

TIP   *It is not necessary to use parentheses or brackets to combine the pairs of coordinates; the browser automatically takes them in pairs. However, you might find it easier to follow your own code if you add an extra space between pairs of coordinates. The browser ignores the white space, and you'll find it easier if you ever have to go back in and edit your code.*

Plot a Circle

Plotting a circle is a little different from plotting a rectangle. Instead of going to the upper-left corner of the circle (a difficult proposition, as there is no corner), you start by estimating the circle's center. You don't need to be perfectly precise here. Just get as close as you can. Again,

13

you might find it easier to enlarge the image to help you make a better estimate. When you've eyeballed the center of the circle, note the coordinates. The next number you give will not be a pair of coordinates, but rather the *radius* of the circle.

To find the radius of the circle:

1. Place the cursor on the left side of the circle, as near the middle as possible and note the horizontal (first) coordinate.

2. Move the cursor to the right side. Watch the coordinates to make sure the vertical (second) coordinate does not change.

3. Note the second horizontal coordinate.

4. Subtract the smaller number from the larger.

5. Divide the result in half, and you will have the radius.

After you have determined the center coordinates and the radius, plot your circle like this (the first two numbers are the center; the third is the radius):

```
<area shape="circle" coords"184, 164,  57"
href="circle.htm" />
```

The coordinates in the preceding line are taken from the circle in the practicemap.htm image displayed in Figure 13-1. If you download this file from the author's site (www.jamespence.com), you will be able to practice along with the text in this chapter.

Plot Polygons

A polygon is any shape that requires multiple corners, angles, and points of reference. For example, a polygon could be something as obvious as the triangle or hexagon in Figure 13-1. It would also be the arrow in the same figure, the shapes of the four states in the vacation image, and even the outlines of the two children in the photo image map. All of these various shapes would be plotted as polygons, which is why it is the default value for the <area /> element.

To plot a polygon, use the upper-left corner as your starting point. If the image doesn't have a corner as such, choose the uppermost left point. Note the coordinates for that point and move clockwise to the next angle or corner. Also note those coordinates and proceed to the next angle until you have moved around the outside of the image and back to your starting point.

Plot a Triangle   To plot the triangle in Figure 13-1, begin at the top corner and note the coordinates: 281, 259. The coordinates for the bottom-right corner are 320, 316, and those on the bottom left are 242, 316. Now, apply those coordinates into the <area /> element like this:

```
<area shape="poly"
      coords="281,259,  320,316,  242,316,"
      href="triangle.htm" />
```

Plot a Hexagon   The hexagon in the upper-left portion of Figure 13-1 presents a slightly more complex shape to plot. If you simply remember to start at the uppermost left corner and move clockwise from angle to angle, you'll find that it's not much more difficult.

For the hexagon, beginning at the upper-left corner, the coordinates are displayed in this illustration:

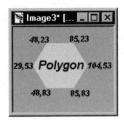

To turn the hexagon into a hot spot, take the preceding coordinates and list them in order, moving clockwise, as in the following line of code:

```
<area shape="poly"
      coords="48,23, 85,23, 104,53, 85,83, 48,83, 29,53,"
      href="hexagon.htm" />
```

Plot an Arrow Shape   The only shape yet to be plotted on practicemap.gif is the arrow in the bottom-left of the picture. Even though this is the most complicated shape you've had to deal with in this chapter, by now you should find it very easy. Begin at the upper-left corner of the arrow and plot each angle in a clockwise direction. Just as you did with the other shapes, include them in the <area /> element. The coordinates in this code come reasonably close to defining the rounded edges of the arrow. Be careful not to omit any commas, or it could throw your entire scheme off.

```
<area shape="poly"
      coords="70,275, 101,295, 74,315, 67,314,
              72,300, 26,300, 22,294, 32,288,
              70,288, 65,283"
      href="arrow.htm" />
```

13

NOTE   *It is not necessary for your coordinates to be precise unless you want the clickable area to coincide exactly with the shape on the screen. The general principle is this: The more precisely you want the shape defined, the more coordinates you need. Generally, though, you'll do fine with fewer measurements.*

Complete the Image Map

Now that you have plotted the coordinates for practicemap.gif, all you need to do to finish your image map is write the rest of the code for your page. Open template.htm and save it as *imagemap.htm*. Then follow these steps to turn practicemap.gif into a functioning image map:

1. In the <body> section of the page, insert the <map> element.

```
<body>
<map> </map>
</body>
```

2. Modify the opening <map> tag by adding the name=" " attribute, with practicemap as the value.

```
<body>
<map name="practicemap"> </map>
</body>
```

NOTE   *If you want to use the XHTML Strict DTD, or write XHTML 1.1, then you need to substitute the* id *attribute for* name.

3. Add the area elements you have already written. There should be one <area /> element for each shape you have defined, and they all should be nested inside the <map> </map> element.

```
<body>
    <map name="practicemap">
        <area shape="rect" coords="221, 27, 320, 79" <
            href="rectangle.htm" />
        <area shape="circle" coords="184, 164, 57"
            href="circle.htm" />
        <area shape="poly" coords="281,259, 320,316, 242,316,"
            href="triangle.htm" />
        <area shape="poly" coords="48,23, 85,23, 104,53,
            85,83, 47,83, 29,53," href="hexagon.htm" />
        <area shape="poly" coords="70,275, 101,295, 74,315,
            67,314, 72,300, 26,300, 22,294,
            32,288, 70,288, 65,283"
            href="arrow.htm" />
    </map>
</body>
```

4. Add the <img /> element to insert your map on the page. You also will insert the usemap=" " attribute with the name #practicemap so the browser will know the image is an image map.

```
<body>
    <map name="practicemap">
        <area shape="rect" coords="221, 27, 320, 79" <
            href="rectangle.htm" />
        <area shape="circle" coords="184, 164, 57"
            href="circle.htm" />
        <area shape="poly" coords="281,259, 320,316, 242,316,"
            href="triangle.htm" />
        <area shape="poly" coords="48,23, 85,23, 104,53,
            85,83, 47,83, 29,53," href="hexagon.htm" />
        <area shape="poly" coords="70,275, 101,295, 74,315,
            67,314, 72,300, 26,300, 22,294,
            32,288, 70,288, 65,283"
            href="arrow.htm" />
    </map>
    <img src="practicemap.gif" alt="Practice Image Map"
        usemap="#practicemap" />
</body>
```

TIP *To see how the image map really works, create five HTML pages and name them rectangle.htm, circle.htm, triangle.htm, hexagon.htm, and arrow.htm. Save them in the same directory as your imagemap.htm file. That way your links will actually take you somewhere.*

Now load imagemap.htm into your Web browser and move your mouse over each of the images. You'll notice that the status bar at the bottom of the browser window changes as the cursor goes over each different shape. If you click on each shape, it should take you to the page you created for that part of the image map.

Understand Image-Mapping Software

Although it is possible to create an image map with nothing more than a Web browser for plotting coordinates, it can be a long process, particularly if you are mapping complex shapes. Also, if you are trying to create and maintain more than one Web site, creating image maps this way is simply too time consuming. Just as HTML editors and WYSIWYG programs can make creating Web pages easier, image-mapping software can speed up the process of creating image maps.

13

NOTE *Many WYSIWYG programs, such as FrontPage, feature image-mapping software as part of the total package*

There are a number of different programs available; most are in the $20–$60 range. Although you might not feel like investing in an image-mapping program for just a few images, if you plan to do a lot of Web design and work on multiple sites, these can be great timesavers. A few of the most popular programs are listed in Table 13-1, with the URL for the publisher and an approximate price. These programs are available as trial downloads.

Image-mapping software makes your job easier by allowing you to click various portions of an image while the software plots the coordinates and writes the code for you. Some of the programs, such as MapEdit, are quite simple. Others are more complex and include the capability to add advanced features such as mouse rollovers and so on. To get a feel for working with image-mapping software, try downloading one of the sample programs and creating some complex image maps.

CAUTION *Unless you are creating a site for a closed network (Intranet), you should always provide some alternative form of navigation at the top, bottom, or sides of your page. This isn't only to accommodate those who might be using nonvisual browsers (for example, Braille and aural browsers). It's also a courtesy to those who don't want to take the time to decipher what an unclear image map might mean.*

Use Image-Mapping Software for Complex Tasks

Earlier in this chapter you saw how a simple line drawing of four states could be used as an image map. Because of the complex shapes involved, turning that image into an image map would be a tedious process. However, with a program such as MapEdit, the job is greatly simplified.

Begin the process by creating your Web page and placing your images just as you normally would. When your page design is complete, open MapEdit and begin the process of converting the image into an image map. The software will bring up a dialog box asking you to open the page you want to work on; then it will give you another box with a list of images on that page.

Image-Mapping Program	Publisher Web Site	Approximate Price
CoffeeCup Image Mapper	www.coffeecup.com	$20
MapEdit	www.boutell.com	$10
CuteMap	www.globalscape.com	$20

 TABLE 13-1 Low-Cost Image-Mapping Software

You can choose whichever image you wish to map. After the image is selected, MapEdit will bring it up in a window, as in the following illustration:

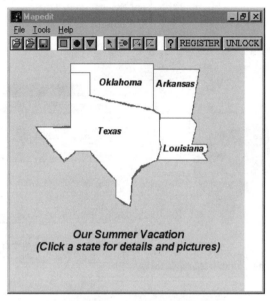

In the toolbar at the top, you can choose from a rectangle, circle, or triangle (polygon) button. Choose the polygon and then simply left-click around the borders of one state (in this case, Oklahoma). Click at each point where you want a set of coordinates fixed. When you're finished, click the right mouse button and another dialog box will appear. This one gives you options for the URL you want to link to, ALT text, advanced options for mouseovers, and so on.

13

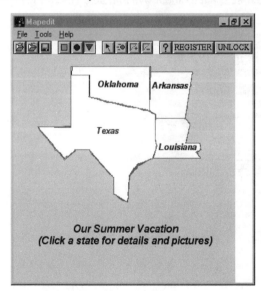

After you have clicked around the borders of all four states, MapEdit allows you to test your hot spots by selecting the arrow tool. With this button selected, when you click a hot spot it will highlight it and bring up the dialog box you filled out for that spot. This gives you the opportunity to make any edits you need before you save the image map.

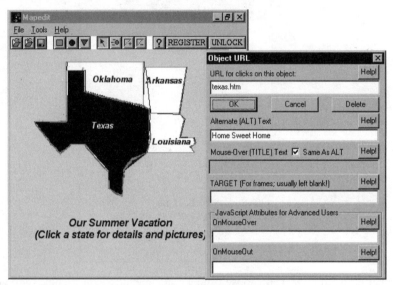

When you are satisfied with the map, links, and any other features you have added, simply click Save and MapEdit will write the HTML code that creates your image map. With complex shapes such as the ones shown here, you could easily spend a half hour or more mapping out and plotting coordinates. The software reduces the time spent to about five minutes. The following Web page is the result of a very brief session with MapEdit:

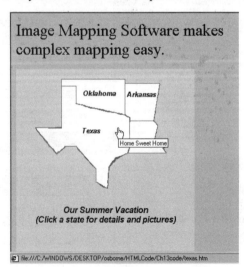

You might wonder why you should bother learning how to do image maps at all if it is so much easier with software. It's the same reason you should learn HTML even though you can create a Web page with a WYSIWYG program: You might just find it necessary to go in and fine-tune your Web pages. If you don't know how an image map works, you won't be able to "get under the hood" and work with it if you need to.

That's why some programs, such as CuteMap, display the code as the software creates it. You can see exactly what the software is doing and make adjustments on the fly, if necessary. This makes it ideal for difficult images such as the two children. You can refine your image map and make it very precise with tools such as what you see here:

Understand the Sliced Image Alternative

Although image maps can be fun to create and can give your site a professional look, you might not want to bother with them. If you are interested in having a similar look without the hassle of plotting coordinates, consider using a program that will slice a single image into several pieces and reassemble it into a seamless table. Then you can make each part of the image into a link, just as you would any other kind of image link. For more on how to slice an image and reassemble it, see Chapter 6.

You can use an image editor to slice an image into pieces, but it's more difficult to achieve precise results when the image is reassembled. It can actually take you more time to do this yourself than if you had done an image map the conventional way. If you are inclined to slice your images, you would be well advised to use an image slicer such as the one included with the CoffeeCup HTML editor (www.coffeecup.com). A sample can be downloaded along with the CoffeeCup HTML Editor as a 30-day free trial. This software slices the image and generates the HTML code necessary for reassembling it. All you have to do is paste it into your document.

Quick Reference: Image Maps

Image maps are fun to create and can give you a real feeling of accomplishment the first time you see them working on your Web site. However, that feeling of accomplishment should not be allowed to cloud some of the problems that come along with image maps. Don't allow yourself to get so carried away with the fun of creating image maps that you forget why they're on your page—to help people find their way around. Make sure that your image maps are easy to understand and always provide an alternate, text-based means of navigation. The following table will help you remember the details of creating image maps:

To Do This	Use This
Define a client-side image map	`<map> </map>`
Assign a name to your map	`<map name="mymap">` (deprecated) or `<map id="mymap">`

Specify coordinates for hotspots on a client-side image map	`<map id="mymap">`
	      `<area />`
	`</map>`

Specify the type of shape you are mapping	`<area shape="polygon" />` (or circle or rectangle)
Specify coordinates for a rectangle	`<area shape="rectangle" coords="x, x, x, x" />` Plot the coordinates for the upper-left and lower-right corners
Specify coordinates for a circle	`<area shape="circle" coords="xx, xx, xx" />` Plot the coordinates for the center of the circle (first two numbers); then do the same for the radius
Plot the radius of a circle	Find the coordinate at the middle-left side of the circle. Repeat for the middle-right side Subtract the smaller number from the larger Divide the result in half

To Do This	Use This
Specify coordinates for a polygon	`<area shape="polygon" coords="x,x, x,x, x,x, x,x "/>` Start at the upper-left point and move clockwise, plotting the coordinates at angles and direction changes
Specify the image you want to use for your image map	`<img src="image.gif" usemap="mymap" />`

Use your web browser to plot coordinates for an image map	`<a href="nolink.htm">`
	`   <img src="image.gif" ismap="ismap" />`
	`</a>`

13

Chapter 14

Add Interactivity with Forms

How to…

- Understand form elements
- Create a simple guestbook
- Create a survey form
- Use tables for form structure
- Understand CGI
- Locate and use CGI resources

If you are content with creating a static Web site, such as an online brochure or a family album, and you don't really care whether your visitors have the opportunity to respond to you, you can skip this chapter without missing much. On the other hand, if you want to enable your visitors to interact with you and respond to your site, you might want to stick around and read about XHTML forms. With XHTML form elements you can add a guestbook, put a menu on your site, add a search engine, create a survey, construct a catalog, develop an order form, and much more. Best of all, forms are easy to create—when you've sorted out the various elements involved. The process of getting a form to actually work (deliver information to you) is a bit trickier, but once you learn how to take advantage of the available resources, you'll soon be creating and using forms like a pro.

Understand Form Elements

When creating a form with XHTML, whether it's a guestbook, a catalog, an order form, or an e-mail form, you need the <form> element along with a combination of *controls*. As you would expect, the <form> element creates the form, whereas the controls determine what kind of information your visitors can send you. The kind of form you want to create determines the types of controls you choose to include in it.

Project 21: Create a Simple Guestbook Form

Before you experiment with different form controls, try creating a simple guestbook for your Web site. This form will provide a text box where your visitors can write you a note that will be e-mailed to you when they press Submit. Open template.htm and save it as *formsample1.htm*; then create a form by adding the <form> element to your code, like this:

```
<body>
   <form>
   </form>
</body>
```

If you save and view this page in your browser, you'll get a blank page. You must add the form controls before you will see anything. However, before you begin adding the controls to your form, you must include some attributes in the <form> element that tell the browser (and the server) what to do with the data your visitors type in. To do this, use the action and method attributes.

Understand the action Attribute

The action attribute tells the browser where to send information in the form. Most of the time it tells the browser to use a *Common Gateway Interface (CGI)* program to process the data. (The CGI program then sends the information to you—it's the information handler.) CGI is covered later in this chapter, so you needn't be too concerned with it at this point. For now, just keep in mind that for a form to work, you must store a CGI program on your Web server.

Because we haven't covered CGI in detail yet, for this exercise you will use the mailto: protocol as your action. This tells the browser to e-mail the contents of the form directly to you. This isn't really the best way to handle form data, although it is unquestionably the easiest. Because not all browsers allow you to use the mailto: protocol for form processing, if you plan to use a lot of forms, you will want to learn how to use CGI scripts. However, mailto: is a great tool for learning how to work with forms. To add the action attribute and mailto: protocol to your form, modify the opening <form> tag to read as follows:

```
<body>
   <form action="mailto:my_e-mail@my_server.com">
   </form>
</body>
```

Why Do You Need CGI?

Did you know?

14

If you want your form to work, you need to use a CGI program because XHTML is not a programming language. XHTML is a markup language that was created to structure documents and enable them to be shared easily. To process data, you need more programming power than XHTML has. CGI programs usually are written in Perl or some other programming language and pack a little more punch than XHTML. If you know how to program, you can write your own CGI programs (usually called *scripts*). If the idea of programming causes you to break out in hives, don't despair. Plenty of CGI scripts are available online and many are free of charge. Later in the chapter, you'll learn how to incorporate a pre-written CGI script into a form. Check out the table at the end of this chapter for sources of ready-to-use CGI scripts.

Once you've specified the action, you're almost ready to begin designing your form. However, before you begin adding buttons, menus, and text boxes, you must tell the browser how to handle the data it receives. To do this, add the method attribute to the opening <form> element.

Understand the method Attribute

Whereas the action attribute tells the browser where to send the information collected from a form, the method attribute tells it how to send it. You have two possible choices (values) with this attribute: *get* or *post*. The get value simply tacks the information on to the end of the URL where the information is to be sent. Post sends the information separately to the specified location. Each method has its pros and cons; for the most part, you will want to stick with post.

To add the method=" " attribute to your sample form, modify the opening <form> tag as in the following listing:

```
<body>
   <form action="mailto:my_e-mail@my_server.com"  method="post">
   </form>
</body>
```

Use Tables to Add Structure to Your Form

Before you begin adding controls, you will want to define some type of structure for your form. Although the table element is not supposed to be used for layout purposes, it remains the easiest way to give structure to your form. Using tables enables you to create a balanced and dependable layout for your form. If you skip this step, your form's appearance will be at the mercy of every browser that displays it—and often will turn out looking pretty ragged.

TIP *If you are going to use a table to structure your form, you might find it helpful to sketch your table layout on a piece of paper before you write your code. You also might find it helpful to put an x inside each of the table cells to get them to display before you add your form elements.*

To insert a table inside your form, simply nest a set of <table> tags in between the <form> tags; then create whatever cells you need to give the form the design you want it to have. The following code creates a simple four-row single-column table to contain your guestbook form:

NOTE *Some other presentation adjustments have been made by using the <style> and <div> elements. These are in bold type, along with the table elements you will be adding.*

```
<!DOCTYPE HTML PUBLIC "-//W3C//DTD XHTML 1.0 Transitional//EN"
"http://www.w3.org/TR/xhtml1/DTD/xhtml1-transitional.dtd">

<html xmlns="http://www.w3.org/1999/xhtml">
```

```
<head>
   <title>Forms Sampler</title>
      <style type="text/css">
         body     {background-color: white;}
         table    {background-color: aqua;}
      </style>
</head>
<body>
   <div align="center">
      <p style="font-size: 2em">Sample Guestbook Form</p>
      <form action="mailto:my_e-mail@my_server.com"
          method="post">
         <table>
            <tr><td> </td></tr>
            <tr><td> </td></tr>
            <tr><td> </td></tr>
            <tr><td> </td></tr>
         </table>
      </form>
   </div>
</body>
</html>
```

Add Controls to Your Guestbook Form

For a simple guestbook form, you need only a few controls: an input line for your visitor's name, a text box for a brief note, a Submit button, and a Reset button. As you add these controls, you will be learning the basics of using the <input> element and its numerous attributes. The <input> element enables you to create a form specifically suited to your needs. Along with input, you will use the type attribute to tell the browser what kind of controls to display.

Add Lines of Text with <input type="text" />

To add lines for text input (for names, addresses, and so on), use the <input /> element with the type="text" attribute. Input is an empty element, so you don't need to include a closing tag. (Don't forget to put the slash at the end of the tag.) The type attribute specifies the type of control you want to place in the form. By choosing text as a value for the type attribute, you are telling the browser to create a small, one-line text box.

You can tell the browser how many characters to accept by adding the size attribute and supplying a number. For example, a value of 40 allows a visitor to input 40 characters. The id attribute is used to assign an identifying name to the information that the user inputs. This is the name by which the information will be identified when it is relayed to you. When you create your form, choose the values you put in the id attribute carefully so you won't have difficulty understanding or sorting your data. And remember that each id value may be used only one time. IDs are like fingerprints; no two should be alike.

To add a text input line for visitors to insert their names, modify the table in your guestbook form to look like the following code listing:

In HTML, you would use the name attribute to assign an identifying name to user input. However, because the name attribute is deprecated in XHTML 1.0 and dropped entirely from XHTML 1.1, you are encouraged to use id instead of name. Keep in mind that every id must be unique.

```
<tr><td>Please sign my guestbook.</td></tr>
<tr><td>Name: <input type="text" id="visitor-name"
                      size="15" maxlength="30"/></td></tr>
```

If you want a text window to accept more characters than it actually displays, use the maxlength attribute. For example, if you set a text box to read size="15" maxlength="30", only 15 characters will display. However, your visitor will be able to enter up to 30 characters.

Add a Text Box with <textarea>

The next item your guestbook will need is a larger text box for your visitors to use when writing comments about your site. Although you could do this with a text line as in the preceding example, a text line would not allow your visitors to view more than one line at a time while they wrote their messages. Therefore, instead of using the <input /> element with a type="text" attribute, you will use the <textarea> element.

The <textarea> element allows you to create a larger working space for your form data. You tell the browser how large to make the text box by using the rows=" " and cols=" " attributes. For example, if you want to display a text box with 10 rows and 45 columns, you would add the attributes as in the following listing:

```
<textarea id="message" rows="10" cols="45"> </textarea>
```

Notice also that even though <textarea> has a closing tag, it functions as an empty element. Nothing goes in between the two <textarea> tags. All the information necessary to create the text area goes inside the opening tag.

After you have added your text box, you must create a way for your visitors to send you the information they have entered. Also, you must provide them with a way to clear the form and start over—just in case they don't like what they've written. You do this by adding Submit and Reset buttons.

Add Submit and Reset Buttons with <input />

Creating buttons for your forms is easy. As you'll see later in the chapter, you have quite a bit of room for creativity when you put buttons into your forms. However, if you just want to add

Submit and Reset buttons, you can do it simply by using the <input /> element with the type attribute set either to submit or reset. You can add these buttons to your guestbook by modifying the bottom data cell in your form/table to read like the following listing:

```
<input type="submit" /> <input type="reset" />
```

TIP   *You can add white space between your buttons by adding space between the <input /> elements.*

When you have added the various lines described in the preceding paragraphs, you will have a simple guestbook form that will work with many browsers. If you post it on your site and someone clicks the Submit button, it should send you the data by using your visitor's e-mail server. If you haven't done it already, try adding the form elements just described to formsample.htm. Then save and display it in your Web browser. It should look something like the illustration that follows the code listing:

```
<form action="mailto:my_e-mail@my_server.com" method="post">
    <table>
        <tr><td>Please sign my guestbook.</td></tr>
        <tr><td>Name: <input type="text" id="visitor-name"
                 size="15" maxlength="30" /></td></tr>
        <tr><td><textarea name="message" rows="10" cols="45">
                </textarea></td></tr>
        <tr><td><input type="submit" /> <input type="reset" />
                </td></tr>
    </table>
</form>
```

Sample Guestbook Form

Please sign my guestbook

Name: [   ]

[   ]

[Submit Query] [Reset]

14

 **Add a Search Engine to Your Site**

Would you like your visitors to be able to search your site and search the Web *from* your site? If so, Google provides an easy solution. Just go to www.google.com/searchcode.html and you will find three pre-written HTML forms that you can copy and paste into your own site. One form adds a simple Google search engine form. The second form is designed to provide a "safe" (that is, no pornographic or explicit content) search. The third form enables your visitors to search your site in addition to the Web search. The form code is free and can be a great addition to your Web site.

Project 22: Create a Visitor Survey

Now that you have created a simple form and have a feel for how forms work, you will want to discover the other form tools available in the XHTML toolbox. There are so many to choose from; the best way to learn how to use them is to build a form that is useful (so all this work won't be wasted) but allows you to use all the various form elements. The form that will best accomplish these goals is a visitor survey.

Plan Your Survey

A visitor survey is self-explanatory: It is nothing more than a form on your site that asks your visitors to share their opinions. For example, if you have a site devoted to cooking, you could survey your visitors about their favorite cookbooks, cooking shows, spices, recipes, and so on. You could even create a guestbook that would allow them to add recipes to your site for other visitors to use. In other words, a visitor survey can be whatever you want it to be.

For the purposes of learning to create XHTML forms, a visitor survey will allow you to experiment with most of the different form elements. The survey you will create in this project is geared toward readers and book lovers. If you want to modify the form so that it will better fit your own needs, simply change the information in the form elements to ask for different information. By modifying this form rather than merely copying the code, you'll find that you will learn how to use forms even more quickly.

The first step in creating your survey is to decide what information you want to collect from your visitors. If you are developing a survey for book lovers, you will want to obtain basic information such as names, ages, where your visitors live, and so on. You also will want to collect specific information about their reading and purchasing preferences. As you develop a list of the information you want to collect, you might come up with some of the following possibilities for a book-lovers survey:

- Your visitors' names
- Where they live

- Their ages
- Male or female, married or single
- Reading preferences (fiction or nonfiction)
- Fiction genres (mystery, romance, thriller, historical, and so on)
- Nonfiction topics (computer, cooking, parenting, history, and so forth)
- How/where they buy books (online, bookstores, used books)
- Favorite authors
- Comments on their favorite book this year

You could come up with other possible options, but these will give you enough to create a form using most of the possible form elements. To begin building your form, open template.htm and save it as *formsample2.htm*. Add a set of <form> tags to create the form, like this:

```
<body>
    <form action="mailto:my_e-mail@my_address.com" method="post">
    </form>
</body>
```

Build Your Survey

There are many different ways you can structure a visitor survey; the simpler it is, the better. Arrange the elements logically so your visitors will not have to spend time trying to understand your form and what you are asking for. Also remember to use tables to help develop a pleasing layout for the survey.

Add Text Input Lines with <input type="text" />

Because you have already practiced adding a text line to your form, this part will be easy. Because you are surveying only your visitors' opinions, it won't be necessary to collect complete address information. However, you might want to at least know the part of the world where your visitors live. Thus, the first part of your form will be primarily text-input lines. Remember that to add these lines you use the <input /> element with the type="text" attribute. Add the following lines to formsample2.htm:

```
First Name: <input type="text" id="fname"
                  size="15" maxlength="20" />
Last Name: <input type="text" id="lname"
                  size="15" maxlength="20" />
City: <input type="text" id="city"
                  size="15" maxlength="20" />
State: <input type="text" id="state"
              size="2" />
Country: <input type="text" id="country"
                size="15" maxlength="20" />
```

14

TIP *As you write the code for the form, be sure to observe how each attribute functions in the <input /> element. You might even want to experiment by adjusting some of the values. The more you play with the code, the faster you'll learn how it works.*

When you save this form and display it in your browser, you will understand why most forms are laid out with tables. Simply using form elements without some way to give them structure leads to a form that works but is not visually appealing. For example, the preceding code produces a form that looks something like this:

First Name: [   ]   Last Name: [   ]   City: [   ]   State: [ ]   Country:
[   ]

When you enclose the code in a table, you can add structure and a pleasing appearance to your form. Notice how different the same data fields look when they are put into a table, as in the code listing and illustration that follow:

```
<table>
   <tr>
      <td style="text-align: left">First Name:</td>
      <td style="text-align: right">
         <input type="text" id="fname"
                size="15" maxlength="20" /></td>
   </tr>
   <tr>
      <td style="text-align: left">Last Name:</td>
      <td style="text-align: right">
         <input type="text" id="lname"
                size="15" maxlength="20" /></td>
   </tr>
   <tr>
      <td style="text-align: left">City:</td>
      <td style="text-align: right">
         <input type="text" id="city"
                size="15" maxlength="20" /></td>
   </tr>
   <tr>
      <td style="text-align: left">State:</td>
      <td><input type="text" id="state"
                size="2" /></td></tr>
   <tr>
      <td style="text-align: left">Country:</td>
      <td><input type="text" id="country"
                size="15" maxlength="20" /></td>
   </tr>
</table>
```

First Name:
Last Name:
City:
State:
Country:

Offer a Single Choice with Radio Buttons

When you want your visitors to select a single item from a list of possible choices, you'll want to use radio buttons. If you are familiar with older cars, you won't have much trouble figuring out why these controls are called "radio buttons." Old car radios usually had a series of five or six buttons for preselected stations. When you wanted to go to a favorite station, you simply pushed the appropriate button. One thing you obviously could not do with the radio buttons was to select more than one station at a time. Likewise, the radio buttons you use in a form allow your visitors to choose only one option. The following list demonstrates how a single radio button element can be constructed:

1. To add radio buttons to your form, use the <input /> element with the type=" " attribute set to *radio*.

   ```
   <input type="radio" />
   ```

2. Be sure to give all of your radio buttons the same id attribute. That's how the browser knows to associate all the choices. Because these radio buttons are used to ask your visitors' ages, the most logical value for id is *age*.

   ```
   <input type="radio" id="age" />
   ```

3. You also need to assign a value with the value element. You didn't need to do this with text boxes because your visitors add their own values when they input text. With radio buttons and other controls where *you* supply the choices, you also must add the values.

   ```
   <input type="radio" id="age"  value="31-40"  />
   ```

4. To preselect an option, add the checked attribute to one of the <input /> elements. In the days of HTML, this attribute did not require a value. All you needed to do was add the word *checked* inside the tag. However, with XHTML's stricter rules, you must add a value to the checked attribute. Although it may seem redundant, you would write it this way: checked="checked".

   ```
   <input type="radio" id="age" value="31-40" checked="checked" />
   ```

14

For example, if you want your visitors to specify their ages by choosing from a series of age ranges and want the 31–40 age range preselected, you could write something that resembles the following listing and illustration:

```
<p style="font-size: 1.1em;">Your age (choose one):</p>
13-18 <input type="radio" name="age" id="age" value="13-18" /><br />
19-30 <input type="radio" name="age" id="age2" value="19-30" /><br />
31-40 <input type="radio" name="age" id="age3" value="31-40"
          checked="checked" /><br />
41-50 <input type="radio" name="age" id="age4" value="41-50" /><br />
51-60 <input type="radio" name="age" id="age5" value="51-60" /><br />
61-99 <input type="radio" name="age" id="age6" value="61-99" />
```

TIP *The line break element, <br />, is placed at the end of each of the input elements to move the next one to a new line on your page. If you want the options to display side by side, simply omit the line breaks.*

Use Check Boxes for Multiple Choices

If you want to provide a visitor with multiple choices, you need check boxes rather than radio buttons. In the book-lovers' survey you are building, you will want to ask your visitors about their reading preferences. Obviously this is a situation in which you should provide more than one option. With check boxes, your visitors can choose as many items as they like.

To create a check box, you again use the <input /> element. However, this time you must add the type attribute with the value set to *checkbox*. As with radio buttons, if you want to preselect an item, simply add the attribute checked="checked" to the <input /> element. As in the preceding example, you need to assign the same id to all of your options. You also need to specify a value for each option. The code for a series of check boxes might look something like the following code and illustration:

```
Fiction Preferences:<br />
(Choose as many as you want.)<br />
<input type="checkbox" id="fictionpreferences"
       value="historical" />Historical<br />
<input type="checkbox" id="fictionpreferences2"
       value="literary" />Literary<br />
<input type="checkbox" id="fictionpreferences3"
       value="mystery" />Mystery<br />
```

```
<input type="checkbox" id="fictionpreferences4"
      value="romance" />Romance<br />
<input type="checkbox" id="fictionpreferences5"
      value="thriller" />Suspense/Thriller<br />
<input type="checkbox" id="fictionpreferences6"
      value="western" />Western<br />
<input type="checkbox" id="fictionpreferences7"
      value="horror" />Horror<br />
```

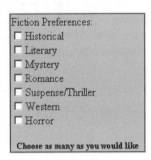

Create Pull-Down Menus with <select>

If space is a consideration or if you want to add a bit of variety to your form, you can create a pull-down menu for your visitors to choose from. These menus are easy to create, and they can function either as single choice lists (like radio buttons) or as multiple option lists (like check boxes). Although constructing pull-down menus is not difficult, the elements you use are somewhat different from those you've worked with so far.

To build a pull-down menu, use the <select> element instead of <input />. You add choices with the <option /> element and use the id=" " and value=" " attributes. To see how easy it is, add a pull-down menu to the survey that allows your visitor to select from either *male* or *female*. You would write your XHTML code like this:

```
<p>Your Gender:</p>
<select id="gender">
    <option value="male" >Male</option>
    <option value="female" >Female</option>
</select>
```

NOTE *Because Internet filters often block access to sites that use the word "sex," it's a good idea to use the word "gender" if you are asking whether a visitor is male or female.*

To create a list with several options or a list that displays more than one choice at a time (sometimes called a scrolling list), you must add the following attributes to the opening <select> tag:

■ **Size** The size attribute, with a numerical value added, tells the browser to display more than one option in the pull-down list. For example, size="4" displays four choices simultaneously.

14

■ **Multiple**   The multiple attribute allows for more than one selection to be made from the list (similar to check boxes). As with the checked attribute, you should write this as follows: multiple="multiple". Keep in mind that for your visitors to actually be able to select more than one option with a menu list, they probably will have to hold down the CTRL key while clicking. It's good to add an instruction to your form, in case they don't know how to do this.

In the sample form you are building, perhaps you want to find out where your visitors buy their books. Although you could do this with a series of check boxes, a scrolling menu also works well. By typing in the following code, you create a menu that displays five bookstores and allows the visitor to scroll down to display more. They also will be able to select more than one option because the multiple="multiple" attribute has been added.

```
<p>Bookstore Preferences</p>
<select id="bookpurchasepref" multiple="multiple" size="5">
<option value="amazon">Amazon.com</option>
<option value="bncom">bn.com</option>
<option value="bn">Barnes and Noble</option>
<option value="borders">Borders</option>
<option value="halfcom">half.com</option>
<option value="hastings">Hastings Entertainment</option>
<option value="walden">waldenbooks</option>
<option value="hpbooks">Half Price Books</option>
<option value="powells">Powells Books</option>
</select>
<p>For multiple selections, hold down the Control key while
    clicking.</p>
```

Bookstore Preferences

 In HTML, the <option> element often was used without its closing tag. Although your form will work properly if you write it this way, it's not good XHTML. For well-formed XHTML you must always use either closing tags or (in the case of an empty element) a slash at the end of the opening tag, like this: <empty_element />.

Give Your Form Structure with a Table

Now that you have designed your form controls, create a simple table to give the form some structure. Your table should have six cells arranged in two rows with three cells each. After you have created the table, follow these steps:

TIP   *Give your table a border (border="1") to make it easier for you to visualize your layout.*

1. In the first cell (top left), nest the table you created for name and address info.

2. The second cell (top center) should hold the radio buttons for Age information.

3. Place the Fiction Preferences check boxes in the third cell (top right).

4. The fourth cell (bottom left) should hold the Male/Female drop-down menu.

5. Place the Bookstore Preferences controls in the fifth (bottom center) cell.

6. In the sixth cell (bottom right), add a Submit and Reset button so that your form can be submitted or cleared.

When you have finished, your completed form should resemble the following illustration. If you are having difficulty getting your form to match the illustration, the complete code for the form is reproduced in the Quick Reference section at the end of this chapter.

14

The form controls you have covered thus far in this chapter are those you will use most often. They will enable you to create virtually any kind of form you need. However, there are some other controls that enable you to add more specialized functions to your form.

Use Special Form Controls

The following form controls enable you to add password boxes to a form, create customized buttons, and much more. You might not use these all the time, and some of them (such as the password box) require a script to make them work, but it's good to have them in your form-designing arsenal:

■ **<input type="password" />** By using the password value with the <input /> element, you can create a password input field. If you've spent more than five minutes on the Web, you have encountered a password field. What makes it distinctive is that the characters typed in are masked to keep your password secret. An asterisk (*) displays for each character entered.

```
<input type="password" size="10" />
```

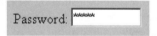

> NOTE   *Just using the password field does not mean you will have a password-protected or -encrypted page. You also need a CGI script to accomplish that task. The password field merely works with the script to help get the job done.*

■ **tabindex** If you've filled out forms on Web pages, you've probably discovered that you can move from field to field by using the TAB key. What you might not know is that, as a form designer, you can tell the browser in which order you want your visitors to be able to tab through your forms. By inserting the tabindex attribute in each field and adding a numerical value, you can set the priority for your form fields. To see how this works, put the following code inside a set of form tags, save the page as *tabindex.htm*, and then tab through the fields:

```
First name: <input type="text" id="fname"
                    tabindex="1" size="10" /><br />
Last name: <input  type="text" id="lname"
                    tabindex="3" size="10" /><br />
Mother's name: <input type="text" id="momname"
                    tabindex="5" size="10" /><br />
Father's name: <input type="text" id="dadname"
                    tabindex="4" size="10" /><br />
Cat's name: <input type="text" id="catname"
                    tabindex="2" size="10" /><br />
```

First name: FIRST
Last name: THIRD
Mother's name: FIFTH
Father's name: FOURTH
Cat's name: SECOND

■ **type="hidden"**   There will be times when you need to add hidden fields to your forms. These cannot be seen or altered by your visitors, and generally they are used to provide necessary information to the CGI program on your server. You do this by using the <input /> element with the type attribute set to hidden.

```
<input type="hidden" />
```

■ **type="image"**   If you want to be creative with your forms and use images as buttons, one way you can do it is with the type="image" attribute. Used with the <input /> element, this attribute allows you to convert any image into a clickable button.

```
<input type="image" src="mybutton.gif" id="surprise" />
```

■ **type="button"**   You can create a more conventional-looking custom button with the type attribute set to the button value. This creates a generic button that has no function itself. However, as you'll see in Chapter 15, you can assign functions to the button with JavaScript or other scripting languages.

```
<input type="button" value="CustomButton" id="surprise2" />
```

The text that displays on the face of the button is created with the value *attribute.*

TIP

14

■ **<button>**   The newest (and preferred) way to create buttons is with the <button> element. With this element, you can convert images and even text to buttons. By using the type attribute, you can assign a value to your buttons that allows them to function as

Submit or Reset buttons, or (as with the preceding example) to respond to script-related functions.

```
<p><button value="button"><img src="mybutton2.gif" />
     </button></p>
<p>(This is a generic button created with the
     button element<br />and with mybutton2.gif.)</p>
<p><button value="submit">This is a submit button<br />
   created with the button element.</button></p>
<p><button value="reset">This is a reset button<br />
   created with the button element.</button></p>
```

(This is a generic button created with the button element and with mybutton2.gif.)

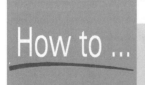

Thus far you have learned how to create a form, how to tell the browser what to do with it, and how to add form controls. Then you saw some special form elements in action. All along, you've been working to build a survey form that collects information from your readers. However, at this point your form is about as useful as a car without an engine. It might look nice, but it won't actually do anything. If you want your form to work, you have to venture from the safe and comfortable harbor of XHTML into the uncharted waters of CGI.

How to ...   Use PayPal to Receive Payments Online

If you are planning to set up an online business, you will want to provide a form for your customers to send payment online through a credit card, debit card, or bank draft. If you've investigated online payment processors, you've probably found that accepting credit cards online can be an expensive proposition. An inexpensive, but secure, alternative is to use PayPal. Now a part of eBay, PayPal is rapidly becoming the primary solution for online payment processing. After you sign up for a free PayPal membership (www.paypal.com), you can click on the Merchant Tools tab, which takes you to a page where you can copy and paste the form code to channel your payments through their server and into your merchant account. For their fee, PayPal takes a small percentage of each payment you receive through them.

Make Your Form Work with CGI

What is CGI and why do you need it? CGI stands for the *Common Gateway Interface,* a fancy name that describes another protocol. If you remember from Chapter 5, a protocol refers to how information is exchanged on the Internet. CGI is a protocol that deals with the exchange of information from your visitor's Web browser (the client) to your Web host (the server) and, ultimately, to you (the Webmaster). The best way to understand why you need CGI is to learn what CGI does.

Understand CGI

As was mentioned earlier in this chapter, XHTML is wonderful, but is limited in its scope. Even though XHTML can collect information through forms, it was never intended to process that information. For that, you need a program (generally called a *script*) that resides on the Web server in a special location (usually what's known as a *cgi-bin*). When a visitor (client) fills out your form and clicks Submit, the information on the form is sent by the client browser to your cgi-bin, where the script processes the data and sends it on to you, usually by e-mail. The script can be written in one of several different programming languages, but usually it's done in a language called Perl. Is this beginning to sound complicated? It can be. That's why some beginning Webmasters might want to consider alternatives to using CGI.

Consider Alternative Form Processing

If you want to collect information from your visitors but don't want to deal with the headaches of using the Common Gateway Interface, there are some alternatives. Unfortunately, they all tend to have their own problems. Some possible ways to avoid CGI include the following:

- **Avoid forms altogether.** If your site does not depend on collecting information from your visitors, don't worry about CGI. Remember, just because you *can* do something with XHTML doesn't mean you *have* to do it. Forms are like any other element of Web design: If you don't need them, don't bother with them.

- **Use the mailto: protocol.** At the beginning of this chapter you learned how to have form data e-mailed to you with the mailto: protocol. The main drawback to this approach is that not all browsers support it. Thus, you might exclude some of the visitors who want to use your forms. Another issue is security. When someone sends you information this way, they reveal their e-mail address to you. In these security-conscious days, people

14

are increasingly hesitant to allow personal information to be revealed to someone they do not know. The following illustration shows the prompt that comes up when a visitor clicks Submit on a mailto: form:

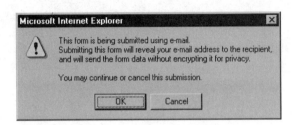

■ **Locate a form-processing service.** If you are willing to pay a fee, there are services that will handle your forms for you. In this case, all you have to do is link to them, and all the form processing is handled from their end. If forms are a must for you, you might consider this an option. You can find them by doing a simple search on Google or another search engine using the keywords "form hosting." Table 14-1 lists some free and fee-based form-processing services you might want to explore.

If these options don't sound appealing to you or if you just like a challenge, put on your waders and step into the sometimes-intimidating waters of the Common Gateway Interface.

Understand CGI Form Processing

If you already know how to program and can understand how to work in Perl or a similar language, you're way ahead of the game. However, knowing how to program isn't absolutely necessary as long as you know what kind of script you need, where to look for it, and how to

Form-Processing Service	URL
My Secure Form (If you need a secure or encrypted form server)	www.mysecureform.com
Response-o-Matic Free Form Processor	http://response-o-matic.com
fireDancer TECHNOLOGIES	www.firedancer.com/services/formhosting.html
TipJar Generic Form Handler (Free)	www.tipjar.com/generic.html
FormSite.com HTML Form Builder	www.formsite.com
DBApp	http://server.com/siteapps/dbapp/index.html
i-Depth	www.i-depth.com
Bummer Form Hosting	www.bummerforms.com/index.shtml
CGISpy.com	www.cgispy.com/info/feedback.shtml
DataTrend Software CGI Scripts	www.datatrendsoftware.com/cgi.html

TABLE 14-1   Form Processing Services

implement it. So if the thought of CGI and programming in Perl makes you break out in a cold sweat, relax. You don't have to *write* the script; you just have to find it and install it.

Find a Script

To figure out what kind of script you need to make your form work properly, you must ask yourself what you want the form to do. Is it a guestbook form? If so, you need to look for a guestbook script. Is it an online catalog or order form? Look for a shopping cart script. Is it a survey or general information form? If so, you will want a simple form script.

There are many sources for free CGI scripts on the Web. Although these scripts are generally copyrighted, most of the time the only requirement is that you leave the header portion of the script (which contains information about the author) untouched. Others might not want you to make any modifications to the script (other than what is necessary to make it functional for your pages). A handful of the sources for CGI scripts are listed in Table 14-2.

NOTE   *There are many different kinds of CGI scripts. As you explore some of these script archives, you might decide to have some fun experimenting with more than just form processing.*

When you have found the script that meets your needs, download it and unzip it (if necessary). Depending on the kind of script you are going to use, you might find that you have been given a CGI script, written in Perl (filename.pl), perhaps one or two HTML files, and usually a *ReadMe* file. The ReadMe file has the instructions you need to get your script up and running. When you have sorted out your files, you are ready to begin phase two of your CGI experience: configuring the script.

Script Source	URL
The CGI Resource Index	www.cgi-resources.com
Dream Catchers Free CGI Scripts	www.dreamcatchersweb.com/scripts/
ScriptSearch.com	www.scriptsearch.com
Free CGI	www.free-cgi.com/freecgi/index.asp
Free-Scripts	www.free-scripts.net
Matt's Script Archive	www.scriptarchive.com
FreeScripts.com	www.freescripts.com
BigNoseBird.com	www.bignosebird.com
TuCows	www.tucows.com (Search for "cgi scripts")
Free Dynamic CGI Scripts	www.websitestop.com/dynamic

TABLE 14-2   Online Sources for CGI scripts

14

Configure Your Script

Obviously, a generic script is not likely to fit your form perfectly. After you have downloaded your script, you will need to tailor it to meet the needs of your form. In some cases (as with a form script), you might also need to tweak your XHTML file, or copy the code from the file you downloaded into your own page. It all depends on what your script needs to work properly.

Because every script is different, and your forms and Web accounts will be unique to you, it's difficult to give precise instructions for configuring a script. That is why the ReadMe file included with your script is essential to setting it up properly. You also might need to contact your Web host to find out about how to use CGI on its server.

Another part of the configuration process that might or might not be necessary is that of adjusting the form, guestbook, and so on, to meet your needs. Often the scripts you download are zipped files that include the basic Web pages you need to execute them. However, you probably will prefer to custom-tailor the Web page to fit the look of your site. Most of the time that can be done by either modifying the page directly, cutting and pasting the relevant code into one of your own pages, or by linking the page to a style sheet you have created. After you have done that, you can turn a plain form page into a customized page that fits the look of your site, as in the illustration that follows:

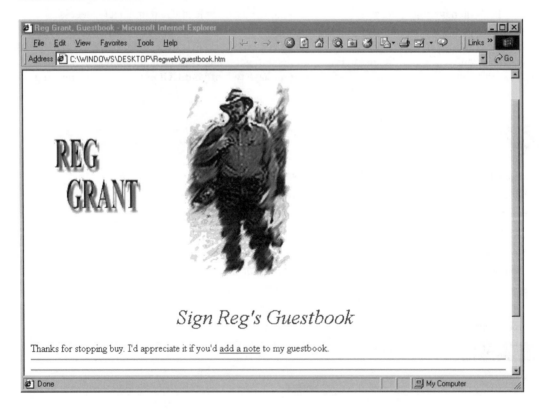

Not All Web Hosts Support CGI

Because CGI raises some security issues, some servers do not support it. It's important to check with a prospective Web host to learn whether you will be allowed to use CGI. For example, Yahoo Geocities free server does not allow you to use CGI scripts. If forms and other server-side applications will be important to your site, be sure to find out whether you can use CGI before you commit your funds to setting up a site on a particular server.

Upload Your Files

When you have configured your script (and your form, if necessary), the next step is to upload the files to your server. This is the easiest part of the whole process. You use your FTP program just as you would for any of your other Web pages. All you need to remember is that your CGI script needs to go into the cgi-bin directory, and that you should put the other files in the location you specified when you configured the script.

Change Permissions

Perhaps the most confusing—and scary—part of using some CGI scripts is that you might have to change some of the security settings for the files on your server. For example, with a guestbook program it is necessary to configure the server to allow your visitors to leave messages that will be added to a Web page. That means that people who visit your site are given permission to write information onto your server's hard drive. Are you beginning to grasp the security implications? What if someone with a little know-how decided it would be fun to make some modifications you (or your server) had not planned on? That is why not all servers allow you to use CGI. If you need to change permissions (and, remember, not all CGI scripts require it), you can contact your server's technical support to find out exactly how to go about it.

 CGI guestbooks are easy targets for spammers who load your pages with phony comments and links pointing to commercial—and often pornographic—sites. Unless you plan on checking your guestbook regularly (that is, every few days), you might find it better to use the mailto: *protocol for guestbook entries and then post them to your Web site yourself.*

Test Your Form

After you have configured your files, uploaded them, and made any changes to the file permissions, you are ready to test your form. Log on to your site, fill out your form (or guestbook), and press Submit. Hopefully, you won't receive an error message; instead you'll be celebrating the first successful addition to your Web site's guestbook.

14

Quick Reference: Forms

HTML forms enable you to add interactivity to your page. With a form you can create surveys, guestbooks, e-mail pages, order forms, and so on. The basic form elements and attributes are included in the following table. Because form construction and design can be very involved, you might want to sketch out your form on paper before trying to build it. If you do have problems or receive an error message, re-read the ReadMe file that came with the CGI script or contact your server's tech support. Generally the problem is simple and can be solved without much difficulty.

To Do This	Use This
Create a form	`<form> </form>`
Tell the browser how to handle the content	`<form method="post">` (or "get")
Tell the browser what to do with the content	`<form action=" "> </form>` (You can use the mailto: protocol or refer to a CGI script)
Create an email form with the mailto: protocol	`<form method="post" action="mailto:me@myemail.com"> </form>`

Create an input field	`<form>`
	`    <input />`
	`</form>`

Add a unique id to an input field	`<input id="unique-id" />` Remember: IDs are like fingerprints; no two should be alike
Specify a value for an input field	`<input value="xxxxx" />`
Choose the order in which fields may be tabbed through.	`<input tabindex="1" />` (Numeric value indicates the order in which a user can tab through fields)
Use an image for a button	`<input type="image" src="image.gif" />`
Create a custom button	`<input type="button" value="button-text" />`
Create a button with the `<button>` element	`<button value="button-text"> </button>` Note: This element generally requires a script to assign it a function
Create an image button with the `<button>` element	`<button value="button"><img src="image.gif" /></button>`
Create a Submit button	`<input type="submit" />`
Create a Reset button	`<input type="reset" />`
Create a radio button	`<input type="radio" />`
Pre-select a button	`<input type="radio" checked="checked" />`
Create a check box	`<input type="checkbox" />`
Create a hidden field	`<input type="hidden" />`

To Do This	Use This
Create a password field	`<input type="password" />`
Create a pull-down menu	`<select> </select>`
Allow multiple choices in a pull-down menu	`<select multiple="multiple"> </select>`

Add menu options	`<select>`
	`    <option> </option>`
	`</select>`

Preselect an option	`<option `**`selected="selected"`**`>` This is preselected`</option>`
Add a text input area	`<textarea rows="#" cols="#"> </textarea>`

Code for Project 22

Creating forms can be a rather complex task. If you're having difficulty getting your form to match the illustration for Project 22, the complete XHTML code for the project is reproduced here. Compare your code to the following to see if you can track down the problem:

```
<!DOCTYPE html PUBLIC "-//W3C//DTD XHTML 1.0 Transitional//EN"
"http://www.w3.org/TR/xhtml1/DTD/xhtml1-transitional.dtd">
<html xmlns="http://www.w3.org/1999/xhtml">
    <head>
        <title>Sample Survey</title>
        <meta http-equiv="Content-Type"
            content="text/html; charset=iso-8859-7" />
    </head>
    <body>
        <form action="mailto:my_e-mail@my_address.com"
            method="post">
<!-- Begin Name and Address Info -->
        <table border="1" style="text-align: center">
            <tr>
                <td>
                    <table>
                        <tr>
                            <td style="text-align: left">
                                First Name:</td>
                            <td style="text-align:right">
                                <input type="text" id="fname"
                                    size="15" maxlength="20" /></td>
                        </tr>
```

14

```
                    <tr>
                    <td style="text-align: left">
                        Last Name:</td>
                    <td style="text-align:right">
                       <input type="text" id="lname"
                         size="15" maxlength="20" /></td>
                    </tr>
                    <tr>
                       <td style="text-align: left">City:</td>
                       <td style="text-align: right">
                          <input type="text" id="city"
                            size="15" maxlength="20" /></td>
                    </tr>
                    <tr>
                       <td style="text-align: left">State:</td>
                       <td style="text-align: right">
                           <input type="text" id="state"
                              size="2" /></td>
                    </tr>
                    <tr>
                       <td style="text-align: left">
                           Country:</td>
                       <td style="text-align: right">
                          <input type="text" id="country"
                             size="15" maxlength="20" /></td>
                    </tr>
                  </table>
              </td>
<!-- Begin Age Fields -->
                  <td><p style="font-size: 1.1em;">
                       Your age (choose one):</p>
13-18 <input type="radio" name="age" id="age" value="13-18" /><br />
19-30 <input type="radio" name="age" id="age2" value="19-30" /><br />
31-40 <input type="radio" name="age" id="age3" value="31-40"
                    checked="checked" /><br />
41-50 <input type="radio" name="age" id="age4" value="41-50" /><br />
51-60 <input type="radio" name="age" id="age5" value="51-60" /><br />
61-99 <input type="radio" name="age" id="age6" value="61-99" />
                  </td>
<!-- Begin Fiction Preferences -->
                  <td style="text-align: left">
                     <p>Fiction Preferences</p>
```

```
<input type="checkbox" id="fictionpreferences"
        value="historical" />Historical<br />
<input type="checkbox" id="fictionpreferences2"
        value="literary" />Literary<br />
<input type="checkbox" id="fictionpreferences3"
        value="mystery" />Mystery<br />
<input type="checkbox" id="fictionpreferences4"
        value="romance" />Romance<br />
<input type="checkbox" id="fictionpreferences5"
        value="thriller" />Suspense/Thriller<br />
<input type="checkbox" id="fictionpreferences6"
        value="western" />Western<br />
<input type="checkbox" id="fictionpreferences7"
        value="horror" />Horror<br />
                </td>
            </tr>
<!-- Begin M-F Menu -->
            <tr>
                <td><p>Your gender:</p>
<select id="gender">
   <option value="male" >Male</option>
   <option value="female" >Female</option>
</select>
                </td>
<!-- Begin Bookstore Preferences -->
                <td>
                    <p>Bookstore Preferences</p>
<select id="bookpurchasepref" multiple="multiple" size="5">
   <option value="amazon">Amazon.com</option>
   <option value="bncom">bn.com</option>
   <option value="bn">Barnes and Noble</option>
   <option value="borders">Borders</option>
   <option value="halfcom">half.com</option>
   <option value="hastings">Hastings Entertainment</option>
   <option value="walden">waldenbooks</option>
   <option value="hpbooks">Half Price Books</option>
   <option value="powells">Powells Books</option>
</select>
   <p>For multiple selections, hold down the Control key while
   clicking.</p>
                </td>
                <td>
```

14

```
<input type="submit" /><br />
<input type="reset" /><br />
                </td>
            </tr>
        </table>
    </form>
  </body>
</html>
```

Chapter 15

Improve Interactivity with JavaScript

How to...

- Understand scripting languages
- Write a script that identifies your browser
- Write a script that displays the date and time
- Add a "Last Modified" line to your page
- Understand events and event handlers

Have you ever gone to a Web site and noticed that part of the site changed when your mouse cursor moved over it? No doubt you have. Have you ever filled out a form incorrectly and had it "kicked back" to you with a request for additional information? Maybe you've hit a site where the Web page told you what kind of browser you were using and suggested a different one. Did you ever wonder how it knew? Chances are it was all done with JavaScript.

Understand Web Page Scripting

Although you can accomplish much in the area of Web design with XHTML, many of the exciting things that make Web sites come alive are far beyond XHTML's scope. Even with the added power of Cascading Style Sheets, you are still bound by XHTML's limitations as a markup language. Because it is not a programming language, XHTML cannot enable you to do much more than create static Web pages. If you want to create pages that your visitors can interact with, or pages that change dynamically, or even pages that are generated on the fly, you'll need to give XHTML a shot in the arm. Although there are many ways you can do this, one of the best—and most popular—places to start is with JavaScript.

Before you begin working with JavaScript, you'll find it helpful to understand a little about Web page scripting. Chapter 14 introduced the term *script* when dealing with the Common Gateway Interface (CGI). If you read that chapter, you might have noticed that sometimes the text referred to a CGI program, whereas other times it was called a CGI script. Although sometimes the two terms are used interchangeably, there is a distinct difference between a program and a script.

> TIP
>
> *For more information on JavaScript, check out the following online resources:*
> *http://javascript.com*
> *www.webreference.com/js*
> *http://devedge.netscape.com/library/manuals/2000/javascript/1.5/guide*

A script is a program, but it differs from other types of programs in that it cannot stand on its own—you can't download a script and run it on your computer like you can a spreadsheet, word processor, or computer game. For a script to function, it must work hand-in-hand with another application (such as a browser).

The CGI script mentioned in Chapter 14 is a *server-side* script. That means it remains on and works through your Internet server's computer. JavaScript is used for *client-side* scripting. This type of script works on your visitor's (the client's) Web browser and uses that computer to process information. How does it get to your visitor's computer? It is either downloaded as part of the Web page (like an inline or embedded style sheet) or can exist on your server as a plain text file that the browser reads whenever necessary (like an external style sheet).

Scripts Speed Information Processing

Why are scripts useful? For one thing, because they operate on your visitor's computer, they can speed up the processing of information. For example, say you have a catalog and an order form on your site, and you want your visitors to see a tally of their orders before they submit them. You could do this using a CGI script, but then the browser would have to send the information to the server. After it had the data, the server would have to process it and then send it back to your visitor's computer. All that takes time.

With a client-side script, all that processing can be done on your visitor's computer without the need to send anything to the server, which saves your visitor time and might result in a happier customer. Additionally, not only can scripts speed things up, but they can make your pages more interesting, too.

Scripts Add Interactivity

Buttons that change when a mouse moves over them, pictures that display when your cursor hovers over a link, Web pages that seem to "talk" to your visitor—all this and more is possible when you use a script. How is this interactivity accomplished? It is done largely with *events*. What, exactly, is an event? Basically, an event is something that happens; however, in Web page scripting, the term means a lot more than that. An event is something that happens on your visitor's browser. For example, when they move their mouse cursor over a button, that's called a *mouseover* event. When the cursor is removed from the button, that's called a *mouseout* event. When an event occurs, it can be used to activate an *event handler*. An event handler is what you use to program your page's response to certain events.

Web page scripts enable you to anticipate different events and use event handlers to plan a response. The event acts like a trigger, causing the event handler to spring into action and do whatever you told it to. For example, for a mouseover event, you would use the onMouseover event handler. Likewise, for the mouseout event, you would use the onMouseout event handler. Sound pretty complicated? Perhaps the best way to see how these work is by a little experimentation.

NOTE   *There are many more event handlers than onMouseover and onMouseout. Later in this chapter you will find a chart listing all the event handlers.*

15

To see an event handler in action, try writing a simple script using the onClick event handler. Open template.htm and save it as *clickevent.htm*, then follow these steps:

1. Create a button with the <input /> element and type="button" attribute.

```
<input type="button" />
```

2. Put some text on the button itself. You do this with the value=" " attribute. With a button, you now have a possible "event" on the page.

```
<input type="button" value="Trigger an Event" />
```

3. Add an event handler—in this case it will be onClick. By using this event handler, you are telling the browser that something is to be done whenever the button is clicked.

```
<input type="button" value="Trigger an Event" onClick=" " />
```

4. Tell the browser what to do when the event occurs. For this illustration you will tell it to bring up an alert box with a message.

```
<input type="button" value="Trigger an Event" onClick="alert('Good Job!');" />
```

 Whereas HTML is very forgiving, scripting languages are not. If even a quotation mark is out of place, you will receive an error message. Some things you need to watch for will be covered later in the section "Avoid Common Errors in Coding." For now, make sure you copy the code exactly as written.

After you have put the preceding line of code (from Step 4) on your page, save it and display it in your browser. You should see a button in the upper-left corner of your screen that reads "Trigger an Event." When you click the button, an alert window should pop up with the message "Good job!" as in the following illustration:

The creative use of events and event handlers enables you as a Web author to add a dimension to your pages that simply is not possible with HTML alone. However, speed and added interactivity are not the only benefits of using a scripting language. A Web page script also can extend HTML's capabilities.

Scripts Can Give HTML a Boost

As a markup language, HTML is essentially limited to creating a document and defining its structure. For example, as demonstrated in Chapter 14, you can collect data with an HTML form but for the form to actually do anything with the data it receives, you need a CGI script. However, Web page scripting can give HTML a boost by extending some of its capabilities. For example, you can use a script to validate a form (make sure it has been correctly filled out) before it is sent off. If your visitors fail to fill out one of your required fields, they'll receive a prompt that encourages them to try again, as shown next.

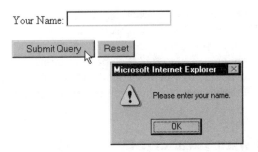

Scripts Have Their Disadvantages

There are certain disadvantages inherent in Web page scripting. First, scripting languages are considerably more complex than HTML or even CSS. Remember, even though they are limited in their application, scripting languages are programming languages—which implies that if you plan to write your own scripts, you will have to think (and write) like a programmer. In other words, you will need to think step-by-step through the task that you want the script to accomplish and then choose the appropriate commands to bring about the desired results. You can avoid this problem by using prewritten scripts. However, even with these you'll need to understand the script well enough to debug it if you have a problem.

Another disadvantage of scripting is that a script can interfere with a search engine's capability to *index* your site. Many search engines use automated programs that browse your site and index it according to the words they find near the top of the document. A large script, placed in the <head> </head> portion of your page, can skew the results because it will have a lot of text that is unrelated to the purpose or subject of your site.

> **TIP** *If you decide to use scripts and want to avoid problems with search engines, save them as text documents (myscript.txt) and link to them. You'll learn how to do this later in this chapter, in the section "Link to an External Script."*

Also, some older browsers do not support Web page scripts. Thus, your page can suffer doubly when such a browser loads it. The script will not run and, if the script is in the <body> of the page, the browser will ignore the <script> tags and treat the script as text to be included in the Web page. The results are not very attractive, as is shown here:

```
function CheckForName() { if (document.Name.fname.value < 1){alert("Please enter your name.");}}

Your Name: [                    ]

[ Submit Query ]   [ Reset ]
```

Another disadvantage with scripts is that your visitor is not required to make use of them. This is just another reminder to you as a Web author that you do not have ultimate control over how your page is displayed when it arrives on your visitor's browser. Visitors can turn off images, specify their own fonts and colors, use their own style sheets, and even disable JavaScript if they want to. Thus, if you have a page that is heavily dependent on scripts and someone visits you with their browser's script option set to "off," your page's functionality might suffer.

All things considered, you are likely to find Web page scripting to be a useful addition to your Web authoring toolbox. It enables you to accomplish many things on your site that you couldn't do otherwise. With that in mind, by now you might be wondering which scripting language you should use.

Project 23: Work with JavaScript

Although JavaScript is not the only language to choose from, it is without a doubt the best supported. The other alternatives are VBScript, which is based on Microsoft's Visual Basic programming language, and JScript (Microsoft's counterpart to JavaScript). However, because JavaScript is supported on all the major browsers (Internet Explorer, Netscape, and Opera), it should be your language of choice.

Although it is beyond the scope of this book to teach you to program in JavaScript, it is possible to give you a chance to experiment with it. By doing so you will at least develop a feel for how Web page scripts work and what you can do with them. To begin with, you need to know how to include JavaScript in your Web page properly.

Add a Script to a Web Page

As with Cascading Style Sheets, there are multiple ways to put a script into a page. Sometimes a script can be included as part of an HTML tag and other times as part of the <body> of the page. A script also can be placed in the page's <head> portion or saved as a separate text file and linked to the page. If your script is going to be inline or embedded, you will need to use the <script> element to identify it and to let the browser know not to display it as part of the page. Try adding a script with the script element by opening template.htm, saving it as *js1.htm*, and following these steps:

1. Type the opening <script> tag.

```
<script>
```

2. Add an opening HTML comment tag just below the <script> tag.

```
<script>
<!--
```

3. Add the *language* attribute to identify what scripting language you are using. In this case, it will be language="Javascript".

```
<script language="Javascript">
<!--
```

4. Add the *type* attribute to give the MIME type for the scripting language you will be using. For JavaScript, you will write type="text/javascript".

```
<script language="javascript" type="text/javascript">
<!--
```

5. Add a closing comment tag.

```
<script language="javascript" type="text/javascript">
<!--
-->
```

6. Type the closing </script> tag.

```
<script language="javascript" type="text/javascript">
<!--
-->
</script>
```

7. Insert a line of script on the line between the comment tags.

```
<script language="javacript" type="text/javascript">
Your line above has "javacript" and so is missing the letter s.
<!-- document.write("My first JavaScript script");
  -->
</script>
```

Save the file and display it in your browser. As in the following screen shot, you should see a page with the line "My first JavaScript script." Not very exciting, perhaps, but it's a start.

TIP *Use comment tags (<!-- -->) to hide your script from older browsers. Browsers that do not support JavaScript will ignore the script lines, whereas browsers that do support scripts will ignore the comment tags and execute the lines.*

15

Link to an External Script

An *external* script, like an external style sheet, is a plain text file that contains a script for use on one or more Web pages. If you plan on doing a lot of Web page scripting, this is definitely the way to go, as it frees you from having to write the same script again and again. Instead, you often can write one script and then just link to it. In the following exercise you will see just how easy it is to link to an external script.

This exercise modifies your first JavaScript page (js1.htm) to include an external script that sets the background color to yellow and adds a line of text with the <h1> </h1> element. The first steps in linking to an external script are creating the script itself and saving it as a text file. You don't need to use <script> tags when writing an external script; you need only the commands that you want the browser to execute. Open Notepad, Wordpad, or another text editor and type the following lines on the blank page. Remember, you must type the lines exactly as they are here:

```
document.bgColor = "yellow";
document.write("<h1>This is from an external script.</h1>");
```

When you have typed the lines, save the file as a plain text file with the name *extscript.js*. To link to this file, first you must add the <script> element to your page. Open js1.htm and save it as *js2.htm*. The body of your page should look like this code listing:

```
<body>
    <script language="javascript" type="text/javascript">
        <!-- document.write("My first JavaScript script");
        -->
    </script>
</body>
```

To modify this code to link to the external script, add a second set of script tags. They can be placed either in the <head> or <body> portion of the page, as long as they are not inside or overlapping the other script tags. In the following listing, the additional script tags have been placed in the <head> of the page:

```
<head>
    <script language="javascript" type="text/javascript"
            src="extscript.js">
    </script>
</head>
<body>
    <script language="javascript" type="text/javascript">
        <!-- document.write("My first JavaScript script");
        -->
    </script>
</body>
```

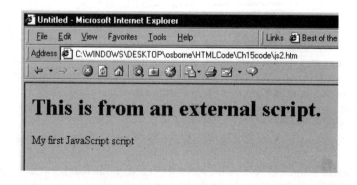

Understand Key JavaScript Concepts

When you know how to put a script on a page, you are almost ready to begin having some serious fun with JavaScript. However, before you start, it's good to nail down some of the key concepts that make this language work. With HTML you learn to work with elements, attributes, and values. In CSS you use selectors, properties, and values. With JavaScript, your primary tools are *objects, properties,* and *methods.* Understanding these concepts will take you a long way toward being able to use JavaScript. Consider the following explanations of the key JavaScript concepts:

- **Objects**   JavaScript is an *object-oriented* language, which means that when you work with JavaScript, you must think in concrete rather than abstract terms. For example, the browser is an object. The HTML page you are creating is the *document object.* If you want a new window to open, you are going to work with a *window object.* If you create a form, you will have made a *form object.* Although the hierarchy of objects is very complex, it's important to be object-oriented in your thinking so you know how to construct the commands that make your script work.

- **Properties**   A property is a characteristic of an object. For instance, in the preceding example, you set the background color of a page to yellow with the following line: document.bgcolor = "yellow";. What you did, in JavaScript terms, was modify the background color *property* of the document *object.*

- **Methods**   A *method* is an action that is taken with respect to an *object.* In previous examples, the line document.write("text"); used the method write to cause text to be written to the document object.

Now, if all this seems a bit fuzzy, perhaps a practical illustration would help. You might tell your son or daughter to wash the car. In this case, the car is the object, and wash is the method. What if you have three cars—one red, one white, and one teal—but you want only the red car washed? You throw in a property to clarify things. You tell your child to wash the red car. If you wrote the command in JavaScript, it might look like this: car.red.wash("Now!");. This might be an oversimplification, but it should help you better grasp the idea of objects, properties, and methods.

Avoid Common Errors in Coding

Writing any kind of computer code is tricky because programming languages are not at all forgiving. Be prepared to have to "debug" your JavaScript, because no matter how careful you are, errors will slip in. However, if you keep in mind some of the more common errors, you should be able to catch most of them:

- JavaScript is case-sensitive. Always make sure you are consistent in how you write and capitalize.

- Every JavaScript line should end with a semicolon (;).

- You shouldn't break up a single line of code into multiple lines. You can do this with HTML, but JavaScript will treat it as an error.

- Many parts of your code will have to be contained in quotation marks. You can use either single or double quotation marks, but if you put one set inside another, you must alternate them.

15

```
"This 'is an' acceptable construction."
"This construction "is not" acceptable."
```

If you plan to use JavaScript in your Web design, you will find it helpful to test your pages on a Netscape browser. Although both Internet Explorer and Netscape let you know when you've got an error in your code, IE merely gives you an error message in an alert box, as in the following illustration:

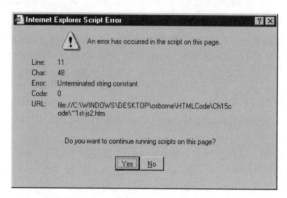

On the other hand, Netscape helps you debug the code. If you run a page that has a JavaScript error, a message on the status bar at the bottom of the browser instructs you to type **"javascript:"** in the location bar (where you normally type the Web addresses). This brings up a JavaScript console that actually shows you where the error(s) occurred.

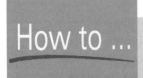 **Add Hidden Comments in JavaScript**

You've already learned how to add "hidden" or invisible comments with the XHTML comment tags: <!-- comment -->. But what if you want to add a comment to your JavaScript? You'll find that XHTML comment tags will not work for this purpose. Instead the browser will misinterpret them as code, and your script will not work. There are two ways to add comments to JavaScript. If your comment will be on a single line, then just add two slashes (//) and then your comment. If your comment will cover more than one line, then open it with a slash followed by an asterisk (/*). Close the comment by using an asterisk followed by a slash (*/). Thus your JavaScript comments will look like this: // single line comment /* multiple line comment */.

Of course, you still need to know enough about JavaScript to know how to correct the errors in your code, but at least you won't waste a lot of time trying to find them.

Project 24: Experiment with JavaScript

A good way to begin working with JavaScript is with some easy but practical applications. These will not only get you used to writing JavaScript, they will give you some useful tools for your Web pages as well. You will also gain a better understanding of objects, methods, and properties as you apply them in the following exercises.

Write a "Last Modified" Script

You have undoubtedly seen a line at the bottom of many Web pages that reads, "This page was last modified on," and then the page included the date on which the Webmaster made changes to it. You might have wondered if the Webmaster had to go in and adjust that line every time the page was changed. Actually, there is a way to have the date line correct itself automatically, and it takes only a few lines of JavaScript to do it. Open template.htm and save it as *lasmod.htm*; then add the <script> element and comment tags (<!-- -->) to the <body> portion of the page. When your code looks like the following listing, you'll be ready to add your script:

To write a one-line JavaScript that will add a "last modified" line to your page, follow these steps:

1. Because you are going to be writing to your HTML document, you will be using the document object and the write method to instruct the browser to write a line of text. Insert it in your code like this:

```
<script type="text/javascript" language="javascript">
document.write( );
</script>
```

15

2. Inside the parentheses you will put a property that causes the browser to display the date and time the document was last modified. In this case, use the document object with the lastModified property. If you save the page and view it in your browser, you will see a line at the top left of the screen that displays the date and time (of the last modification).

```
<script type="text/javascript" language="javascript">
document.write(document.lastModified);
</script>
```

CAUTION *Don't forget to write lastModified exactly as you see it. In JavaScript, when two words are put together, a capital letter is often used to distinguish where one ends and the other begins. Because JavaScript is case sensitive, your browser will not understand what you are asking for if you write lastmodified, LastModified, or Lastmodified.*

3. Because your visitors will not necessarily understand what that date and time refer to, you will want to add an explanatory note, such as "Date last changed:". To add your text, enclose it in quotation marks and put it inside the parentheses, along with your document.lastModified.

```
<script type="text/javascript" language="Javascript">
document.write("Date last changed:" = document.lastModified);
</script>
```

Save the page and display it in your browser. As shown in the following illustration, you should see a line displaying the time you saved the document (down to the very second). It might not be attractive, but you can change that by adding a little HTML.

Date last changed: 03/27/2010 14:48:36

By putting your script inside a table cell and adding a little HTML to the command, you can dress up the display. The HTML for creating such a design is in the following listing. Modify your page to include the changes, then save it as *lastmod2.htm*. As in the illustration that follows the code, your "last modified" display will look a little more pleasing.

NOTE *The line of JavaScript in the following listing has been broken into two lines because of this book's layout. However, it's important to remember that it should be written on a single line. Otherwise, the browser will think it is two separate statements and will return an error.*

```
<head>
    <title>Last Modified</title></head>
    <body style="background-color: white">
    <div align="center">
      <table border"1">
        <tr><td>
          <script type="text/javascript" language="javascript">
```

```
    <!-- Comment tags to hide script from older browsers
        document.write("<h5>Date last changed: " +
        document.lastModified + "</h5>");
    -->
    </script>
  </td></tr></table>
</div>
</body>
```

```
Date last changed: 03/27/2010 14:50:48
```

Write a Script that Identifies Browsers

In JavaScript the browser is considered an object. Identified as a *navigator* (remember, JavaScript was developed by Netscape), the browser object allows you to design a page that gathers information about the browser that is viewing it. After you get comfortable with JavaScript, you can even design your code to load different pages depending on which browser your visitor is using. To see the capabilities of the navigator object, open template.htm and save it as *navigator.htm*. After you've added a set of script and comment tags, add the following lines of JavaScript:

1. Add a line that identifies the browser that is displaying the page.

```
document.write("Your browser is: " + document.appName +
"<br />");
```

2. Add a line that displays the browser's version number.

```
document.write("The version is: " document.appVersion +
"<br />");
```

3. Write an instruction that displays the type of platform (computer) on which the browser is running.

```
document.write("Your platform is: " + document.platform +
"<br />");
```

4. Your finished code should look like the following code listing:

```
<script language="javascript" type="text/javascript">
<!-- document.write("Your browser is: " + navigator.appName +
"<br />");
document.write("The version is: " + navigator.appVersion +
"<br />");
document.write("Your platform is: " + navigator.platform +
"<br />");
-->
</script>
```

15

To see this script in action, you should try it on different browsers. Your results will be different for each different browser, version, or system on which the page is displayed. For example, if you view this page with Netscape, your results will look like this:

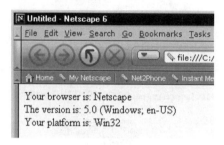

However, if you use Internet Explorer to display the page, your results will be different. As in the following illustration, the application name and version number will change to reflect the browser with which the page is being displayed:

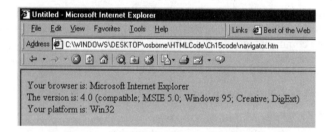

Because most people already know which browser they are using to surf the Net, you might be wondering what possible use that little bit of JavaScript can be. Granted, as just an informational tool it's not all that exciting. However, you also can use the navigator object to analyze the kind of browser a visitor is using and then display an appropriate page.

For example, say you want to use some aspects of CSS that were supported in Netscape but not in Internet Explorer. You don't want to exclude your faithful visitors who might not be using Netscape. So to alert your viewers that they will gain the most benefit from the page if they use Netscape, you can write a code that tests the browser and returns a special prompt if it is not Netscape. Open template.htm and save it as *navtest.htm*; then add the following script to the page:

```
<script language="javascript" type="text/javascript">
<!-- Comments hide script from older browsers
document.write('<p style="font-size: 1.5em">You are using ')
     if(navigator.appName == "Netscape")
          {document.write("Netscape. Proceed</p>")}
     else{(document.write( "a non-Netscape browser.</br>
          This page is best viewed with
          Netscape.</p>"))};
// You can stop hiding the script, now. -->
</script>
```

Don't get too confused by some of the unfamiliar parts of the script; the best way to understand the script is to examine it line by line.

1. The first line should look somewhat familiar. In it you use the write method and the document object to have the browser write the phrase "You are using." Note the addition of the <p> element inside the quotes, along with the style attribute and font-size property. Be sure to observe that the document.write statement is enclosed in single quotes. This is because you will need to use double quotes for the style information.

TIP *Remember that in JavaScript, single and double quotes are interchangeable. You just can't overlap them, and you must use them in pairs.*

```
document.write('<p style="font-size: 1.5em">You are using ')
```

2. Next you set up a condition that the browser should look for with an "if, else" statement. The idea is that the browser should look for a certain condition. "If" it is true, the browser is instructed to take one action. If the condition is not true ("else"), it is to take a different action. This line sets up the condition the browser is to look for. Notice the use of a double equal sign. In JavaScript, a single equal sign is used to assign a value to something. To convey the idea of one thing being equal to another, you must use two equal signs, as shown here:

```
if(navigator.appName == "Netscape")
```

3. The next line tells the browser what to do if it is a Netscape browser. In this case it uses the document.write command to write a line that says "Netscape. Proceed." Note that the entire statement is contained in curly braces:

```
{document.write("Netscape. Proceed</p>")}
```

4. The final line of the script gives the "else" condition. This statement tells the browser what to display if it is not a Netscape browser. Notice again that, after the else command, the entire statement is enclosed in curly braces:

```
else{document.write("a non-Netscape browser.<br />This page is
best viewed with Netscape.</p>")}
```

CAUTION *Remember that the preceding statement must be written on a single line.*

15

When you have typed the script, save it and display it in Netscape. Your results should look something like the following illustration:

You are using: Netscape. Proceed

If you try viewing the page in Internet Explorer, you should see a different display, as is reflected here:

> **You are using a non-Netscape browser.**
> **This page is best viewed with Netscape.**

Write a Script that Displays the Current Date

Have you ever visited a site that displayed the current date and time? This is easy to do with JavaScript. It also gives you the opportunity to work with the date object. To see how easy it is to use JavaScript to display a date, open template.htm and save it as datetime.htm; then follow these steps:

1. Add your script and comment tags.

```
<script language="javascript" type="text/javascript">
<!-- Hide your code from older browsers
// Stop hiding -->>
</script>
```

2. Create a date with the date object. You will assign the name "Today" to the date. You can name it whatever you want to, but "Today" seems appropriate.

```
Today = new Date( );
```

3. Tell the browser to display the date by using the document.write command. Notice that you use the name (Today) that you assigned to the date object. The phrase "Today's date is:" is enclosed in quotation marks because it is a text string. The two are connected with a plus sign (known as a *concatenating operator*).

```
document.write("Today's date is: " + Today);
```

4. Your completed script should look like this:

```
<script language="javascript" type="text/javascript">
<!-- Hide your code from older browsers
Today = new Date( );
document.write("Today's date is: " + Today);
// Stop hiding your code -->
</script>
```

If you save this page and display it in your browser, you will see the current date and time displayed in the upper-left corner of the page. The following illustration shows what you should see:

> Today's date is: Sat Mar 27 19:58:30 CST 2010

Realistically, you would want to display the date in a slightly more conventional manner. It's not much more difficult to do that; you just need to instruct the browser to display only certain parts of the date. Using the getMonth, getDay, and getYear methods, you can make your display more specific. Each method is connected with a period to the date (Today) you already defined. Your line of JavaScript would be modified to read like the following listing:

```
Today = newDate();
document.write("Today's date is: " + Today.getMonth() + "/"
+ Today.getDay() + "/" + Today.getYear());
```

The three methods mentioned above are connected with the plus sign (+), and a slash is added between the parts of the date by enclosing it in a set of quotation marks ("/").

Also, using style sheets, you can enhance the appearance of the JavaScript display. Consider the difference it makes when you add some CSS style rules to improve the look of your page. Modify your code to match the following listing. As the illustration after shows, your date display can be made to look quite attractive.

```
<!DOCTYPE html PUBLIC "-//W3C//DTD XHTML 1.0 Strict//EN"
    "http://www.w3.org/TR/xhtml1/DTD/xhtml1-strict.dtd">
<html xmlns="http://www.w3.org/1999/xhtml">
    <head>
        <title>JavaScript Date Display</title>
<meta http-equiv="Content-Type"
        content="text/html; charset=iso-8859-7" />
        <style type="text/css">
body    {background-color: tan;}
table   {background-color: peach;
           border-style:outset;
           border-color: yellow;}
td         {font-family: arial;
           font-size: 12pt;
           font-weight: bold;
           color: brown;}
        </style>
    </head>
    <body>
        <table>
            <tr>
                <td><script type="text/javascript">
<!-- Hide your code from older browsers
Today = new Date( );
document.write("Today's date is: " + Today.getMonth() + "/"
+ Today.getDate() + "/" + Today.getYear());
```

```
// Stop hiding your code -->
                </script>
            </td>
         </tr>
      </table>
   </body>
</html>
```

NOTE   *The preceding code validated against the XHTML 1.0 Strict DTD.*

Today's date is: 2/27/2010

Work with Events and Event Handlers

By now you're either very excited about JavaScript or thoroughly intimidated by it. Realistically, not everyone finds programming an easy thing to do. Fortunately, a number of the more impressive things JavaScript can do are also some of the easier things to accomplish.

Earlier in this chapter you read about events and event handlers. To refresh your memory, an *event* is something that happens on your visitor's browser, generally in response to an action the visitor has taken (for example, loading a page, unloading it, clicking on something, and so on). An *event handler* is a JavaScript statement that is triggered by a particular event. Table 15-1 lists some of the most commonly used event handlers and the events that trigger them.

Event	Event Handler
Visitor stops a page that is loading.	onAbort
Visitor tabs out of a form field.	onBlur
Visitor tabs into a form field.	onFocus
A page loads into the browser.	onLoad
Mouse cursor moves over a part of the page.	onMouseOver
Mouse cursor moves away from a button or other part of the page.	onMouseOut
Visitor clicks the Submit button.	onSubmit
Visitor clicks the Reset button.	onReset
Visitor holds the mouse button down.	onMouseDown
Visitor releases the mouse button.	onMouseUp
Visitor clicks on part of your page.	onClick

TABLE 15-1   Some Events and Event Handlers

Experiment with Event Handlers

Event handlers enable you to create a page that responds to the actions of your visitor. Whether it is through mouseovers, keypresses, or simple clicks, you can use event handlers to create a responsive environment on your Web site. The best part about event handlers, though, is that they are easy to use.

Create a "Ticklish" Button

To see how easy it is to use event handlers (and to have some fun doing it), try creating a "ticklish" button. This little JavaScript effect demonstrates how you can make a page change dynamically in response to a visitor's actions. The effect begins by displaying a button that says "Click for a surprise." When you move a mouse over the button, it triggers the onMouseOver event handler and the button changes to read "That Tickles!" If you move the mouse off the button, the onMouseOut event handler changes the button to read "Come Back." Then, if you hold the button down, it triggers the onMouseDown event handler, which alters the button to read "Ready for the surprise?" Finally, when you release the button, it disappears and the word "Surprise!" appears in its place.

The code for the ticklish button is reproduced in the following listing. As you type it in, note that you do not use the <script> element. Often event handlers are placed right inside an HTML element, as in the code here. For the ticklish button, all the event handlers are in the same <input /> element.

```
<head>
    <title>The Ticklish Button</title>
    <style>
body {background-color: white; color:navy}
    </style>
</head>
<body>
    <div align="center">
    <h1>The Ticklish Button</h1>
    <form>
        <table border="1"><tr><td>
<input type="button" value="Click for a surprise."
    onMouseOver = "value='That tickles!'";
    onMouseOut = "value='Come back!!!'";
    onMouseDown = "value='Ready for the surprise?'";
    onMouseUp = "document.write('<h1>SURPRISE</h1>')"; />
        </td></tr></table>
    </form>
    </div>
</body>
```

15

When you have typed the code, save it as *ticklish.htm* and open it in your browser. The opening screen will resemble the following illustration. However, when you move your mouse over the button and back out, the button should respond to your movements.

The Ticklish Button

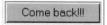

Create a Rollover

A more practical use of event handlers is with mouse rollovers for navigation buttons. To create a simple rollover effect, you must create two buttons that are nearly identical. For this illustration, two buttons, hibuttonoff.gif and hibutton.gif, differ only in the color of the text, as is shown in the following illustration:

These two buttons will be used to create your rollover. To try this for yourself, open template.htm and save it as *hibutton.htm*. Then follow these steps to use the onMouseOver and onMouseOut event handlers:

1. Create a simple image link using the hibuttonoff.gif image.

```
<a href="falselink.htm"><img src="hibuttonoff.gif" /></a>
```

2. Add the name=" " attribute to the image element to assign a name to the image. For this exercise, the name will be "hiThere".

```
<a href"=falselink.htm"><img src="hibuttonoff.gif"
    id="hiThere" /></a>
```

3. Modify the anchor <a> </a> element to add the onMouseOut event handler. The event handler will refer to the name that you assigned to the image (hiThere).

```
<a href="falselink.htm" onMouseOut="hiThere.src='hibuttonoff.gif'">
<img src="hibuttonoff.gif" id="hiThere" /></a>
```

4. Add the onMouseOver event handler to the <a> element.

```
<a href="falselink.htm"
onMouseOut="hiThere.src='hibuttonoff.gif'"
onMouseOver="hiThere.src='hibuttonon.gif'">
<img src="hibuttonoff.gif" id="hiThere" /></a>
```

Save the code and display it in your browser. Your complete page should resemble the illustration that follows:

```
<body>
<a href="falselink.htm"
   onMouseOut="hiThere.src='hibuttonoff.gif'"
   onMouseOver="hiThere.src='hibuttonon.gif'">
<img src="hibuttonoff.gif" id="hiThere"/></a>
</body>
```

Quick Reference: Scripting with JavaScript

Unless you are familiar with programming, you have encountered a number of unfamiliar ideas and constructions as you've worked with JavaScript. Although this chapter cannot go into every possible detail, some of the aspects of JavaScript "grammar" you have used thus far are reviewed in the following table:

To Do This	Use This
Add a single-line comment to JavaScript	// Your comment goes here
Add a multiple-line comment to JavaScript	/* Your comment goes here */
Hide JavaScript from HTML	<script> <!-- script goes here --> </script>
End a complete JavaScript statement	Use a semicolon (;)
Use a method or function. The method or function's *arguments* go inside parentheses (Arguments are the specific actions a method or function performs.)	method( ) function( ) document.write("Hello")
Connect multiple JavaScript statements	Enclose in curly braces { }

15

To Do This	Use This
Connect (concatenate) groups of literal characters (strings)	Use the "plus sign" (concatenate operator) `"string" + "string" + "string"`
Say that something is "equal to" something else (as in 2 + 3 = 5)	Use double equal signs (= =) `if {date = = Today}`
Assign a value to a variable (something that can change)	Use a single equal sign (=) `var = Variable`

Chapter 16

Understand the Future of XHTML

How to...

- Understand XML
- Understand XHTML 1.1
- Create a page with XML
- Create a style sheet for your XML page

If you've been working through this book chapter by chapter, you have observed firsthand the similarities between XHTML and its predecessor HTML. You have learned about XHTML's stricter requirements and what must be done to write well-formed and valid documents. However, so far you've seen only hints about XHTML's potential for expansion—its *extensibility*. In this chapter, you will learn how skilled XHTML authors can actually extend this language with new elements and attributes.

Understand XHTML Modularization

In the Web markup world you have two extremes. HTML is an easy-to-learn language, but it isn't extensible. You're stuck with it as it is. On the other hand, there is XML, which is more difficult to learn but gives you the freedom to create your own markup language from scratch. But as you think about it, you might begin to wonder if using XML is worth the trouble. After all, HTML might not be perfect, but it does provide pretty much everything you need for doing Web pages. Why should you "reinvent the wheel" by trying to create your own markup language? Isn't it better to stick with something that has already been developed?

Well, what if you could have the benefits of HTML markup (most of it, anyway) along with the ability to extend it by adding your own elements? That's what you have in XHTML 1.1 or *Module-based XHTML*.

Understand XHTML 1.0

The first version of XHTML (1.0) could have been called *Transitional* XHTML, because it was designed to begin moving users of HTML in the direction of XML. Of course, the W3C didn't want to make the change too suddenly. That's why they instituted the three different DTDs you learned about earlier: Transitional, Frameset, and Strict. By doing this, they were able to slowly phase out the presentational elements and attributes by deprecating them. However, these three DTDs were never intended to be ends in themselves. They were intended to be stepping stones, as it were, to a much different method for creating Web pages.

Understand XHTML 1.1

XHTML 1.1, or XHTML Modularization, is the current recommendation of the W3C. This specification contains a number of significant changes from the original version of XHTML. For starters, the deprecated attributes and elements have been dropped entirely. In other words, there is no longer a "transitional" DTD that allows you to work with those presentational elements and attributes you may have grown to love. A second difference is that the lang attribute has been removed for all elements and replaced with the xml:lang attribute, and the name attribute has been removed from the <a> and <map> elements in favor of id. Perhaps the most significant change of all has been the grouping together of related elements into modules.

Understand the Concept of XHTML 1.1 Modules

To understand XHTML modules and how they can be extended, think of a toolbox. Instead of providing an alphabetical listing of elements and attributes, the elements of module-based XHTML are organized into related subgroups. Each module is a tool for accomplishing a particular task. For example, all the table elements are grouped together in the Tables Module, form elements are combined into a Forms Module, and so on. Thus, you can create your own custom markup language by choosing only the tools (modules) you need. You can also design your own modules and add these in to your customized markup language. Table 16-1 lists the different modules of XHTML 1.1 and the elements that are contained in each.

NOTE   *A module is usually a collection of related elements. However, a module can also be a collection of other modules.*

Understand How Modules Work

What makes an XHTML module different from an ordinary collection of HTML elements? It has to do with the XHTML 1.1 DTD. A *DTD* (*Document Type Description*) is the blueprint for any markup language created in XML. The module-based XHTML DTD is broken up into smaller, subset DTDs that can be referenced individually. For example, in developing your own markup language you can choose to include the Forms Module but to ignore the Tables Module. You can also write a list of your own elements and attributes—in other words, your own DTD—and save it as a module. This is what enables you to extend XHTML to include your markup. The downside is that you must be able to write your own DTD. Sound complicated? Well, actually, it is.

HTML is intuitive and easy to learn. Its immediate successor, "transitional" XHTML, is also easy to learn. Granted, the rules are a bit stricter, but they are not daunting. Unfortunately, ease of use ends with XHTML 1.0. Although XHTML 1.1 is a great concept, its complexity has moved it out of the realm of the casual page author. It is unlikely that the "Mom and Pop" users who have created Web pages with HTML will be able to make the jump to modular-XHTML without special software. On top of that, XHTML 2.0 (currently in the working draft stage) moves even *further* away from its HTML predecessor. Virtually all presentational elements will be removed—for example <img />—and the markup will be stripped back to a bare minimum.

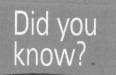

There Are Four Required Modules

If you want to create truly module-based pages based on the XHTML DTD, you must include the four *core* modules: Structure, Text, Lists, and Hypertext. If you do not include the core modules, your document cannot be considered part of the XHTML family of documents. It may be a perfectly valid XML document but not truly XHTML.

16

Module Name	Includes These Elements
Structure Module	`<body>`, `<head>`, `<html>`, `<title>`
Text Module	`<abbr>`, `<acronym>`, `<address>`, `<blockquote>`, ` `, `<cite>`, `<code>`, `<dfn>`, `<div>`, `<em>`, `<h1>`, `<h2>`, `<h3>`, `<h4>`, `<h5>`, `<h6>`, `<kbd>`, `<p>`, `<pre>`, `<q>`, `<samp>`, `<span>`, `<strong>`, `<var>`
Hypertext Module	`<a>`
List Module	`<dl>`, `<dt>`, `<dd>`, `<ol>`, `<ul>`, `<li>`
Applet Module (deprecated in favor of the Object Module)	`<applet>`, `<param />`
Presentation Module	`<b>`, `<big>`, `<hr />`, `<i>`, `<small>`, `<sub>`, `<sup>`, `<tt>`
Edit Module	`<del>`, `<ins>`
Bi-directional Text Module	`<bdo>`
Forms Module	`<form>`, `<input />`, `<select>`, `<option>`, `<textarea>`, `<button>`, `<fieldset>`, `<label>`, `<legend>`, `<optgroup>`
Basic Forms Module	`<form>`, `<input />`, `<label>`, `<select>`, `<option>`, `<textarea>`
Tables Module	`<caption>`, `<table>`, `<td>`, `<th>`, `<tr>`, `<col>`, `<colgroup />`, `<tbody >`, `<thead>`, `<tfoot>`
Image Module	`<img />`
Client-side Image Map Module	`<a>`, `<area />`, `<img />`, `<input />`, `<map>`, `<object>`
Server-Side Image Map Module	`<img />`, `<input />`
Object Module	`<object>`, `<param />`
Frames Module	`<frameset>`, `<frame />`, `<noframes>`
Target Module	`<a>`, `<area>`, `<base>`, `<link>`, `<form>`
Iframe Module	`<iframe>`
Intrinsic Events Module	`<a>`, `<area>`, `<frameset>`, `<form>`, `<body>`, `<label>`, `<input>`, `<select>`, `<textarea>`, `<button>`
Metainformation Module	`<meta />`
Scripting Module	`<noscript>`, `<script>`
Stylesheet Module	`<style>`
Link Module	`<link />`
Base Module	`<base />`
Name Identification Module	`<a>`, `<applet>`, `<form>`, `<frame>`, `<iframe>`, `<img>`, `<map>`
Legacy Module	`<basefont>`, `<center>`, `<dir>`, `<font>`, `<isindex>`, `<menu>`, `<s>`, `<strike>`, `<u>`
	The following elements have some of their deprecated attributes restored in this module:
	`<body>`, ` `, `<caption>`, `<div>`, `<dl>`, `<h1-h6>`, `<hr>`, `<img>`, `<input>`, `<legend>`, `<li>`, `<ol>`, `<p>`, `<pre>`, `<script>`, `<table>`, `<tr>`, `<th>`, `<td>`, `<ul>`

TABLE 16-1 The Modules of XHTML 1.1

Users will have no choice but to design a good portion of their markup. To give you a taste of what that will be like, the final project for this book will be to create a page in XML.

> **TIP** *If you want to make sure your documents are ready for the change to XHTML 2.0, you can move a long way in this direction by following the principles laid out at the end of this chapter.*

Project 25: Create a Page with XML

Now that you've learned some XHTML, as you start to explore XML you'll find that you are on familiar ground from the very beginning. An XML document is built with elements, attributes, and values, just as the HTML documents you are familiar with. The primary difference is that the elements, attributes, and values are unique because authors can create their own tags. For example, the following code listing provides an example of how the markup in an XML document might look:

```
<webpage>
  <heading>Welcome to my XML page</heading>
  <paragraph1>This is my page of the future.</paragraph1>
  <logo> <!-- This will display a logo --> </logo>
  <paragraph2>It is written in XML.</paragraph2>
  <closing>Good bye!</closing>
</webpage>
```

To see how an XML page comes together, open a text editor and type in the preceding code listing. Save the page as a text file named *webpage.xml*.

> **TIP** *If you want to view your XML page, you will need to have at least Internet Explorer 4 or higher, Netscape 6, or Opera.*

Create a Document Type Description (DTD)

A DTD is where you write down the rules for your new markup language and define your elements. You also decide what attributes and values you want each element to accept. Then, when a *validating parser* loads your document, it checks your DTD, reads the rules, and interprets the page accordingly. The following code listing shows what a simple DTD for our webpage.xml would look like:

```
<!ELEMENT webpage (heading, para1, para2, closing)>
<!ELEMENT heading (#PCDATA)>
<!ELEMENT para1 (ANY)>
<!ELEMENT logo (ANY)>
<!ELEMENT para2 (ANY)>
<!ELEMENT closing (#PCDATA)>
```

For the sake of simplicity, this particular DTD is keeping to the very basics: elements. No attributes, values, or entities were defined, although they could have been. If you look at the DTD line by line, it's not difficult to figure out what each line is doing:

- **<!ELEMENT webpage (heading, para1, logo, para2, closing)>**   The first statement is made up of three parts: the ELEMENT declaration, the element name (webpage), and the element's "children" (other elements that must be nested inside it).

16

TIP
The first element declaration is arguably the most important part of your DTD because in it you define your root element. You can have only one root element in an XML document, and all the others must be nested within it. For example, in an HTML page, the root element is <html>. All other elements must go inside it. For the page described in the preceding example, the root element is <webpage>.

- **<!ELEMENT heading (#PCDATA)>**   This line defines the <heading> element. Again, it has three parts: the ELEMENT declaration (this tells the parser that you are defining an element), the element's name (heading), and the type of data it can receive (#PCDATA). The #PCDATA statement stands for *parsed character data*, which simply means that text can be contained in that element.

- **<!ELEMENT para1 (ANY)>**   By now you should be getting a feel for what these lines are doing. This line declares and defines the <para1> element. The main difference in this line is that, instead of #PCDATA, this element can accept any data. For example, this element can also contain other elements, whereas the preceding <heading> element cannot. Although all the lines in this DTD are virtually identical, except for the element names and data types, in a more complex DTD you will have various types of elements (other than the #PCDATA type), attributes, values, and even entities.

With a clearly written document type description, your XML page is nearly complete. However, two more components must be added before it is ready to display: an XML declaration and a document type declaration.

Add an XML Declaration

The XML declaration is simply a line at the beginning of the file that identifies your document as an XML document. Strictly speaking, you don't have to add this line, but again, it's a good idea to include it. To add an XML declaration to the beginning of our "webpage" document, you add a line at the very top that looks like this:

```
<?xml version="1.0"?>
```

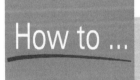

Understand the Difference Between Nonvalidating and Validating Parsers

When discussing how XML documents are dealt with, you normally hear the term *parser* used rather than *browser*. This is because XML deals with more than just Web pages. There are two basic kinds of parsers: validating and nonvalidating. A nonvalidating parser merely checks to make sure your XML document is "well-formed," then it displays the page. A validating parser also checks your document against a DTD to see if it conforms to the DTD's specifications.

With the addition of an XML declaration, the "webpage" document is almost ready to display. However, another optional but helpful addition is a *document type declaration.*

Add a Document Type Declaration

There are two ways to include a document type declaration. The first is used to link to an external DTD, which is basically the same idea as linking an HTML page to an external style sheet or JavaScript. The statement is made up of three parts: the !DOCTYPE statement, the name of the DTD that you want the parser to use (the name of the root element), and the location of the DTD (so the parser can find it). For example, if you plan on saving your DTD as a separate file and linking the page to it, the document type declaration for the "webpage" document might look like this:

```
<!DOCTYPE webpage SYSTEM "webpage.dtd">.
```

The SYSTEM keyword identifies the URL of the document type definition. Notice that the "webpage.dtd" is identified in quotation marks following the system keyword.

> **TIP** *As is the case with style sheets, it's a good idea to save your DTD as a separate file and link to it. This way you can use it with more than one document. If you embed it in the document itself, you tie it down to that one page.*

If, as in the "webpage" sample, your DTD is relatively simple and you want to embed it in the document, you actually include it as part of the document type declaration. You do this by enclosing the entire DTD in square brackets *inside* the document type declaration tag. Because you are not linking to an outside document, you can leave out the SYSTEM keyword. With the document type declaration included in the "webpage" sample, the completed code will look like the following listing:

```
<?xml version="1.0"?>
<!DOCTYPE webpage [<
<!ELEMENT webpage (heading, para1, para2, closing)>
<!ELEMENT heading (#PCDATA)>
<!ELEMENT para1 (ANY)>
<!ELEMENT logo (ANY)>
<!ELEMENT para2 (ANY)>
<!ELEMENT closing (#PCDATA)>
]>>
<webpage>
  <heading>Welcome to my XML page</heading>
  <para1>This is my page of the future.</para1>
  <logo> <!-- This will display a logo --> </logo>
  <para2>It is written in XML.</para2>
  <closing>Good bye!</closing>
</webpage>
```

16

Save this page and then open it in Internet Explorer 4 or higher, and you will see your first XML page displayed. You might be surprised at how it looks. As shown in the following illustration, it appears to be displaying your XML code:

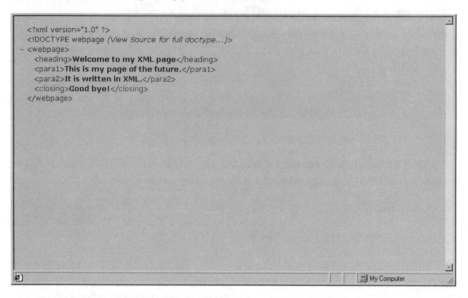

If you were writing HTML and your page displayed like this, you would wonder what went wrong. However, in this case, the page is displaying exactly as it is supposed to. In fact, if you made even the slightest error, the page simply would not have displayed at all, as the following illustration demonstrates:

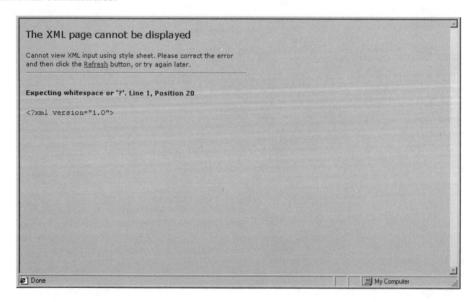

You see, whereas HTML is "forgiving," XML is not. Your code must be written correctly, down to the last quotation mark. If it isn't, an XML browser or parser will not display it. There's no room for sloppy coding with XML. However, that doesn't answer the question of why your XML code displayed instead of the Web page you may have been expecting. The reason is that there is one more "component" an XML page *must* have: a style sheet.

Create a Style Sheet for Your XML Page

When you write your XML code and display it, only the structure of your data will display. If you want your page to look like a Web page, you have to write a style sheet for it. Fortunately, you are again on familiar ground because you can use CSS to create the styles for your XML page. There are other style sheet languages you can use, such as *eXtensible Stylesheet Language* (XSL), but because you are familiar with CSS already (if you've been working through this book), CSS will be fine for this example.

Design Your Style Sheet

You design the style sheet for your page essentially the same way you would for an HTML page but with a few differences. The primary difference is that you will be specifying styles for your own selectors (elements) rather than for HTML elements. Another important difference in using style sheets with XML is that you can't take anything for granted. You must specify how you want each element to display, where it should be positioned, how large the margins are, and so on. If you leave the browser to itself, it will display everything in a linear fashion, as in the following illustration:

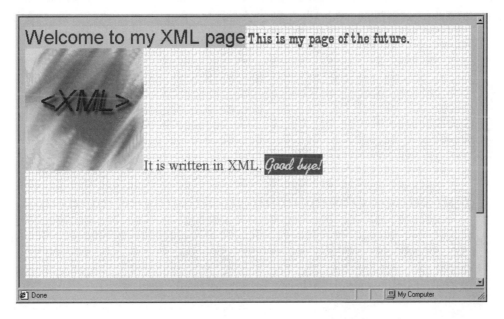

To avoid this problem, you need to use CSS to position the elements on the page.

As you go through the following steps, you will need a background image to include on the page, as well as an image for the logo.

NOTE   *As with each chapter, you can find the files you need on the author's Web site at www.jamespence.com.*

The following style rules are in the order the elements occur on the page, but you can write them in whatever order you want:

■ For your "root" element, "webpage," specify a background color of white (#ffffff) and include a background image for the page. Set the background image to repeat, so that it will function as "wallpaper," and set the background attachment to "fixed." A width and height set to 100% will fill the browser screen. Set the display property to "block." Add a little space to the bottom margin by setting it to 20px (pixels):

```
webpage   {display: block;
background-color: #ffffff;
background-image: url(weavetile2.gif);
background-repeat: repeat;
width=100%;
height=100%;
margin-bottom: 20px;}
```

■ For the <heading> element, set the display to "block" and set a font family, size, and color for the <heading> element. Align the text to the center of the page. For fun, give it a border and its own background color. As a final touch, add a margin of 10 pixels all the way around:

```
heading   {display: block;
font-family: arial;
font-size: 2em;
color: maroon;
text-align: center;
border-style: inset;
border-color: brown;
background-color:#ffcc99;
margin: 10px;}
```

■ For the <para1> element, set the display property to "block." Use the CSS position property set to a value of "absolute," and the z-index property set to a value of –3. A bold "fantasy" font will give this element a little different look. Don't use a background color for this element, but set the text color to "brown." Also, make some adjustments to the top, left, and bottom margins to better size and position the element:

```
para1      {display: block;
position: absolute;
z-index: -3;
font-family: fantasy;
font-weight: bold;
font-variant: italic;
font-size: 1.5em;
color: brown;
margin-top: 15px;
margin-bottom: 10px;
margin-left: 50px;}
```

■ For the <logo> element, the only settings that are unique are the "top" and "left" properties, which refer to the position of the logo image, and the "height" and "width" properties, which specify its size. A z-index of "1" ensures that the logo does not overlap any of the text in either the <para1> or <para2> element:

```
logo       {display: block;
position: relative;
z-index: 1;
top: 55px;
left: 280px;
height:200px;
width:200px;
background-image: url(xmllogo.gif);
background-position: center;
background-color: white;}
```

■ For the <para2> element, set the font size to 1.5 ems and the text to dark green. Align this text with the right margin, but add 50 pixels to the right margin to move the text toward the left:

```
para2      {display: block;
position: relative;
z-index: 2;
font-family: Times-New-Roman;
color: #336600;
font-size: 1.5em;
text-align: right;
margin-top: 15px;
margin-bottom: 15px;
margin-right: 50px;}
```

16

■ For the <closing> element, set the font to cursive, the font size to 1.75 ems, the text to yellow, and the background color to brown. Align this text in the center of the page. A little padding on the top and bottom gives the text some breathing room:

```
closing  {display: block;
font-family: cursive;
color: #ffff66;
font-size: 1.75em;
background-color: brown;
text-align: center;
margin-top:30px;
margin-bottom: 10px;
margin-left: 100px;
margin-right: 100px;
border-style: inset;
border-color:#ffff66;
padding-top: 10px;
padding-bottom: 10px;}
```

Your completed style sheet should look like this:

```
webpage  {display: block;
background-color: #ffffff;
background-image: url(weavetile2.gif);
background-repeat: repeat;
background-attachment: fixed;
width=100%;
height=100%;
margin-bottom: 20%;}

heading  {display: block;
font-family: arial;
font-size: 2em;
color: maroon;
text-align: center;
border-style: inset;
border-color: brown;
background-color:#ffcc99;
margin: 10px;}

para1    {display: block;
position: absolute;
z-index: 3;
font-family: fantasy;
```

```
font-weight: bold;
font-variant: italic;
font-size: 1.5em;
color: brown;
margin-top: 15px;
margin-bottom: 10px;
margin-left: 50px;}

logo      {display: block;
position: relative;
z-index: 1;
top: 55px;
left: 280px;
height:200px;
width:200px;
background-image: url(xmllogo.gif);
background-position: center;
background-color: white;}

para2     {display: block;
position: relative;
z-index: 2;
font-family: Times-New-Roman;
color: #336600;
font-size: 1.5em;
text-align: right;
margin-top: 15px;
margin-bottom: 15px;
margin-right: 50px;}

closing   {display: block;
font-family: cursive;
color: #ffff66;
font-size: 1.75em;
background-color: brown;
text-align: center;
margin-top:30px;
margin-bottom: 10px;
margin-left: 100px;
margin-right: 100px;
border-style: inset;
border-color:#ffff66;
padding-top: 10px;
padding-bottom: 10px;}
```

Save your style sheet as *webpage.css*. Remember to save it as a plain text file, particularly if you are writing it in a word processor. When you've saved your style sheet, your next step is to link your XML page to it.

Link to Your Style Sheet

To link to the style sheet you just created, you need to add one more line to your XML file. Like the XML declaration mentioned earlier in this chapter, this is a processing instruction, so it begins with a question mark (?) followed by an instruction that identifies the tag as a "link" to a style sheet: <?xml-stylesheet?>. Next add a hypertext reference (href=" ") that points to the location of webpage.css. Finally, define the type of style sheet by adding the type=" " attribute. The value should be text/css. Your style sheet link should look like this:

```
<?xml-stylesheet href="webpage.css" type="text/css"?>.
```

This line should be inserted in your webpage.xml document just below the XML declaration, as in the following listing:

```
<?xml version="1.0"?>
<?xml-stylesheet href="webpage.css" type="text/css"?>
<!DOCTYPE webpage [<!ELEMENT webpage (heading, para1, logo, para2, closing)>
<!ELEMENT heading (#PCDATA)>
<!ELEMENT para1 (ANY)>
<!ELEMENT logo (ANY)>
<!ELEMENT para2 (ANY)>
<!ELEMENT closing (#PCDATA)>
]>>
<webpage>
  <heading>Welcome to my XML page</heading>
  <para1>This is my page of the future.</para1>
  <logo> </logo>
  <para2>It is written in XML.</para2>
  <closing>Good bye!</closing>
</webpage>
```

After you've included the style sheet link, save the page. Make sure that the image you chose for your background image is located in the same directory as your XML page, and you're ready to display it in your browser. When you bring it up, it should look something like this:

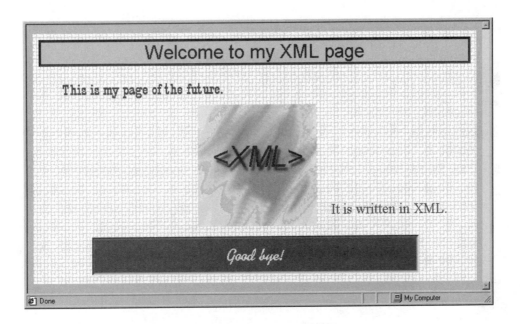

Write XHTML Standards-Compliant Pages

So how do you sort out XHTML 1.0, 1.1, and 2.0? Will you have to learn how to create your own modules to be standards compliant? Eventually, perhaps, but not just yet. It will still be some years before browsers eliminate their "backward compatibility," so you needn't be in a rush to learn how to create XHTML modules or develop DTDs. However, the more standards compliant your documents are, the less maintenance they will require in the future. So there are definite advantages to learning how to adhere to the Strict DTD.

What should you do to make sure that your pages are ready for the future? The following principles will help you write well-formed and valid XHTML pages:

- ■ **Always include closing tags.**   No exceptions. If an element takes an opening tag and a closing tag, always use both.

- ■ **Empty elements must always have a closing slash.**   If you use an *empty element* (an element that does not enclose content), always make sure that you include a space and a closing slash in the tag, like this: <img />.

- ■ **Always include a value with an attribute.**   There are a few instances in HTML where you didn't need to add a value to an attribute. Usually this is because the attribute is self-explanatory. For example, using radio buttons, you could specify an option as preselected by adding the word "checked." Checked was an attribute, but it didn't take a value. Now you need, even in these cases, to include a value with the attribute, as in checked="checked".

16

■ **Enclose all attribute values in quotation marks.**   In the past, you could get away with leaving these out, but not anymore. When you include an attribute value, put it in quotes, like this: attribute="value". No exceptions.

■ **Write your code in lowercase.**   XHTML is case-sensitive. By getting in the habit of writing all your code lowercase, you'll be a long way down the road toward compatibility with the new standard.

■ **Use the id attribute instead of name.**   The name attribute is on the way out, being replaced by id. As much as possible, use id instead of name.

■ **Make sure your tags are all correctly nested.**   No overlapping tags, period.

■ **Check your documents to be sure they are well-formed.**   With HTML your documents *should be* well-formed (correctly written); with XHTML they *must be* well-formed.

■ **Include a <!DOCTYPE> declaration in every document.**   Ideally, you should use the Strict DTD. That way your pages will have to conform to the stricter standards that are coming.

TIP   *If you need some help remembering how to write a <!DOCTYPE> declaration, check out Chapter 7.*

■ **Always Validate your HTML documents.**   Use the W3C's validation service (or somebody else's) to make sure your documents are not only well-formed but that they also conform to the XHTML Strict DTD. The corrections you receive from the validator are great tools to help you learn how to improve your code.

■ **Use CSS for style.**   Learn to use Cascading Style Sheets. Browser support for CSS is growing, and soon the compatibility issues that have made them a mixed blessing will no longer be a problem. In fact, sooner or later you'll *have* to use them anyway. Learn how to do it now.

■ **Stop using presentational elements and attributes.**   Define your presentation with style sheets, not HTML.

Like it or not, the stricter standards of XHTML are the future of the Web. If you begin to write standards-compliant code now, future browser versions will have little or no trouble interpreting your code, even if you aren't writing in XHTML 1.1 or 2.0.

Throughout this book you have learned how easy it is to create pages in XHTML. You have learned how to place the proper emphasis on structure in your markup and use CSS for style and design purposes. Most important, you have discovered that Web authoring isn't some mystical process that can be undertaken only by "techies." You now have the tools you need to create good, functional Web sites. However, keep in mind that if you don't use these tools, you'll probably lose (forget) them. XHTML markup is simple and intuitive, but if you are to become proficient as a Web author, you need to practice. So don't close this book and put it on the shelf. Keep it handy—and start designing Web sites.

And don't forget to have fun!

Index

INTERNATIONAL CONTACT INFORMATION

AUSTRALIA
McGraw-Hill Book Company
Australia Pty. Ltd.
TEL +61-2-9900-1800
FAX +61-2-9878-8881
http://www.mcgraw-hill.com.au
books-it_sydney@mcgraw-hill.com

CANADA
McGraw-Hill Ryerson Ltd.
TEL +905-430-5000
FAX +905-430-5020
http://www.mcgraw-hill.ca

GREECE, MIDDLE EAST, & AFRICA
(Excluding South Africa)
McGraw-Hill Hellas
TEL +30-210-6560-990
TEL +30-210-6560-993
TEL +30-210-6560-994
FAX +30-210-6545-525

MEXICO (Also serving Latin America)
McGraw-Hill Interamericana Editores
S.A. de C.V.
TEL +525-1500-5108
FAX +525-117-1589
http://www.mcgraw-hill.com.mx
carlos_ruiz@mcgraw-hill.com

SINGAPORE (Serving Asia)
McGraw-Hill Book Company
TEL +65-6863-1580
FAX +65-6862-3354
http://www.mcgraw-hill.com.sg
mghasia@mcgraw-hill.com

SOUTH AFRICA
McGraw-Hill South Africa
TEL +27-11-622-7512
FAX +27-11-622-9045
robyn_swanepoel@mcgraw-hill.com

SPAIN
McGraw-Hill/
Interamericana de España, S.A.U.
TEL +34-91-180-3000
FAX +34-91-372-8513
http://www.mcgraw-hill.es
professional@mcgraw-hill.es

UNITED KINGDOM, NORTHERN,
EASTERN, & CENTRAL EUROPE
McGraw-Hill Education Europe
TEL +44-1-628-502500
FAX +44-1-628-770224
http://www.mcgraw-hill.co.uk
emea_queries@mcgraw-hill.com

ALL OTHER INQUIRIES Contact:
McGraw-Hill/Osborne
TEL +1-510-420-7700
FAX +1-510-420-7703
http://www.osborne.com
omg_international@mcgraw-hill.com

Sound Off!

Visit us at **www.osborne.com/bookregistration** and let us know what you thought of this book. While you're online you'll have the opportunity to register for newsletters and special offers from McGraw-Hill/Osborne.

We want to hear from you!

Sneak Peek

Visit us today at **www.betabooks.com** and see what's coming from McGraw-Hill/Osborne tomorrow!

Based on the successful software paradigm, Bet@Books™ allows computing professionals to view partial and sometimes complete text versions of selected titles online. Bet@Books™ viewing is free, invites comments and feedback, and allows you to "test drive" books in progress on the subjects that interest you the most.